LEADING AS A
PUBLIC-MINDED MANAGER

LEADING AS A
PUBLIC-MINDED MANAGER

People, Politics, Purpose

JOHN CLAYTON THOMAS

Georgia State University

Melvin & Leigh, Publishers

IRVINE, CALIFORNIA

For Bill Bolling,
the finest public-minded managerial leader I've known.

Leading as a Public-Minded Manager: People, Politics, Purpose
© 2020 by John Clayton Thomas
All Rights Reserved.

Published by Melvin & Leigh, Publishers
6 Curie Court
Irvine, CA 92617
orders.melvinleigh@cox.net
www.melvinleigh.com

Cover design by Jesse Sanchez
Production by Stacey Victor

ISBN: 978-1-73393442-8

Printed in the United States of America on mixed recycle paper

Visit our home page at www.melvinleigh.com

Table of Contents

Preface vii

Chapter 1: Introduction: Thinking About Leading as a
Public-Minded Manager 1

Chapter 2: What's Different About the Public Realm? 15

Chapter 3: Building the Personal Foundation 32

Chapter 4: Preparing for a Political World 48

Chapter 5: Becoming a Manager 68

Chapter 6: Managing and Motivating People 79

Chapter 7: Developing Relationships with Subordinates 98

Chapter 8: Making Decisions—With and Without Others 120

Chapter 9: Leading Small-Group Teams and Meetings 138

Chapter 10: Looking Upward and Outward 161

Chapter 11: The Ultimate Challenge: Leading
Organizational Change 186

Chapter 12: Conclusions: The Politically Skilled
Public-Minded Managerial Leader 205

References 217

Index 233

About the Author 245

Preface

This book originated from a perception that, amid a wealth of scholarly and popular writing on leadership, relatively few books focus specifically on leadership *skills,* on what people can learn that will translate to their becoming more effective leaders. Even fewer books focus on the narrower topic of leading as a manager in the public realm, including any organization where public or community purposes loom large, a description that encompasses the public and nonprofit sectors plus substantial parts of the private sector.

With those holes in the literature in mind, I wrote this book to explore various skills that managerial leaders may find useful, especially skills for persuading others to join in the pursuit of public ends. These are sometimes termed "people skills" because they focus on working with subordinates, peers, and superiors internal to organizations as well as stakeholders external to organizations. This book does not speak to many other skills managerial leaders also need in such areas as budgeting and finance, strategic planning, performance measurement and management, and so on. Those topics receive ample attention and explanation elsewhere.

In addressing the book to practicing and aspiring managerial leaders, I reject the distinction sometimes drawn between leading and managing. As explained in more detail in Chapter 1, I believe that an effective manager has to be an effective leader, too, that one cannot manage effectively without leading effectively, and vice versa. That is why this book talks about managerial leaders and, given its concern with the public realm, even more specifically about public-minded managerial leaders.

My work on this book essentially began with my becoming responsible for master's level courses on leadership and later leadership and organizational behavior. That started by chance, the luck of the draw of a newly untenured faculty member being asked to fill an open teaching slot for a management and leadership class in a Master of Public Administration program. That experience has now extended off and on for several decades but most intensively for the past decade or so. I am appreciative to the many master's students whose reactions to my ideas have helped enormously in the development of my thinking. Many of them have since become effective public-minded managerial leaders, mostly through applying their own skills and values, but also in part, I hope, through experimentation with the skills explored here.

Around the same time I began these courses, personal experience as an academic administrator, in my home universities and larger professional associations, provided insights into the kinds of skills leaders need and presented opportunities to practice those skills. I am grateful to colleagues at Georgia State University and earlier at the University of Missouri-Kansas City for tolerating my sometimes-ham-handed experimentation with these skills. That experimentation was also tolerated by colleagues at the Urban Affairs Association and the American Society for Public Administration as well as contributors, editorial board members, and fellow editors during my time as an editor of the *American Review of Public Administration,* to all of whom I am also grateful.

My experience has fortunately extended to observations of and reading about a wide array of effective public-minded managerial leaders. This book draws on the stories of many of them to illustrate various aspects of leadership. I have especially benefited from observing and listening to Bill Bolling, the founder and long-time Chief Executive Officer of the Atlanta Community Food Bank, and the person to whom this book is dedicated. I benefited earlier from the mentoring of Bill Eddy, former dean of the Henry W. Bloch School of Management at the University of Missouri-Kansas City, who opened my eyes to the techniques and benefits of collaborative decision making.

Beyond those personal experiences, I must acknowledge my intellectual debts to the many scholars, only some of whom I know personally, whose ideas have shaped my thinking about leadership. Those debts begin with three late luminaries and pioneers of thinking about leadership and management—Warren Bennis, John Gardner, and Leonard Sayles. Without the work of any of them, the insights I am able to offer here would be much more limited.

Beyond those three, I have benefited from the work of many other scholars of managerial leadership in general and that leadership in public administration and public management specifically. Among the former, those who have exerted the most influence on my thinking include Lee Bolman and Terrence Deal; Gary Yukl; John Kotter; Jeffrey Pfeffer; Chris Argyris and Donald Schon; Victor Vroom, Philip Yetton, and Arthur Jago; Cass Sunstein and Reid Hastie; Robert Axelrod; James Surowiecki; and Michael Doyle and David Strauss. Within public administration specifically, my thinking has been shaped most by Hal Rainey by himself and with a number of coauthors (most notably, Barry Bozeman, Sergio Fernandez, and James Thompson); John Alford; John Bryson and Barbara Crosby; Charles Goodsell; Don Moynihan; Jim Perry; Norma Riccucci; Lois Wise; and Brad Wright. Ideas from all of these authors—and others too numerous to mention—proved invaluable in the writing of this book and always for the better. If I have misinterpreted the work of any of them (as seems likely), I apologize. More generally, any mistakes in this book are my responsibility alone.

I must give special thanks to colleagues Guy Adams and George Reed, who originally planned to join as coauthors of this book. Other priorities pulled them elsewhere, but my thinking on leadership and on the possibility of this book benefited enormously from the time the three of us spent discussing what a book on leadership should look like.

I am also grateful to those graduate research assistants who have assisted with various parts of this book, especially Hala Altamimi and Matteo Zullo.

I have also benefited from the encouragement of my publisher, Harry Briggs. Harry assisted enormously with my last book, and has been just as supportive and patient with the development of this book.

Chapter 4 and, in part, Chapter 10 are adapted from articles previously published in *Public Administration Review* (Thomas 2017, 2013). I am grateful to anonymous reviewers for their helpful counsel on both articles.

Finally, I am pleased once again to thank my wife, Marilyn, for all her help. In addition to serving as my life partner, enough of a task in itself, she has served as, literally, my "in-house" editor, reading and commenting on every part of this book. Marilyn has a great eye for seeing the larger issues that can arise in my writing—like a chapter's conclusion that reads better as the chapter's introduction (I refuse to divulge for which chapter(s) that was the case)—as well as the many minor, but crucial errors that escape my eye, but not hers. Thanks, Marilyn, for all you have given and continue to give me.

Chapter 1

Introduction

Thinking About Leading as a Public-Minded Manager

Charles Rossotti became the Commissioner—the boss—of the U.S. Internal Revenue in 1997 at a low point in the history of an agency that, at its highest points, has never been much loved. It was a time when the IRS had "problems to match its vast size and complexity," problems that had persisted for decades through ongoing controversy and frequent legislative action (Rainey, and Thompson 2006, 598). Only five years later, Rossotti would leave office at the end of his term to the sound of "sincere praise" from virtually "every group or authority with which he dealt." That praise came in spite of Rossotti having led "a major, challenging reorganization" of the IRS that stepped on many toes and imposed costs on many people both inside and outside the IRS.

In a different kind of public domain, from beginning in a soup kitchen in the basement of an Atlanta church in 1979, Bill Bolling built one of the first and eventually one of the largest nonprofit food banks in the world. Unlike Rossotti, Bolling did not face a hostile environment, but, also unlike Rossotti, he started with no formal power; he had no position of authority and none of the resources such positions bring. Bolling had only the informal power of his personality, especially his commitment to the problem of hunger and his tenacity in seeking solutions. Yet, over the course of the next several decades, Bolling built an Atlanta Community Food Bank which, a year before he stepped down as its Executive Director in 2015, distributed more than 50 million pounds of food through a network of more than 600 local and regional partners covering all of Georgia's 159 counties (Davis 2015, D4). Bolling had also become a leader—the most prominent leader, by many accounts—in the national food bank movement.

Charles Rossotti and Bill Bolling, one in the public sector and the other in the nonprofit sector, exemplify the idea of leading as a public-minded manager. They led by making choices for how their enterprises should proceed, they managed by implementing strategies to make those choices a reality, and they did both from a public-minded perspective. This book examines how that can be done, how, that is, someone can lead effectively as a public-minded manager.

Leading as a Public-Minded Manager Defined

A definition of leading as a public-minded manager must address three elements: (1) leadership, (2) management, and (3) public-mindedness. This could be problematic since some writers draw a sharp distinction between the first two components, leadership and management, arguing that the two do not combine well in the same person. As Bennis and Nanus (2007) have asserted, "Managers do things right. Leaders do the right thing." Or, as Yukl (2013, 6) expanded on the distinction, "Managers are concerned about how things get done, and they try to get people to perform better. Leaders are concerned with what things mean to people, and they try to get people to agree about the most important things to be done."

It is the difference, according to Bennis (1994, 44), "between those who master the context and those who surrender to it." Managers supposedly surrender to the organizational and bureaucratic context, seeing their role as "to solve problems . . . in ways that conform with existing rules and regulations" (Rainey 2014, 175). Leaders, by contrast, are described as taking the role as "not to solve problems, but to increase the ability of employees to solve them collaboratively. . . ." Based on that distinction, some scholars contend, as Yukl (2013, 6) summarizes their perspective, "that leadership and management are qualitatively different and mutually exclusive." After all, the individual who surrenders to a context would hardly seem to be the same person who could master it.

This book takes a very different perspective, beginning from a belief that organizations run most effectively when those in charge combine the skills of leadership *and* management. From this perspective, leaders cannot succeed at doing the right thing without some managerial ability to also do things right. And, what good are managers who can do things right if they cannot first determine if they are doing the right thing? To be effective in running an organization or some part of it requires skills for both making the right choices and knowing how to put those choices into operation.

The examples of Charles Rossotti and Bill Bolling are instructive. Consistent with the Bennis and Nanus sense of leadership, Rossotti (2005, 598) had a clear vision of what was the right thing to do at the IRS, focusing especially on providing service to taxpayers and helping them understand their responsibilities. To make that vision a reality, however, Rossotti also had to manage effectively, doing things right by creating and implementing a plan entailing extensive involvement of employees and other stakeholders. Bolling, too, had a leader's vision of what he wanted to accomplish through the Atlanta Community Food Bank, but, starting from scratch, he had to be able to manage in order to achieve that vision.

Following the Rossotti and Bolling models, this book focuses on management *and* leadership in combination, in other words, on managerial leadership. Managerial leadership seeks to influence the behavior of others toward accomplishment of some end valued by the organization. That influence will affect choices on what to do (doing the right thing), strategies for putting those choices into operation (doing things right), and, most often, both in combination.

Moving to the third component, for managerial leaders to also be public-minded, they must embrace "a sense of stewardship" for some common good for a community or larger public (Keohane 2012, 39). That sense of stewardship should begin with the organization and its members, with public-minded managerial leaders feeling responsible for the well-being of both. It should also include a concern for goals that extend beyond an organization's boundaries, goals such as preserving the environment, promoting civil rights, or improving the lot of the disadvantaged. A public-minded managerial leader, as the late John Gardner (2012, 290) once suggested, "serves the individual human goals that our society values so highly."

That sense of stewardship also holds implications for how influence will be exerted and achieved. A true sense of responsibility for the well-being of others requires that public-minded managerial leaders learn what others feel about their own well-being, allowing those who might be led to speak to the directions that those leaders may ask them to follow. To do that, these leaders must be substantially facilitative in their approach, involving others in setting and pursuing goals, rather than being predominantly directive.

Combining these several elements, public-minded managerial leadership can be defined, following the examples of Gary Yukl and Nannerl Keohane, as (1) "the process of influencing others to understand and agree about what needs to be done and how to do it, and the process of facilitating individual and collective efforts to accomplish shared objectives" (Yukl 2013, 7), where (2) the shared objectives focus on "providing solutions to common problems or offering ideas about how to accomplish collective purposes, and mobilizing the energies of others to follow these courses of action" (Keohane 2012, 19). Or, more succinctly, public-minded managerial leadership entails working with and influencing others to achieve public value. It is this public-minded managerial leadership that is the concern of this book.

Nothing in that definition limits public-minded managerial leadership to the public and nonprofit sectors. Many in the private sector undoubtedly seek to lead and manage with a sense of stewardship for their subordinates, their organization, and collective societal purposes, thereby also qualifying as public-minded managerial leaders. It is not the issue of a profit motive but the degree of interest in broader public goals that determines whether a managerial leader qualifies as a *public-minded* managerial leader.

The Fantasy and Reality of Managerial Leadership

Popular stereotypes picture leaders barking orders that others readily obey. In this view, leaders know what to do and, acting on that knowledge, are not shy about making demands of subordinates. Those subordinates for their part move quickly to comply, recognizing that, were they to balk, they might shortly be poring through help-wanted ads, having lost their jobs due to insubordination. As Gardner (2012, 288–289) once summarized this viewpoint, "The popular notion of top leadership is a fantasy of capricious power: The top man presses a button and something remarkable happens; he gives an order as the whim strikes him, and it is obeyed." This is traditional bureaucracy operating in its theoretically purest form: Power rests at the top of the hierarchy and, when exercised, results in lockstep compliance at lower levels.

If organizations really worked like that, the tasks of managerial leadership would be so straightforward and readily achievable that a book on public-minded managerial leadership might not be needed. Managers would need only to decide the right things to do and how to do them, issue orders for how subordinates should put those plans into operation, and then sit back and watch as their plans came to fruition.

Contemporary reality departs sharply from that stereotype. Leaders on their own seldom have knowledge sufficient to frame sensible orders; that is, orders which, if followed, they can be confident will enhance their organizations' performance. In a world where information is now widely dispersed, leaders must gain access to information held by others in order for their decisions to be well-informed. Nor typically do they hold enough formal authority to force others to comply. Using Gardner's (2012, 289) words again, "Most leaders are hedged around by constraints—tradition, constitutional limitations, the realities of the external situation, rights and privileges of followers, the requirements of teamwork, and most of all the inexorable demands of large-scale organizations, which do not operate on capriciousness." Managerial leaders are constrained in what they can command in the first place as well as limited in their ability to influence others to comply with their commands. They may be even more constrained in the public realm where restrictions can be more common (Sayles 1979). In this world where power is broadly shared and constrained, leaders must find techniques other than formal power to gain the support necessary for their decisions to be effectively implemented.

The fantasy of omnipotent managerial leaders pairs well with the illusion of their work being largely thoughtful and reflective, with most of their time devoted to strategizing for how to make their organizations function better. Managerial work is envisioned as resembling "the studied, analytical, persisting work pattern of the professional who expects and demands closure: the time to do a careful and complete job that will provide pride of authorship" (Sayles 1979, 17).

Here, too, fantasy bears little resemblance to reality. Far from being reflective and systematic, managerial work tends to be "hectic and fragmented," requiring "the ability to shift continually from person to person, from one subject to another" (Sayles 1979, 14). Managerial leaders engage in many activities, each often of only a few minutes' duration, with interactions frequently initiated by others, placing leaders more often in a reactive than a proactive role (Yukl 2013, 24-25). Instead of regularly issuing commands, these leaders may have difficulty finding the time even to reflect on what to command. As one manager observed, "I usually come to my office in the morning without any plans as to what I am going to do that day. Any minute something can happen that upsets the works" (Sayles 1979, 15).

That reality of managerial leadership can be difficult for new managers—and not-so-new managers—to deal with. As Sayles (1979, 4) observed decades ago, "Not knowing how to do it, what managerial life would be like, and what the 'process would feel like,' typical managers are shocked and dismayed by what they find. The reality of being a manager is far different from the expectations."

The difficulties are exacerbated by the tendency for many people to be promoted to managerial leadership positions based on their performance as professionals. The best engineer is chosen to lead an engineering agency, the best planner to lead a planning agency, and the most-published scholar to lead a university academic department. Lacking obvious criteria for assessing would-be managerial leaders, agencies often default to professional performance as the best available metric. That choice can easily lead to new managerial leaders who base their approach on what worked for them as professionals.

Can Managerial Leadership Be Taught?

Granting these challenges, a popular perspective holds that the ability to be an effective managerial leader cannot be taught, that "leaders are born, not made." Proponents of this perspective point to many famous historical leaders whose abilities to lead were evident at an early age and endured throughout their lifetimes.

This viewpoint draws the strongest objections from contemporary leaders themselves, from people who have held major leadership positions. Summarizing his interviews of many prominent leaders in American society, Warren Bennis (1994, 5) reported that "they all agree that leaders are made, not born." While all of those leaders might have had personal traits conducive to leading, they were emphatic that their leadership abilities were developed rather than being innate. Many people may be born with inherent talents for leadership, but the evidence strongly suggests that effective leadership will not result from these talents alone.

Even if leaders are actually made, the question remains of how they are made, in particular, whether some of the how involves being taught (as, for example, by reading this book). The leaders who Bennis (1994, 5) interviewed appeared skeptical, mostly asserting that they were "made more by themselves than by any external means." Skepticism is also implied by the common belief that leadership is "more art than science" (Cronin and Genovese 2015, 308). It is not clear, after all, whether "art" can be taught.

This book disputes that premise, contending that there are teachable skills that can enhance the ability to lead as a public-minded manager. To be clear, these skills cannot be taught as, say, facts might be taught; that is, here they are, remember them. The skills that can be taught—and learned—are more in line with athletic skills. Students can receive instruction on athletic—and managerial leadership—skills from a book or in the classroom, but they must also practice the skills on the field, reflect on success or failure there, and then repeat the process regularly until the skill is, to a substantial extent, learned.

Take the abilities that are required for running small-group meetings, one of the subjects of Chapter 9. It is the rare individual who can lead a small-group meeting effectively without any preparation or practice. It may be equally rare that someone could be effective in that role based on reading alone or on reading combined with classroom instruction. The ability to run effective small-group meetings likely develops best through reading and/or instruction, followed by practice in actually running meetings, followed by reflection and more practice, and so on. The same rule holds with the other skills explored later, from developing a vision to building personal power to motivating employees, as a few examples: Practice is likely essential for developing these skills but reading and instruction can be invaluable to know *what* to practice and *how*.

This line of thinking suggests how managerial leaders could be both "made more by themselves than by any external means," as Bennis's leaders described themselves, yet have the ability to learn leadership and management skills, too. On the one hand, they can truly *learn* skills only by choosing to practice and to reflect on that practice, but, on the other hand, they can learn *about* specific skills to practice through reading and other educational techniques. The hope is that this book can assist would-be public-minded managerial leaders in following such a process, gaining ideas here for what to practice and how, before actually practicing and reflecting to build specific skills.

In taking this approach, the intent is to chart a different path from that taken by most books on leadership and management. As anyone who has looked at books on leadership knows, the choices are many, leadership being one of the few scholarly topics to sometimes gain its own section in commercial bookstores. Those choices include many popular books typically focusing on specific aspects or approaches to leadership, as well as an ample supply of scholarly books mostly focusing on academic leadership theories.

In contrast to most of those books, the goal of this book is to provide preparation in a range of skills of managerial leadership, especially skills for working with and leading people. If successful, the book will provide current and prospective public-minded managerial leaders with (1) an understanding of a number of specific managerial leadership skills and (2) strategies for developing the skills. As such, the best measure of this book's success with any given reader might not be the individual's *improvement* as a public-minded managerial leader, but the individual's *plan* for developing in that role.

The Skill Domains: People, Politics, Purpose

The skills of interest here focus mostly on working with people to develop solutions and plan their implementation to achieve public ends. These skills pertain to the three principal domains of the work of those who lead as public-minded managers: people, politics, and purpose. People refers to those who would be led or, in any event, whose support is needed; politics refers to how that support might be gained; and, purpose refers to the goals that might be pursued by public-minded managerial leaders.

People

For anyone to lead, others must follow. It is the *sine qua non* of leadership, that leaders can motivate others to follow as desired. Yet, as suggested earlier, few leadership or management positions come with any guarantee that will happen. To the contrary, ample scholarship and practical experience counsel that would-be managerial leaders will inevitably face challenges in motivating others to follow, starting with the fact that they usually lack much formal power over subordinates (Kotter 1985). Gaining the support of subordinates may typically require more than simply telling them what to do.

The formal authority of managerial leaders is even more limited with the many other actors with whom they must work: superiors, leaders of related agencies in the public realm, various other public, private, and nonprofit actors, and citizens. Yet, in what Crosby and Bryson (2005) characterize as a "shared-power world," the success of public-minded managerial leaders will frequently depend on their ability to gain the support of the other actors.

To do so requires the development of an array of what are often termed "people skills," skills for working with and gaining the cooperation of others. These include skills related to: (1) listening and understanding, (2) gaining credibility, (3) recruiting and retaining high-quality employees, (4) motivating, and (5) making decisions collaboratively. Work with external actors calls additionally for skills such as political mapping and networking. Most of this book focuses on these and other skills for working with people, including both how to develop and how to apply the skills.

Politics

Leading effectively as a public-minded manager demands an understanding of and ability to work in the often-confusing world of organizational politics. Many managerial leaders view organizational politics as distasteful or even unethical and, for those and other reasons, do their best to avoid any involvement. They make that choice at the risk of undermining their own ability to influence organizational decisions and outcomes.

The better choice is to accept organizational politics as a reality and then to strategize on how to work effectively in that reality. That will entail, for one thing, recognizing the importance of power as the currency of organizational politics; those who hold more power can use that power as currency to "buy" influence, as by persuading others to follow their lead. By contrast, managerial leaders who disdain politics and power may find themselves severely constrained in what they can accomplish. Accepting organizational politics as a reality should also entail learning how to develop and apply power, learning, in other words, how to compete in a political world.

Embracing organizational politics and political skills and techniques need not mean compromising one's principles. Political skills can be and often are used for virtuous purposes, as illustrated through the case of Bill Bolling, discussed in Chapter 4. At its core, politics is about reaching solutions that resolve issues between people; there is nothing inherently wrong in that formulation and much that is potentially good, even virtuous.

Purpose

At the core of wanting to lead as a public-minded manager should lie purpose, the sense of purpose implied in being public-minded. Those individuals who assume this responsibility presumably do so, in part or in entirety, to advance the cause of particular public purposes to which they are committed. The task of leading as a public-minded manager consequently requires a sense of relevant purposes, of possible conflicts between them, and of how best to pursue these purposes.

The relevant purposes take at least three forms. First, and perhaps most obvious, are the purposes of the specific public or nonprofit agency (or sometimes private business), purposes such as preserving environmental quality for an environmental protection agency, achieving effective law enforcement for a police department, or feeding the hungry for a nonprofit food bank. Second, with democratic governments, there are also concerns for values or purposes around agency processes, values like representativeness, transparency, and due process. Third, there are intra-organizational purposes related to how agency employees are treated with regard to fairness, lack of bias, autonomy, empowerment, and the like.

Leading as a public-minded manager requires thinking about these purposes early and on an ongoing basis. Early thinking should focus on the purposes leaders seek, as by developing personal and organizational visions of desired ends (see Chapter 3). But purposes cannot simply be defined, then put aside. They must be regularly recalled and compared to decisions and actions that are being contemplated. Will these actions promote the core purposes we seek?

Managerial Leadership Skills and the Organization of the Book

The book's chapters cover a broad range of skills that can prove useful for leading as a public-minded manager. The order of the chapters roughly parallels the sequence in which each of the skills might arise for a would-be or current managerial leader, culminating in a discussion of how the skills might be combined to attempt transformational organizational change.

The Nature of the Public Realm

As a preface to discussing those skills, Chapter 2 examines what's different about the public realm, the context in which the skills might be applied. The term "public realm" refers to organizations with some degree of concern with public purposes, meaning primarily, but not exclusively, public sector or nonprofit sector organizations. The chapter explores the special constraints and resources of the public realm, as well as what those differences imply for how those organizations function and how public-minded managerial leaders might pursue their goals.

The Personal Foundation

The next two chapters examine how one might prepare to become a public-minded managerial leader. Chapter 3 examines how to build a personal foundation for leadership, looking at four elements: (1) emotional intelligence, (2) a desire to serve, (3) a sense of specific public purposes one wants to achieve, and (4) clear personal and organizational visions. The chapter explores what the different elements entail and how a prospective public-minded managerial leader might develop each.

In the area of emotional intelligence, for example, leaders need (1) self-awareness, an understanding of their own emotional makeup, and (2) self-regulation, the ability to maintain self-control and respond appropriately when under pressure, as well as empathy, social skills, and motivation. To be public minded, too, they must feel the desire to serve, have a sense of the public purposes they want to promote, and formulate a vision of what they want to achieve and how.

Preparation for a Political World

Building on the political perspective introduced earlier in this chapter, Chapter 4 explores how to prepare for working in a political world. Managerial leaders will be severely limited in their potential effectiveness unless they recognize and embrace the political nature of their work world. The chapter speaks essentially to the political element as a fourth element of the personal foundation. Using the example of Bill Bolling, the chapter explains how one might develop informal power in an organization, beginning well in advance of assuming a leadership position.

Becoming a Manager

With this personal foundation and political preparation, would-be public-minded managerial leaders may be ready to assume managerial positions.

Amplifying on discussions earlier in this chapter, Chapter 5 examines the challenges likely to arise when moving into a managerial position and suggests strategies that can help new managerial leaders adapt to their new responsibilities and, potentially, new way of life.

Managing and Motivating People

Managerial effectiveness depends on an organization's human resources: its employees. Chapters 6 and 7 address several topics related to developing relationships with employees. The strongest of these relationships build from a foundation of effective human resource management (HRM) principles, as will be outlined in the first part of Chapter 6. Gaining employee support starts with respecting such HRM principles as (1) hiring the right people, (2) investing in employees after hiring, (3) rewarding good performers, (3) protecting the jobs of effective performers, (4) promoting from within to the extent possible, (5) avoiding in-breeding, (6) seeking diversity, and (7) empowering employees to do their jobs.

Next come issues of motivation. As discussed in the second part of Chapter 6, managers need to understand and be responsive to what motivates their employees. Are they driven principally by public service motivation, by the opportunity to serve others, or are they motivated more by (1) responsible professionalism, the desire to apply their professional skills effectively, or (2) rational economic self-interest, the desire for personal economic gain, or most likely, by (3) by some other factor or combination of factors? Careful consideration of the different sources of motivation for specific employees can prove invaluable in figuring out how to maximize employee and organizational performance.

Relationship Development and Conflict Management

Chapter 7 looks more in-depth at how to develop the manager-employee relationship. As explained in the chapter, effective managerial leaders build relationships with subordinates through focused efforts at interactive communication, where managers and subordinates exchange information and engage in mutual influence. The chapter initially outlines an interactive approach for building partner-like relationships with employees, the kind of relationship that research shows works best for both parties. Given the inevitability of occasional conflict in even the best relationships, leaders must also be able to address disagreements, preferably through a cooperative approach based on a combination of inquiry and advocacy but sometimes, too, through tougher approaches, all of which are explained in the second half of Chapter 7.

Understanding When and How to Involve Others

The next two chapters turn to the principal participatory processes in organizations, starting in Chapter 8 with questions of when, how, and why to involve others in decision making. The need to work with others calls for an ability to determine when others should be involved, whether to involve them as individuals or as groups, and how much authority to share when others are involved. The options are many, including choices of whether to involve as well as how much influence to share when involving others. Too little involvement and the leader may not obtain necessary information or nurture essential acceptance for decisions, while too much involvement could result in decision-making stalling as a consequence of an excess of organizational democracy. By contrast, making the appropriate choices can produce higher-quality decisions with strong organizational support. This chapter offers guidelines for how leaders can walk the fine line required to achieve those outcomes.

Leading Small-Group Teams and Meetings

When managers choose to involve others extensively in decision making, additional questions arise around how to work with the decision-making group. The growing popularity of organizational teams puts a premium on managers being able to structure small-group teams and manage their meetings. With the former, managers need to be able to determine when a team is needed, what capabilities it should have, who can best provide those capabilities, and how to develop that team as an effectively functioning entity. With the latter, managers need skills for planning and facilitating small-group meetings, including skills for setting agendas, sequencing topics, facilitating discussions, addressing conflicts, and moving issues to resolution.

Chapter 9 examines the two core elements of working with small-group teams: (1) developing teams and (2) running small-group meetings. The chapter offers guidelines for making both parts work more effectively, arguing again for the value of political skills in managing teams and small-group meetings.

Looking Upward and Outward

Managers also need skills for working with superiors and external stakeholders, people over whom they hold no formal authority. Chapter 10 pivots from the manager-employee relationships to focus on these relationships with superiors and external actors. To be effective, managerial leaders need skills to gain top-management support and commitment, which is a necessity of everyday management. In an increasingly networked society, leaders must also develop skills to use in nurturing support from actors outside the core organization, external stakeholders who function as the organization's customers, partners, and citizen-owners. As the chapter makes clear, no matter how effective a manager is at developing relationships with subordinates, overall success will require the ability to work effectively with superiors and important stakeholders, too.

Leading Organizational Change

Drawing on all of these chapters, Chapter 11 outlines a strategy for how public-minded managers can lead processes of organizational change, what is often termed "transformational change." The chapter draws from two parallel theories, one for transformational leadership and the other for organizational change, in order to outline a strategy for achieving major organizational change, principally through application of the skills explored in earlier chapters.

The Politically-Skilled Public-Minded Managerial Leader

To be effective in their work, public-minded managerial leaders must consequently develop a range of political skills, including both latent political skills (i.e., the personal characteristics discussed mostly in Chapters 3 and 4) and manifest or operational political skills (i.e., the principal focus of Chapters 6–11). The concluding Chapter 12 summarizes those skills, reviews how they can be developed, considers their value in the often-constrained public realm, and ponders why more public servants do not rise to the challenge of becoming public-minded managerial leaders.

Developing as a Public-Minded Managerial Leader

This book is addressed to current and prospective public-minded managerial leaders, especially but not exclusively in the public and nonprofit sectors. It may interest current or aspiring managerial leaders, whether in the public, nonprofit, or private sector, who desire to lead and manage with a sense of stewardship for their organization, its people, and the public good.

Within that audience, the book will likely have its greatest appeal for those who are inclined toward more facilitative and participatory approaches to leadership since most of the skills discussed tilt in that direction. That said, the approach recommended here is not a wholly "feel-good" or "win-

win" approach. As explained in many points, facilitative and participatory approaches will not always be desirable (see Chapter 8) and can sometimes be manipulated by opportunists (see Chapter 7). Public-minded managerial leaders should be alert to these realities, and prepared to make unilateral decisions as appropriate and to draw hard lines with the resistant as necessary.

The book's chapters are sequenced to fit an individual's possible incremental development for managerial leadership roles, building from initial elements of a personal foundation to becoming a manager through the various skills of managerial leadership. If that sequence works as intended, the would-be leader who reads and practices each chapter, chapter by chapter, should be well-prepared for assuming managerial leadership roles. (To assist in that effort, most chapters include "personal leadership exercises" that can be used for practice.)

At the same time, each of the chapters can stand on its own as a guide to a particular aspect of public-minded managerial leadership. One need not necessarily be well-grounded in how to manage and motivate people (Chapter 6), for example, to be able to benefit from recommendations on when and how to involve others in decision making (Chapter 8) or how to run small-group meetings (Chapter 9).

As the notable exception, Chapter 11 requires understanding of all or most of the other chapters; the challenges of transformational organizational are too daunting to be undertaken by anyone other than a well-rounded public-minded managerial leader. It is this author's hope, though, that many readers will want to grasp the lessons of all or most of the chapters, thus to be able to undertake the transformational organizational change that is so often needed in the public realm.

Chapter 2

What's Different About
the Public Realm?

When it comes to leadership, context matters. Those who seek to lead in the public realm, comprised mostly of the public and nonprofit sectors, face some different opportunities and constraints than do those who lead in the private realm, extending across much of the private sector. The public realm can differ from the private in a number of dimensions, and those differences affect the job of public-minded managerial leaders.

The differences correspond only partially to sector. Publicness is hardly exclusive to the public and nonprofit sectors, and all of its aspects do not apply equally to all entities in those sectors. As Boyne (2002, 113) concluded after a comprehensive review of research on the topic, "the balance of the evidence seldom supports the argument that public organizations are distinctive." Parts of the private sector are more public-like, relative to terms defined later, than are parts of the public or nonprofit sector. A municipal golf course which depends on customer patronage may operate more like a private business than does a private business focused on training the unemployed on a contract with government. The different sectors also appear to be becoming more similar as the "blurring and entwining of the sectors has advanced even further in recent years" (Rainey 2014, 57).

This blurring complicates any effort to draw clear lines between what falls in the public realm and what does not. In the end, the safest conclusion may be that organizations with more aspects of publicness fit more clearly in the public realm, while organizations with fewer of those aspects do not.

For specific public-minded managerial leaders, though, the relevant question may not be in which realm they fall, public or private, but which aspects of publicness fit their situation and what those aspects imply for their work. This chapter examines the various aspects of this publicness in the belief that public-minded managerial leaders will be better prepared to lead and manage if they begin with an understanding of these contextual differences.

The Different Goals of the Public Realm

The differences begin with the goals organizations seek. Organizations in the public realm were mostly created to pursue outcomes different from those private entities pursue. As Rainey (2014, 64) has observed, "In theory, government in the United States and many other nations exists to maintain systems of law, justice, and social organization; to maintain individual rights and freedoms; to provide national security and stability; to promote general prosperity; and to provide direction for the nation and its communities." Similarly, nonprofit agencies were typically created to pursue social or public service missions, missions distinct from those of most parts of the private sector.

The differences are often summarized in the contrast of a focus on the public interest as opposed to private profit. In Graham Allison's (1983, 78) words, "Governmental managers rarely have a clear bottom line, while that of a private business manager is profit, market performance, and survival." The differences also often extend to how the public realm accords a higher priority to the *process* for pursuing its goals, with *how* outcomes are sought and *who* is involved sometimes as important as whether outcomes are achieved. Each of these elements warrants elaboration.

Public-Serving Goals

Although it is an oversimplification to say that organizations in the public realm focus on achieving public values while private enterprises focus on making profits, the two realms clearly lean in those contrasting directions. With respect to the public and nonprofit sectors specifically, their entities typically focus on the pursuit of public values, outcomes that are viewed as unlikely to result from letting market forces operate (e.g., Bozeman 2007). Those public values (and the entities that might pursue them) include:

- Clean air (for an environmental agency).
- Better health outcomes for low-income populations (for a public health agency or nonprofit community health center).
- Protection against external military threats (for a branch of the military).
- Income protection for the unemployed (for an unemployment insurance program).
- Maintenance of at least a minimum quality of life for the elderly (for a social insurance program for seniors or a nonprofit community senior center)

To be sure, many private businesses attempt to address these and other public values (e.g., as private security forces operate in combat zones to supplement the military arm of government), but those efforts are usually designed first to turn a profit, not to provide a service. With the public sector, the emphasis is usually reversed with the service coming first. Still, to the extent a private enterprise seeks public ends, it also falls in the public realm.

That difference in emphasis carries important implications for how managers in the different realms might manage and lead. On the positive side, public-minded managerial leaders should be able to lean more on public values to motivate employees. On the negative side, they will usually face greater difficulties in assessing the achievement of their more subjective goals.

A Priority on Process

The process by which things are done in the public realm, especially in the public sector, can be as or more important than the ultimate intended public-value outcomes. There is, for one thing, the matter of *how* decisions are made—for example, who was consulted and who wasn't? In the words of one senior official who served as a private-sector chief executive before becoming a secretary of a federal agency, "Possibly the most difficult adjustment a business executive who moves into a top job in Washington has to make is learning to live with a far more complex decision-making process, in which just about everyone wants to have his say, and which he can influence but not control" (Blumenthal 1983, 29).

The principal reason for this difference is straightforward. Believing in democratic theory, people see government as "of the people," and consequently are more likely to believe that decisions made by government should reflect the wishes of the people or at least of their elected representatives. Whose opinions are solicited and heard during decision making can then become salient issues.

As another element of the priority on process, people who make requests of government often value how they were treated—promptly? courteously? fairly?—as highly as whether they ultimately received the product or service they requested. In Fountain's (2001, 58) description, "customers find it difficult to distinguish clearly between the quality of an intangible service and the process by which the service was rendered."

These concerns arise in the private sector, too, but seldom hold the same valence. Citizens are more likely to feel they are owed high-quality treatment by government—because, again, it is "of the people"—than by private enterprise. In addition, since many governmental entities function as monopolies—that is, with no competitors in their jurisdictions—people may legitimately perceive no option to exit if they want to be treated better. Voice in the form of complaining about process may appear the only viable option.

A Value for Diversity and Representativeness

One cannot go very far in reading about the contemporary workplace, regardless of sector, without encountering encouragement to increase workforce diversity. Employers are frequently encouraged to hire more employees from underrepresented groups and to make other organizational changes (e.g., training) as may be necessary to accommodate increased diversity (e.g., Bolman and Deal 2017, 152–153).

Even if diversity and representativeness are becoming societal values, they are still given higher priority in the public realm, especially the public sector. For one thing, democratic systems rest in part on the principle of representativeness. Since decisions can seldom be made by plebiscite, by everyone voting or having the opportunity to vote, elected representatives must make those decisions on behalf of the larger public. Their decisions may be viewed as legitimate only if perceived as accurately representing the public. Private businesses face no comparable challenge.

The administrative side of American government also has a long history of pursuing better representation of the public in its ranks (Krislov and Rosenbloom 1981). The public bureaucracy has always provided a pathway for upward mobility for immigrant groups in the United States, leading to better representation of those groups, dating back at least to Jacksonian democracy in the nineteenth century and its philosophy of "to the victor goes the spoils."

Concerns for representative bureaucracy gained an even higher priority in the public realm about a half-century ago when many observers contended that disadvantaged groups, African Americans in particular, had been largely excluded from much of government employment. Similar complaints soon surfaced from other groups, such as women and Hispanics, prompting calls to improve their representation, too. A variety of programs ensued, with Equal Employment Opportunity and Affirmative Action as perhaps the two most prominent examples, demonstrating the increased importance of diversity as a value for the public realm.

While the changes came earlier and were initially more extensive in the public sector, they soon reached other sectors. The social focus of much of the work of the nonprofit sector meant that diversity and representativeness would quickly become a priority. Even in the private sector, diversity and representativeness eventually achieved salience for many managers, increasing the resemblance of their work to that of public-minded managerial leaders.

The Special Resources of the Public Realm

Public-minded managerial leaders are fortunate to have available a few resources that are mostly unavailable outside the public realm. The first of those derives from those different goals.

Public Service Motivation

Their focus on public-serving goals gives public-minded managerial leaders a potentially invaluable resource. As an immense and growing literature documents, public-serving goals underlie the public service motivation (PSM) that drives the work of many public- and nonprofit-sector and even some private-sector employees. As Wise (2004, 674) has explained the concept, public service motivation "causes individuals to perform acts that contribute to the public good as a way of satisfying their personal needs." PSM explains a lot about why many employees choose the public or nonprofit sector over the private sector in the first place and how well they perform once hired.

PSM holds obvious relevance for public-minded managerial leaders. For one thing, PSM likely represents their own principal personal motivation; one might question why anyone would take a leadership role in either the public or nonprofit sector absent strong personal PSM. After all, the private sector offers more lucrative and often less demanding opportunities. Those who choose instead to labor in the public realm presumably are drawn to the sense of meaning and purpose that public service can provide.

More important for the work of these managers, PSM offers a potential means for motivating employees. By motivating through the nature of the work rather than through material incentives, PSM can even prove "a low-cost driver of job satisfaction" (Homberg et al. 2015). Managers working in either the public or nonprofit sector should consequently consider how PSM might be used to spur better performance from employees (see Chapter 6).

The Authority of Democratic Government

A democratic polity endows public agencies and their leaders with the special authority that derives from its foundation in the consent of the governed. That authority is in part legal or constitutional; an agency can exercise authority delegated to it by elected bodies and officials or by founding documents. This authority may include powers to allocate funds, to issue regulations, and to sanction violations of regulations, sometimes with recourse to the use of force. That represents an impressive range of possible formal powers for managers who work in the governmental area of the public realm.

The public sector also offers access to forums where issues can be debated and authoritatively resolved. These forums include legislative chambers, courtrooms, city council meeting chambers, and various other governmental offices. Carrying the imprimatur of government, these venues often confer a special legitimacy that can add force to any decisions made on their grounds (Ostrom 1990, 100).

Governmental authority is also in part informal: An arm of government often exercises authority in part because the public views that arm—as a part of government—as legitimate. Former Georgia Governor Joe Frank Harris tells the story of a coastal resident who refused requests to vacate in the face of an approaching hurricane. In a last-ditch effort to overcome the man's resistance, the governor instructed emergency workers to tell the man that the governor himself asked him to leave. When they did, the man immediately reversed course, declaring, "If the governor says to leave, I'll leave." That is the power of informal authority in action.

Whether formal or informal or both, that authority represents a resource for public sector leaders. True, they must wield power cautiously since a heavy-handed assertion of formal authority can antagonize even as overreliance on informal authority can smack of empty bravado. Between those extremes, savvy public leaders will find this unique authority a valuable resource for leading.

While not sharing in that democratic authority, nonprofit agencies may benefit from the public's perception of their unique social legitimacy. Skepticism about the effectiveness of government can combine with distrust of the profit motives of the private sector to leave nonprofit agencies by default as the most trusted entities for dealing with social issues. Recent positive public discourse about the value of civil society and social capital likely further enhances the perceived legitimacy of the nonprofit sector.

The Challenges of Public Accountability

Along with its unique goals and special resources, the public realm brings some special challenges, mostly as by-products of its ultimate accountability to the public.

Flawed Political Leadership

The challenges begin with the nature of the political leadership to whom public-minded managerial leaders report. Managers in the public sector, in particular, often encounter difficulties as a consequence of common flaws in the nature of political leadership in democratic systems of government.

"Amateur" political overseers. Although public managers report to elected political overseers who are counterparts to private sector boards of directors, the two types of overseers often differ in important ways. Most notably, elected officials frequently achieve their positions without benefit of training or experience for those positions. Many of these officials ran for office as "outsiders," claiming to be better qualified on the basis of their *inexperience* with the very governments they want to lead. As well, to the extent a career ladder exists for elected officials, its rungs often ascend from one level of government to another, from local to state or state to federal. The resulting movement of elected officials between levels of government limits the expertise they can develop for work at any one level of government. In the private sector, by contrast, executives are more likely to climb corporate ladders by building their relevant expertise as they rise. Term limits, where they limit the tenure of elected officials, exacerbate the problem by forcing officials from office at about the time they may have begun to understand their jobs. As a result, elected officials can lack in-depth knowledge or understanding of the governments they oversee.

That lack of understanding sometimes translates to effective professional management being given low priority. A common complaint holds that "too often elected officials charged with overseeing public organizations show too little concern with effectively managing them" (Rainey 2014, 9). That can leave public-minded managerial leaders without the support they need from higher levels.

Even worse, these amateur elected officials can hamper the work of professional managers by not respecting boundaries between the political and administrative realms, choosing instead to intervene on matters that are traditionally viewed as the prerogative of professional administrators. Often, they do so at the behest of constituents who are dissatisfied with the direct response they received from an agency. At the local level, for example, municipal elected officials are notorious for pressuring their traffic engineering departments to install a traffic light or stop sign where residents, but not the traffic engineers themselves, believe one is needed.

Local school boards can suffer from the same affliction, with critics arguing that the boards are too often comprised of inexperienced lay people who meddle in a complex and technically demanding profession (Sell 2006). Despite regular critiques that school boards are outdated and incapable of properly managing educational reform and student achievement (Land 2002), the boards mostly persist unchanged as another domain for amateur political leadership.

This reality could suggest a need for public-minded managerial leaders to educate their political bosses on the workings of their governments. As one former federal bureaucrat once commented, "The process of education is constantly going on, and learning about the highly technical areas that we have to deal with takes time" (Blumenthal 1983, 29). Choosing to try to educate one's boss is, however, a risky proposition since elected superiors may not welcome instruction from their subordinates. It can be all the riskier if the elected political leader did not hire that public manager in the first place, as is often the case where managers are selected through merit systems and do not exit when newly elected officials arrive. A manager could be in the position of trying to educate an elected superior who, given the choice, might have hired a different manager.

Multiple superiors. Compounding the problem, many public-minded managerial leaders must report to multiple overseers. This description applies to:

- A city manager who, in a council-manager form of government, reports to every city council member (numbering five or more in most cities).
- A county administrator who reports to a county commission (also typically numbering five or more).
- The head of a department of state government who reports to the governor, to members of legislative committees in each of two houses, and perhaps to an official advisory board, too.
- A federal administrator who serves at the pleasure of the president but is also accountable to Congressional committees and/or subcommittees.

Public managers who work with multiple overseers sometimes face difficult balancing acts. On the one hand, keeping their jobs requires that they maintain majority support of their oversight body. As a city manager who worked under a nine-member council once commented to the author, "After each election, I learn to count to five all over again." On the other hand, they must endeavor not to be perceived as overtly political and thereby possibly stepping on the toes of the elected officials to whom they report.

Managers in the private sector sometimes confront similar challenges with their boards of directors, but the challenges appear to be more common for public managers. That tendency likely reflects the difference between democratically elected governing boards with their common amateur composition and mostly appointive boards of directors.

Problematic Goals

The same public-serving goals that can motivate managers and their employees also pose problems. For one thing, as Rainey (2014, 151) has argued, these "goals are always multiple" and "often conflict with one another—maximizing one goal takes away from another goal." Consider the case of public assistance programs, such as the federal Temporary Assistance to Needy Families (TANF) program. While one TANF goal is to improve the economic well-being of recipients through financial assistance, another goal is to place recipients in jobs, thereby increasing their economic self-sufficiency and *reducing* the financial assistance they receive. Pursuit of both goals at once can sometimes result in competition between the two.

These goals draw regular criticism for being "particularly vague and intangible compared to those of private business firms" (Rainey 2014, 151–152). Greater vagueness obviously traces in part to the greater fuzziness of social goals in contrast to the clarity of a focus on profit, but it also reflects the frequently "vague mandates" agencies receive from legislative bodies. Those vague mandates may in turn represent another by-product of flawed political leadership that fails to understand the need to provide clear direction for implementing agencies. Whatever its roots, the vagueness can challenge managers to figure out exactly what they should be trying to achieve.

The Difficulties of Performance Assessment

Lack of goal clarity also creates difficulties for public-minded managerial leaders when they seek to assess the performance of their agencies, programs, and employees. How, after all, can a manager measure performance if the core goals are stated too vaguely to translate easily to specific measures?

Even when the goals are relatively clear, the extent of their achievement can prove difficult to measure. How, for example, might the effectiveness of that public assistance program mentioned earlier be assessed? Assuming a goal of improved economic well-being for program recipients, how might the responsible agency measure the effectiveness of financial assistance and/ or job training on that well-being? If the economy boomed during the time of the program, the effects of the assistance may be difficult to separate from the effects of the boom. The same dilemma arises with almost every public-serving program; program effects are not easily disentangled from the influence of other factors.

Even as public and nonprofit agencies experience more difficulty in measuring their performance than do private businesses, they also face more pressure to do so, with those pressures having grown substantially in recent decades. The 1990s brought two pieces of landmark federal legislation, the Chief Financial Officers Act (CFO)of 1990 and the Government Performance and Results Act (GPRA) of 1993, that together greatly increased the demands on federal agencies for better performance measurement (see Wholey 2010, 654–655). Presidents Barack Obama and George W. Bush both had their own programs pushing for better performance assessment by federal agencies (on the Bush administration initiative, see Moynihan 2013). Similar initiatives have proliferated in state and local governments.

Nonprofit organizations have also felt pressures to improve their performance assessment. Some of those pressures have come indirectly from the same legislative initiatives that catalyzed performance assessment initiatives in the public sector. Growing competition among nonprofits has further increased "the pressure to perform and to demonstrate that performance" (Salamon 2010, 85).

Employees in the public and nonprofit sectors have often resisted the new performance measurement regimes, adding to the challenges for public-minded managerial leaders. At the federal level, performance measurement initiatives have often been "perceived primarily as a compliance exercise rather than an opportunity to generate purposeful performance information" (Moynihan 2013, 502). Worse yet, employees sometimes work to "game" the new systems, devoting more energy to producing data favorable to the agency than to generating data to improve performance (e.g., Heinrich and Marschke 2010). At the extreme, these efforts deteriorate to falsifying data, as happened with performance testing in the Atlanta, Georgia, school system (e.g., Charles 2018).

The gaming may be understandable, if not justifiable, as a reaction to the difficulty of achieving the goals sought in the public realm. Many of the tasks that fall to government and the nonprofit sector are difficult societal problems, such as educating disadvantaged children and addressing hard-core poverty, that the private sector would not or could not address. The public and nonprofit employees who are on the front lines of trying to address such seemingly intractable problems may consequently be tempted to fudge the results of their efforts.

For public-minded managerial leaders, these realities of performance measurement initiatives carry difficult implications. At a minimum, the initiatives will require substantial managerial time, yet without any guarantee of actual improvements in performance.

A Bent Toward Self-Regulation

The legislative history behind performance management initiatives illustrates another of the challenges of public accountability, the tendency for public agencies to be hamstrung by extensive self-imposed rules and regulations. In the governmental part of the public realm, in particular:

> Hierarchical and legal accountability exert high degrees of control. The hierarchical form involves imposition of rules, procedures, scrutiny,

and other controls from within an agency. Legal accountability . . . involves high levels of control from external sources, in the form of oversight and monitoring by external authority." (Rainey 2014, 106)

Governmental agencies are constrained, in particular, in their ability to spend money and to hire and fire employees, with many financial and personnel actions requiring so many approvals that administrators hesitate to initiate either (Bozeman and Rainey 2000, 455–456). Ironically, given how much criticism government takes for supposedly overregulating private businesses, its self-regulation may be even more pronounced.

Excessive financial controls result in part from the reaction of amateur elected overseers to occasional well-publicized financial missteps of particular public agencies. Whenever any administrative financial misbehavior or just *perceived* financial misbehavior gains the public's attention, elected officials often respond reflexively by imposing new regulations, believing in the power of more controls to deter future misbehavior. Perhaps blinded by their inexperience, these officials may not recognize how regulations can also stifle innovation and efficiency.

Restrictions on authority over personnel likely have different roots. On the one hand, earlier civil service reforms prescribed detailed rules for hiring and firing to prevent elected officials from hiring their political supporters, regardless of merit. Former New York City Deputy Mayor Stephen Goldsmith (2010, 57) has decried "a civic service system that punishes good workers by rewarding those who are not." As he asked rhetorically: "Do we really need the elongated disciplinary system that protects the incompetent and lazy, thus shoving work on the rest?"

On the other hand, the power of public unions has produced additional rules that further protect employees from being fired or having their jobs changed. In Goldsmith's words (2010, 56), "multiple levels of legal protections create a barrier to collaboration between management and labor." The regulations are sometimes so severe that, "Even talking to employees about how to do things better can be against the rules."

These restrictions do not affect all parts of government, and they mostly do not apply to the nonprofit sector. Where they exist, though, these restrictions unquestionably limit the ability of many contemporary public sector managers to innovate. Whatever their merits historically, many of these rules and regulations have questionable contemporary value.

Financial Constraints

Most of the government and nonprofit sectors must confront all of these challenges amid tighter financial constraints than in decades past. The two sectors both face tighter budgets and more competition for maintaining their roles in the public realm.

Financial austerity. Government and much of the nonprofit sector will likely function for the foreseeable future in a climate of financial austerity. For government specifically, persisting budget deficits imply needs to cut or eliminate programs or, at the least, to adapt and survive without budget growth. At the federal level in the United States, austerity would seem to be assured in light of substantial recent tax cuts in combination with the failure to address the budget overruns and the growing federal debt.

Nonprofit agencies have also recently "confronted a significant fiscal squeeze" (Salamon 2010, 79–80). Financial wounds from the 1980s that appeared to be healing in the 1990s were reopened; first, in the early years of the new century by a combination of tax reductions, economic recession, and increased military and anti-terror spending that caused new cutbacks in health, education, and social welfare spending, and therefore new pressures on nonprofit finances; and second, by the deep recession that struck the nation late in the century's first decade and generated enormous new strains on nonprofit operations.

Increased market exposure. Even as public and nonprofit entities contemplate a future of tight budgets, they also face increased exposure to competitive economic markets, markets that could threaten the traditional domains of these entities. Since the 1980s, various reform initiatives have pushed governments across the globe to become more economically competitive in order to address the perceived inefficiency of monopolistic governmental agencies. As the most prominent of these reforms, the New Public Management pushed governments to operate more like businesses, in part through increased market exposure. As a result, statist economies around the world privatized many industries that once operated as public monopolies. At lower levels of government, as with local governments in the United States, many municipalities either contracted out services that were once wholly government produced and delivered, or put their traditional departments in bidding competitions with private contractors (e.g., Hefetz and Warner 2004).

Nonprofit entities face their own pressures from increased market exposure. A variety of factors appears to "have enticed for-profit competitors into an ever-widening range of fields and to have given them a competitive edge" (Salamon 2010, 82). As a result, for-profit firms have steadily increased their market share relative to nonprofits in many traditionally nonprofit service areas in recent years.

Public and nonprofit managers must consequently cope with the dual threats of tighter budgets and increased competition for the services they provide. They must learn how to lead with a severely constrained financial base, recognizing that new revenues will come only infrequently, even as they must remain alert to possible competition, whether from the private sector or from entrepreneurial actors in the public and nonprofit sectors.

A Skeptical Citizenry

If these challenges were not sufficiently daunting, public-minded managerial leaders must also cope with a skeptical citizenry ready to question much of what they do. That citizenry can find more to question, too, in an era of easier access to information on the operations of public and quasi-public entities.

Pervasive public distrust. This aspect of the public accountability challenge begins with the persistent high levels of public distrust about the work of government and of most other institutions of society. According to a nationwide poll conducted by the Center for Public Leadership at the Harvard Kennedy School, 69 percent of Americans perceive a leadership crisis (Rosenthal 2012). By 2015 "only 19 percent of Americans" said they "trust the federal government always or most of the time" (Malone 2016). Some of that distrust may represent a spillover of cynical attitudes about political institutions, but, whatever its roots, the distrust of the public is a contemporary fact of life for public-minded managerial leaders.

Working in a fish bowl. Governmental work has often been likened to working in a fish bowl in that everything that happens can seem open for all to see (e.g., Allison 1983, 78). Even when not immediately open to public scrutiny, the action of a governmental entity can readily become subject to the glare of public light if someone asks the right question or requests the right embarrassing information.

Two principal factors underlie this greater transparency of the work of the public sector. At the core, the citizenry as the funders of government is more concerned with the appropriateness of governmental activities than with the appropriateness of activities in the private sector. Citizens want to know if government is spending its revenues, the taxes *they* paid, appropriately or wastefully. That principle can produce a similar attitude toward nonprofit agencies: Just as citizens care how government spends the money they paid as taxes, so they also care about how nonprofit agencies spend the money they *gave* as donations. By contrast, they seldom care about how a private business spends its money.

As a second factor, recent freedom of information policies and sunshine laws make the work of government, if not the nonprofit sector, more readily knowable. Here the media play a major role through their tendency, in the words of a former federal bureaucrat, "to look for mistakes, because mistakes are more interesting than normal progress" (Blumenthal 1983, 24). Acting on that tendency, the media use freedom of information policies as a basis for requesting governmental documents that might reveal misbehavior.

Beyond these unique characteristics of the public realm, the Google phenomenon of being able to ask and answer questions with a keystroke or two illustrates how so much more information has become easily accessible to so many. The spread of computers in combination with the worldwide web give many people access to information that was once limited to a few. Where information could be described a generation ago as a "leaky" resource that that was difficult to contain (Cleveland 1975), it might more aptly be described as porous today.

For all of these reasons, working in government—and, to some extent, in the nonprofit sector—can feel more than ever like working in a fishbowl. More of the work of these entities is now open to public scrutiny with more potential critics joining in that scrutiny. Work in the private sector seldom brings a comparable transparency, and evidence of private sector misbehavior seldom receives the same attention or arouses the same public ire.

The Uniqueness of the Nonprofit Sector

The nonprofit side of the public realm faces both similar and different resources and challenges from those faced by the governmental side. The comparison begins with some similar resources:

- Public service motivation. Like the public sector, the nonprofit sector seeks mostly public-serving goals, creating the potential to catalyze employee performance through recourse to public service motivation.
- A unique social legitimacy. In an environment of skepticism about government and distrust of private sector due to its overriding profit motives, nonprofit agencies may gain a unique legitimacy as the most trusted entities for dealing with social issues.

In the realm of challenges, the nonprofit sector faces some issues similar to those faced by the public sector, including:

- Problematic goals. Nonprofit agencies also struggle with goals that are vague, multiple, and conflicting.
- Difficulties with performance assessment. Problematic goals result in difficulties in assessing performance where nonprofit entities, like governments, feel strong pressures to improve their efforts.
- Financial constraints. Also like government, the nonprofit sector

must cope with limited financial resources even as it faces increasing market competition.

- A skeptical citizenry. Nonprofit entities must also be wary of the wrath of a skeptical public, if perhaps not as keenly as is the case for governments.

On the other hand, the nonprofit sector is fortunate not to be troubled by some elements of public accountability that challenge governmental agencies. Nonprofit entities mostly do not encounter issues with:

- Flawed leadership. While leadership issues can arise anywhere, non-profits are at least not subject to the problems of political leadership that are inherent to government.
- A bent toward self-regulation. Nor do nonprofits mostly suffer from a tendency to over-regulate their own activities.

At the same time, the nonprofit sector confronts some unique challenges, of which the most notable may be:

- A movement "from producer to consumer subsidies." Where in the past government support came directly to nonprofits, support in recent decades has "shifted to forms of assistance such as vouchers and tax expenditures that channel aid to the consumers of services instead, thus requiring nonprofits to compete for clients in the market" (Salamon 2010, 80). That shift increases the uncertainty about how much governmental assistance will come to nonprofits.
- The "tepid growth of private giving." Government cutbacks in direct funding for nonprofits have not been offset by increased private giving as that giving has actually declined in recent decades as a share of personal income (Salamon 2010).

Looking across all of these factors suggests, on average, a more promising environment for nonprofit agencies—and thus for their leaders and managers—than for governmental agencies. Still, public-minded managerial leaders in both sectors confront a difficult and challenging context in which to try to lead.

Latitude for Leadership?

Even with the many challenges they face, latitude remains for public-minded managerial leaders to lead and manage effectively. For one reason, none of these leaders is likely to confront all of the challenges at once. The typical public-minded managerial leader will likely need to deal with only *some* of these challenges at any given time. That leader will also likely have access to at least some of the unique resources of the public realm, such as public service motivation and either the authority of democratic government or the unique legitimacy of the nonprofit sector.

Consistent with this thinking, ample anecdotal evidence can be found of public-minded managerial leaders proving effective and successful in the face of these challenges, sometimes even transforming their organizations into more effective vehicles for achieving public-serving goals. The cases of Charles Rossotti and Bill Bolling, both profiled briefly in the opening chapter, are illustrative. Rossotti for his part spearheaded a successful transformation of the U.S. Internal Revenue Service, an agency which, given its checkered history, was likely subject to as many of the challenges of public accountability as any public agency ever is. Working in the somewhat less constrained nonprofit sector but initially without any formal power, Bolling succeeded in building the enormously successful Atlanta Community Food Bank despite having to struggle continuously with the resource stringency that is characteristic of the nonprofit world.

Beyond the anecdotal evidence, broader studies also demonstrate that motivated public-minded managerial leaders can produce positive change in the public realm. Most notably, Sandford Borins (2000) has documented the success of many governmental innovators in achieving "creative solutions to public-sector problems." Their successes mostly came only after overcoming obstacles both internal and external to their agencies, in other words, only by their successfully confronting the challenges of public accountability.

Those successes did require the ability to lead, as by consulting, compromising, and persuading as well as sometimes coaching. Those techniques help to explain how the innovators could gain "support for their ideas from many sources, both inside and outside the public sector" (Borins 2000, 503). The likely route to those successes is the subject of the rest of this book, beginning in the next chapter with how to build the personal foundation to lead.

Personal Leadership Exercise 2.1

What's Different About Where You Work?

Dimension	Low	Medium	High
How important?			
Public-serving goals			
Priority on process			
Value on diversity & representativeness			
Extent of these resources in your agency?			
Public service motivation			
Authority of democratic government			
Extent of these challenges in your agency?			
Flawed political leadership			
Problematic goals			
Performance assessment difficulties			
Extensive self-regulation			
Financial constraints			
A skeptical citizenry			
Working in a fish bowl			

Considering all of your answers, how much latitude do you see to lead in your agency?

Chapter 3

Building the Personal Foundation

Success in leading as a public-minded managerial leader will come more easily to those who have already built a strong personal foundation for leading. Judging from extensive research on leadership and leaders, that foundation should include emotional intelligence, a personal sense of leadership as service, a clear set of values to pursue, and a vision of how to achieve those values.

Any discussion of how to lead should begin with a review of these foundational elements, addressing what the elements include and how would-be or actual public-minded managerial leaders can develop them. With these goals in mind, this chapter will discuss in sequence emotional intelligence, leadership as service, the choice of values leaders will pursue, and the two types of visions leaders should develop to guide their efforts.

Emotional Intelligence: A *Sine Qua Non* for Leadership?

Some of the earliest writing on leadership argued for specific individual traits as the basis for effective leadership. Different scholars emphasized such diverse traits such as intelligence, self-confidence, charisma, and determination, to mention just a few. By the second half of the twentieth century, however, most scholars of leadership had turned their attention elsewhere, in part because the sole focus on immutable inherited traits offered no path for developing leaders. How can leaders develop if their leadership potential is essentially determined at birth?

Yet, when contemplating the personal roots of leadership, there remains value in thinking about traits, or at least about the more potentially changeable "personal characteristics." Starting from that perspective almost a quarter-century ago, Daniel Goleman (1998) proposed that emotional intelligence (EI), a composite of five personal characteristics, represents a *sine qua non* of leadership. Without some minimum of emotional intelligence, Goleman predicted that anyone's potential to lead would be severely limited. In his view, emotional intelligence might be even more important for the ability to lead than is basic intelligence (IQ). Emotional intelligence for Goleman includes these components: (1) self-awareness, (2) self-regulation, (3) empathy, (4) social skill, and (5) motivation. Each of the five merits additional definition.

Self-awareness entails "having a deep understanding of one's emotions, strengths, weaknesses, and drives" (Goleman 1998). People who are more self-aware know what arouses their emotions, what they do well, what they do not do well, as well as what kinds of work they like and do not like. Self-awareness means greater self-understanding, which could increase comfort with one's personal nature. For leaders specifically, the principal value of self-awareness likely lies in the cues it provides for self-development. Becoming aware of personal weaknesses, for example, might lead to efforts to address.

For many people, self-awareness could include a recognition of an aversion to conflict since that aversion is widely shared. Becoming aware of that tendency might prompt an effort to prevent that aversion from becoming a personal limitation. That might be especially important for leaders since a leader who is conflict-averse risks being manipulated by others who are not.

For others, self-awareness might include a sense of difficulty in dealing with authority figures, perhaps tracing back to childhood conflicts with parents. If left unaddressed, that difficulty could result in a would-be leader balking at taking direction from a work superior, potentially a poor choice if that direction is appropriate. The eventual outcome could be, as popular musician John Mellencamp has lamented, "I fight authority, authority always wins."

Self-regulation, the second EI component, refers to an individual's ability to express and control feelings. It does not mean that feelings are suppressed, only that the individual can and does control when and how those feelings are expressed. Nor does it preclude the expression of strong feelings since, if appropriately self-regulated, that expression could have value. Consider this comment made by a former Army general to a class of master's students: "I never lose my temper . . . unless it's intentional." For him, in other words, *appearing* to lose his temper was actually a choice to *show* his temper, calculating—and self-regulating—the show of anger for strategic effect. The same approach could work with positive feelings, with leaders sometimes acting enthusiastic in the hope of motivating or persuading others.

Self-regulation matters for leaders because "people who are in control of their feelings and impulses—that is, people who are reasonable—are able to create an environment of trust and fairness. . ." Such an environment can do wonders for an organization's human resource management because

"Talented people flock to [such an] organization and aren't tempted to leave" (Goleman 1998, 28).

Empathy refers to the ability to understand and "thoughtfully consider others' feelings" (Goleman 1998, 31). Empathic leaders listen closely when others express their feelings, attempt to understand those feelings, and may be more inclined to try to solve problems those others have voiced. At the same time, empathy:

> doesn't mean adopting other people's emotions as one's own and trying to please everybody. That would be a nightmare—it would make action impossible. Rather, empathy means thoughtfully considering employees' feelings—along with other factors—in the process of making intelligent decisions.

Empathy can be an effective means for building support among others, and that support in turn can translate to a willingness to follow. When people feel heard and understood, they typically are more supportive of those who listened and understood (see also Chapters 4 and 5).

Social skill refers to the ability to interact with other people, especially about work-related issues. It has been described as "friendliness with a purpose" where the purpose is the connection to work. As such, it is not simply what was once termed "water-cooler" conversation, where employees make small talk in a common work space, but conversation that links in part to work and to how to do that work more effectively. Goleman (1998, 34) views social skill as "the culmination of the other dimensions of emotional intelligence," grown, as it were, from roots in self-awareness, self-regulation, and empathy.

Social skill holds obvious relevance for the effectiveness of public-minded managerial leaders. In Goleman's (1998, 33) description, "Socially skilled people tend to have a wide circle of acquaintances, and they have a knack for finding common grounds with people of all kinds—a knack for building rapport." That rapport can be invaluable to leaders as they pursue organizational ends.

Social skill may be especially important in organizations that are more team-oriented since that orientation brings a higher organizational value on social interactions. By contrast, social skill appears to be less important, if not unimportant, for leaders in organizations where work is more technical and solitary (Anderson, Spataro, and Flynn 2008).

Motivation, the fifth and last EI component, means for Goleman being "driven to achieve beyond expectations." It includes the two dimensions of (1) having a passion for the work itself, not principally for material rewards (e.g., salary), and (2) being optimistic, expecting and communicating high expectations for the success of the work. The highly motivated, Goleman has argued, will maintain their optimism even when things are going badly.

In reality, while a strong personal foundation for public-minded managerial leadership likely requires motivation, it may not require the degree of motivation that Goleman suggests. It will likely suffice, for one thing, to *desire* to achieve beyond expectations, without needing to be *driven*; the latter could even imply a lack of self-regulation. In addition, leaders sometimes need to recognize that their optimism was misplaced, that things are going badly could mean that an effort should be abandoned. As Daniel Kahneman (2011) has documented, leaders have sometimes let the glow of past successes blind them to the reality of current failures. Effective leaders will not be blinded by unbridled optimism.

True emotional intelligence may include one additional element beyond Goleman's list, an element that is often termed "character." Character refers to an individual's moral makeup and commitments, with people who are perceived as having strong moral values often described as having character. Character may include integrity, meaning honesty and consistency, as well as courage, such as the "courage to make tough and unpopular decisions" (Keohane 2012, 111). A leader who has all of the other elements of emotional intelligence likely would not succeed without having character, too; at the same time, having those other elements might also help to nurture character. Finally, some research suggests that character and competence both contribute to leadership effectiveness (Sturm, Vera, and Crossan 2017).

Judging from Goleman's research, higher levels of emotional intelligence characterize the most effective leaders. These leaders may not be at the high end on every one of the five elements of emotional intelligence, but they are likely to have developed high levels of most of the five. Emotional intelligence is not important only for leaders, either. Ample evidence indicates that greater emotional intelligence also translates to higher levels of job satisfaction for all employees, not just leaders (e.g., Lee 2018).

For would-be public-minded managerial leaders, the importance of emotional intelligence suggests that its five dimensions might be prioritized as personal developmental targets. Potential leaders might contemplate where they fall on each of the five as well as whether to attempt corrective action where they feel themselves lacking. As for how to do that, Warren Bennis (1994, 60–61), one of the giants of leadership research, offers this simple recommendation: "True understanding comes from reflecting on your experience." As Bennis documents, that reflection is a common habit of high-profile leaders. Aspiring public-minded managerial leaders may benefit from developing that habit.

Servant-Leadership Theory and the Desire to Serve

At some point, an opportunity to lead arises for almost everyone and a decision must be made on whether to pursue the opportunity. That question can arise when an agency head is promoted or chooses to step down or when the agency announces a plan to create a new team, requiring selection of a team leader. In any of those scenarios and others, some who work in the agency may ask themselves: Should I throw my hat in the ring for this position?

"Servant-leadership" theory, a prescriptive theory originally developed by retired AT&T executive Robert Greenleaf, counsels that the choice should be driven by whether one wants to serve. According to the theory, those who want to serve—the purposes of the organization or of a cause—should accept or at least seriously consider the opportunity, and those who do not wish to serve should decline. In contemplating leadership roles, in other words, people should ask if they want to serve the organization or the cause to which they would be committing. In Greenleaf's words (2007, 83):

> The servant-leader is servant first . . . It begins with a natural feeling that one wants to serve, to serve *first*. Then conscious choice brings one to aspire to lead. That person is sharply different from one who is *leader* first, perhaps because of the need to assuage an unusual power drive or to acquire material possessions [emphasis in original].

As the second part of Greenleaf's recommendations, people should not accept managerial leadership positions principally for reasons of personal self-interest, such as material gains or a desire for power. From the perspective of the organization, individuals who take leadership positions principally for reasons of personal advancement or enhanced power cannot be expected to think first about what's best for the organization and its purposes, and the organization is consequently likely to suffer. From the perspective of the would-be leaders, those who prioritize self-interest make a poor fit for their organizational roles, likely resulting in personal discomfort.

As well, others in the organization are likely to perceive and perhaps resist their leaders' lack of commitment to the organization's goals, undermining their ability to lead. In Greenleaf's (2007, 81) words again, "the only authority deserving one's allegiance is that which is freely and knowingly granted by the led to the leader in response to, and in proportion to, the clearly evident servant stature of the leader."

In practice, many people undoubtedly ignore these recommendations by taking managerial leadership positions *without* being motivated principally by the desire to serve. That can happen when a leadership opportunity arises unexpectedly, and a candidate finds the potential for career advancement irresistible. Or, an opportunity appears and no one else voices interest, leaving only one candidate as the default choice. In a search for a chair of a university academic department, for example, one candidate was praised by his predecessor, who was stepping down, as having "emerged" as the best candidate. A skeptical colleague suggested sarcastically that, to the contrary, everyone else who might have been a candidate instead "receded," leaving the possible future chair as the only available candidate. For a variety of reasons, in short, organizations often choose leaders who do not accord top priority to pursuing the organization's purposes.

Fortunately, many managers who begin without the primary commitment to serve eventually adopt that orientation. Sometimes the discomfort of being at odds with what a job calls for prompts personal questioning about how to do the job better. Or, the belief in public-serving organizational values that drew those leaders to public service work in the first place may eventually redirect their attention back to the larger purposes of their organizations. Whatever the route taken, public-minded managerial leaders are likely to be more comfortable in their roles and more effective for their organizations if they see service to the organizations as their principal responsibility.

Serving for What? The Purposes of Public-Minded Managers

The idea of a commitment to serve inevitably raises the question of serving for what. What are the larger purposes or public values that public-managerial leaders should seek to enhance through their public service? To lead and manage effectively, leaders must define the specific public values they will prioritize. These values may change over the course of one's career, but, without a clear initial sense of purpose, a leader may lack the foundational values that should drive important decisions.

At the outset of a career or earlier in weighing possible careers, the best counsel for how to define that sense of purpose may come from Dr. Edward Thorp, whose career has encompassed time as a mathematics professor, inventor, entrepreneur, founder of a hedge fund, and best-selling author. Asked by students how to become successful in any of those fields, Thorp offered this advice:

> I tell them not to start out with some goal, like trying to make money.
> Instead, figure out what it is you like to do, because the activity that

you do—call it work, but it won't be work if you choose it right—the activity that you do is going to be a very large part of your life and you want to be happy doing it. So choose something that will make you happy and it's probably something that you're good at. And then, just follow your dreams in that direction and you'll more than likely find out that everything will work out very well for you.

A strong sense of personal values characterizes successful leaders in both public and private realms. In Bennis's (1994, 6) research, "of all the characteristics that distinguished" the leaders he studied, "the most pivotal was a concern with a guiding purpose." Those values could be even more important for leaders in the public realm, as illustrated by this testimonial from Admiral James Loy (Getha-Taylor 2012, 119), the well-respected former Commandant of the Coast Guard:

> values serve not only as guides but also as sources of inspiration. How do you continue to survive, how do you continue to go back to work the next morning in that kind of atmosphere? You better have the foundation that is attendant to core values and character and recognize that in there lies the strength you need to press on with the work you're challenged to do.

As for where these values originate, in American democracy they often begin with three "supreme values": life, liberty, and the pursuit of happiness (Burns 2003). These values derive, of course, from the Declaration of Independence: "We hold these truths to be self-evident, that all men are created equal, that they are endowed by their Creator with certain unalienable Rights, that among these are Life, Liberty and the pursuit of Happiness."

Sources of Public Values

More specific values will likely come from the mission of the public-minded managerial leader's organization, that is, how the organization is charged with serving and providing for the larger community. An environmental agency would likely value protection or enhancement of the environment; a social service agency might give highest priority to improving the lot of the less fortunate; and, a civil liberties organization might focus on protecting freedoms of expression and religion. Relative to Burns's three supreme values, the values of the social service agency might equate to "life," those of the civil liberties organization to "liberty," and those of the environmental protection agency to "pursuit of happiness." These are the kinds of public values that can give public-minded managers, and those they oversee, the sense of contributing to a cause larger than one's self or even the organization.

Public-minded managerial leaders can also find their public values in the codes of professional associations, such as that of the American Society for Public Administration (ASPA 2019). ASPA's code begins by affirming public administrators' "responsibility to develop the spirit of responsible professionalism within its membership and to increase awareness and commitment to ethical principles and standards among all those who work in public service in all sectors," before encouraging its members to uphold eight specific principles:

> *Advance the public interest.* Promote the interests of the public and put service to the public above service to oneself.
>
> *Uphold the Constitution and the law.* Respect and support government constitutions and laws, while seeking to improve laws and policies to promote the public good.
>
> *Promote democratic participation.* Inform the public and encourage active engagement in governance. Be open, transparent and responsive, and respect and assist all persons in their dealings with public organizations.
>
> *Strengthen social equity.* Treat all persons with fairness, justice, and equality and respect individual differences, rights, and freedoms. Promote affirmative action and other initiatives to reduce unfairness, injustice, and inequality in society.
>
> *Fully inform and advise.* Provide accurate, honest, comprehensive, and timely information and advice to elected and appointed officials and governing board members, and to staff members in your organization.
>
> *Demonstrate personal integrity.* Adhere to the highest standards of conduct to inspire public confidence and trust in public service.
>
> *Promote ethical organizations.* Strive to attain the highest standards of ethics, stewardship, and public service in organizations that serve the public.

That code encompasses Constitutional values, democratic values, social values (e.g., social equity), and managerial values (e.g., fully informing and advancing professional excellence), all of which are likely to be central to the value commitments of public-minded managerial leaders.

Finally, these leaders could also look to the now-extensive scholarly literature on public values. Jørgensen and Bozeman (2007, 359–368), in particular, proposed a comprehensive set of public values, divided into seven value constellations:

- The public sector's contribution to society: what a governmental organization seeks to do for society.
- The transformation of interests to decisions: how different perspectives on public action are converted to specific actions.
- The relationship between public administration and politicians: how appointed administrators work with their elected political superiors.
- The relationship between public administration and its environment: how a public-sector agency relates to its external stakeholders.
- Intraorganizational aspects of public administration: how different parts of public agencies relate to each other.
- The behavior of public sector employees: how public employees are treated and are expected to behave.
- The relationship between public administration and the citizens: how public agencies relate to the citizens they are supposed to serve.

Each constellation, in turn, includes many more specific public values, and the list continues to evolve as new research suggests additional dimensions (e.g., Bozeman and Johnson 2015; Bryson, Crosby, and Bloomberg 2014).

Whatever the source, those who aspire to become public-minded managerial leaders are wise to consider what public values will drive their careers as well as their work in specific leadership positions. Ultimately, as the widely-admired former State of Washington tribal liaison Colleen Jollie has argued, "One needs to be moved in one's work by what is right and wrong and by what is just" (King and Beeby 2008, 119).

Developing Visions for the Future

Public-minded managerial leaders also need to develop a vision of what they want the future to look like. With that vision, leaders can set goals for what they want to achieve and chart a path for how to move from the present to a future where those goals have been achieved. That vision should set a strategy for the leader, including a plan for what steps will be necessary to implement the strategy.

Effective leaders will typically develop two types of visions. The first is a personal vision, which sets out what the individual wants to become and how to get there. The second is the organizational or institutional vision, which describes what an organization, or a part of an organization, might seek to become under the individual's leadership.

The Personal Vision

A personal vision spells out an individual's goals and strategy, providing a plan for where that individual wants to go in the near and perhaps distant future. The idea of having a personal vision gained popularity from Stephen Covey's (1989) book, *The 7 Habits of Highly Effective People,* where having a personal vision was part of the second habit. This kind of vision can and arguably should be developed *before* one assumes a leadership position, thus to be available to help in deciding whether to accept any leadership opportunity that might arise.

To develop that vision requires some self-questioning, asking such questions as:

- What are my values (as addressed in the last section)?
- What am I passionate about, including but also possibly in addition to those values? Personal passions could include desired program outcomes (e.g., cleaner air) and desired work processes (e.g., the opportunity to work with teams or, by contrast, the opportunity to write).
- Where do I want to be in the future? What type of job? In a leadership position?
- How do I get there? What steps might be required or desirable?
- What barriers might arise? How might I address them?

The personal vision should draw from answers to the earlier questions about emotional intelligence and the desire to serve. That could include identification of specific elements of EI that need attention for the individual to reach desired goals.

From the answers to those questions should come the components of an individual's vision, including some or all of the following:

- Public or personal values the individual wants to pursue.
- Desired goals relative to those goals.
- Additional skills necessary to achieve those goals.
- How to overcome possible barriers.
- Desirable next steps.
- The kinds of jobs to seek in the future.

Most personal visions will probably not cover all of these elements, but they will address at least personal goals and how to pursue them. Consider the personal vision of Amanda Steinberg, founder of DailyWorth, self-described as "the premier site for women on all things related to money, career, and entrepreneurship." With its focus on helping women and a professed interest in "world peace," DailyWorth as a private business still falls in the public realm. Consistent with the business's focus, Steinberg's personal vision while at DailyWorth was "to use my gifts of intelligence, charisma, and serial optimism to cultivate the self-worth and net-worth of women around the world." While not covering all of the detail suggested earlier, her vision clearly covers her desired values and goals, suggesting a path for the future and linking that path to her specific skill set.

Well-thought-out personal visions typically take time to develop as individuals contemplate what they want out of life. For Bill Bolling, the founder and longtime executive director of the Atlanta Community Food Bank mentioned in Chapter 1, development of a personal vision required a number of visits to the Ebenezer Baptist Church where Martin Luther King Jr. had preached and is buried. For a time, Bolling visited there regularly, knowing that "people would do pilgrimages to places where saints were buried and to holy places that were power centers. I went to the King center as one of those places."

Once there, Bolling walked repeatedly around the King tomb, meditating and asking, "God, what do you want me to do?" And, "what am I willing to die for—because he [King] had died a martyr?" These are what in spiritual practice are termed "repeating questions." As Bolling has explained, "If you keep asking the same question, you've got to go deeper to get an answer. If you get the same answer, you keep asking the question, and you go a little deeper and a little deeper."

Eventually, Bolling found his answer, although, even then, as he recalls, "the answer wasn't go feed the hungry." Instead:

> It was to raise the consciousness, to change hearts and minds about our relationship with each other and God. And that everything is sacred. If everything's sacred, that will inform how you treat things—animals, the trees, oceans, and other people . . . . That is what I came away with, and that was the call to start a community, to have this safe place for different faith groups, different people of different capacities, mental health capacities or whatever.

That vision gave Bolling a sense of direction that would eventually lead to his creation of the Food Bank (see Chapter 4).

Personal visions can also be useful in reducing the likelihood of being pulled off the path charted in the vision. By prioritizing what the individual will try to accomplish, a vision can suggest when to say "no," that is, where to draw the line against possible distractions.

Personal visions seldom, if ever, become fixed entities. To the contrary, they require periodic review, likely once or twice a year as well as whenever new opportunities arise. Circumstances change, one's values, skills, and interests may change, all possibly calling for changes in the personal vision. Questions may also arise on whether new opportunities fit the vision and, if not, whether the opportunities are sufficiently attractive to warrant modifying the vision. Only through a regular review can individuals be assured that their formal personal vision has kept pace with their personal development.

An Organizational Vision

A different kind of vision, an organizational vision, becomes desirable whenever a public-minded managerial leader accepts a new leadership position. An organizational vision spells out what the leader wants the organization to become in the future and how to make that vision a reality. Its development will ideally be one of the first tasks undertaken by a newly-appointed managerial leader.

An organizational vision refers to an idealized picture of what an organization, in the leader's eyes, can and should become. This vision should (1) offer a picture of the future of the organization, (2) include ideas for change, (3) invoke values intended to appeal to key audiences, especially subordinates and external stakeholders, (4) provide a map of how to get from the present to the future anticipated in the vision, and (5) present a challenge to key audiences, a challenge designed in part to motivate (Bolman & Deal 2017; Northouse 2018; Yukl 2013). An effective vision also needs to be attractive, capable of attracting followers, as well as realistic, so those followers see the vision as worthy of their time.

The Peace Corps and the National Weather Service (NWS) provide two public sector examples of brief organizational vision statements, with the Peace Corps seeking "to promote world peace and friendship" and the NWS focused on "saving lives and livelihoods." While neither meets all of the vision statement criteria above, both appear to "invoke values intended to appeal to key audiences" and in a manner that is attractive and realistic. Interestingly, in choosing to invoke those values, both also make no mention of specific agency activities (i.e., Peace Corps field work, NWS weather predictions). That commonality illustrates how effective vision statements emphasize larger values over day-to-day activities.

That same description fits the vision of the nonprofit Atlanta Community Food Bank (see also Chapters 1 and 4), which seeks "to fight hunger by engaging, educating and empowering our community." This statement again invokes potentially inspiring values, in this case the values of fighting hunger and of "engaging, educating and empowering the community." The latter three values also move the vision beyond the day-to-day work of fighting hunger to broader issues of involving the larger community in the fight. Finally, the vision stays realistic by talking only of "fighting" rather than, say, "conquering" hunger.

Organizational vision statements can serve important functions for public-minded managerial leaders. Like personal visions, organizational visions can sharpen the focus for what leaders want to achieve and how they might do so. They can also provide direction and motivation for others, perhaps especially employees but also possibly client groups and the larger public, whose support could be essential for a vision to become a reality.

The visions of specific public-minded managerial leaders should reflect how they have combined their own public values with agency values, while recognizing relevant resources, opportunities, and constraints, to produce goals and a plan for the organization's development. Where leaders are responsible for only part of an organization, their visions will likely echo the vision of the organization as a whole, while perhaps incorporating additional elements specific to their narrower domain.

To develop these visions, public-minded managerial leaders should look to the nature of the positions they are assuming, consider possible goals that position implies, seek ideas from others in and around the organization, before concluding by articulating a vision for the future of their part of the organization. As that description indicates, development of an organizational vision should follow extensive consultation, including with subordinates, superiors, and external stakeholders. All of those actors may offer useful perspectives on what the organization—or a specific part of an organization—is about and might be about in a more expansive future. Asking their input may also increase the likelihood that they will support the eventual vision. (See Chapter 11 for a more detailed discussion of how to develop an organizational vision.)

Given the need for consultation, public-minded managerial leaders will want to develop their organizational visions only *after* assuming a specific leadership role. The literature on organizational behavior is replete with examples of the horrors possible when new management attempts to impose a vision without first consulting with the organization about the substance of the vision (e.g., Bolman and Deal 2017, 361–364). At best, such visions will only encounter resistance; at worst, they lead to an organization's demise.

Whatever the specifics of their approach, public-minded managerial leaders will be more effective if they begin any leadership role by developing a vision of what they hope to accomplish. As with a personal vision, any organizational vision should be viewed as subject to change, especially as leaders learn more about their organizations. At the outset, though, an organizational vision can provide an initial agenda for action by the public-minded managerial leader.

First Steps for the Public-Minded Manager

Ideally, planning for being a public-minded managerial leader should begin long before an individual actually ascends to such a position. Those who begin to plan only as they assume a leadership role risk being overwhelmed by the often-extraordinary challenges that one's first managerial position can bring. To avoid that fate, this chapter proposed a four-step process of preparation.

As the first step, would-be leaders should attempt to build a strong foundation of emotional intelligence, including all of the five elements of self-awareness, self-regulation, empathy, social skill, and motivation. Higher levels of emotional intelligence can prove invaluable for public-minded managerial leaders in gaining the support of subordinates and others, including some who may resist their direction. More emotional intelligence can also ease the strains of organizational life even when one does not face the special challenges of leading and managing.

Emotional intelligence is neither easily nor ever fully developed. Judging from the reports of many well-respected leaders (Bennis 1994), the task of developing emotional intelligence is ongoing, requiring leaders to reflect regularly on what personal experiences tell them about their emotional intelligence and about possible additional "inner work" they may still need to complete.

As the second step in preparing to lead, would-be public-minded managerial leaders need to recognize the servant nature of possible leadership roles. As Robert Greenleaf counseled, leaders should view themselves first as serving the organization or cause that they are charged to lead, devoting their primary energies to how to advance that organization or cause with the help of the people with whom they work inside and outside the organization.

Many people reach managerial leadership positions in the public realm without having grasped this principle. Fortunately, recognition often comes eventually, as when the demands of a job combine with a core strong service orientation to pull naïve leaders toward the servant-leader and public-minded managerial leader model. Some, of course, never get there, and they and their organizations likely suffer for lack of appropriate leadership. The lesson for would-be public-minded managerial leaders is clear: Think carefully about embracing the servant-leader approach before—as well as after—accepting managerial responsibilities.

As the third step, public-minded managerial leaders should consider what public values they want their service to advance. What ends do they want to seek in terms of organizational and programmatic outcomes and managerial processes? The earlier discussion suggested a range of possible purposes that public-minded managerial leaders might usefully consider relative to their specific responsibilities.

That consideration can contribute to the fourth step in preparing to be a leader, the definition of a personal vision for what the individual wants to become and eventually to an organizational vision for what the individual, once in the role of a public-minded managerial leader, wants to achieve. That vision can motivate and guide managers and those with whom they work, ideally facilitating the work of managing and leading. It can also set the stage to strategize for how to lead and manage effectively in a political environment, the topic of the next chapter.

In reality, almost anyone who has assumed a position as a public-minded managerial leader would readily admit to lacking one or more of these components at the time of achieving that status. Leadership roles are often thrust on people before they know to contemplate what the roles might entail. There is also nothing like the challenge of a new leadership role to reveal previously unknown gaps in one's emotional intelligence. As a result, while would-be public-minded managerial leaders are well-advised to prepare for those roles, they should also recognize that preparation does not end with ascension to a leadership role.

Personal Leadership Exercise 3.1

How Do You Rate Yourself on Each of the Following?

Dimension	Low	Medium	High
Emotional intelligence			
Self-awareness			
Self-regulation			
Empathy			
Social skill			
Motivation			
Desire to serve			
Clarity of public purposes you want to pursue			

What aspects, if any, of your emotional intelligence would you like to develop further?

What public purposes do you want to pursue?

What is your personal vision?

What is your organizational vision?

Chapter 4

Preparing for a Political World

Effective managers are effective *political* leaders. Politics refers to "activities taken within an organization to acquire, develop, and use power and other resources to obtain one's preferred outcomes" (Ferris and Treadway 2012, 11). Or, by a slightly different definition, politics can mean a "realistic process of making decisions and allocating resources in a context of scarcity and divergent interests" (Bolman and Deal 2017, 183). In the context of either definition, effective public-minded managerial leaders seek to build power and to develop and exercise political skills to achieve their goals. In short, they engage actively in politics.

The purpose of this chapter is to explain how current and would-be public-minded managerial leaders can prepare for that engagement by building informal personal power and developing political skills. The chapter examines a range of sources of informal power and a variety of political skills, as well as how to use those skills to apply power to achieve organizational ends. Both elements, the power and the skills, are illustrated through the story of Bill Bolling, former Executive Director of the Atlanta Community Food Bank, whose path to success shows the potential for practicing an effective, but also virtuous, political strategy.

The Debate Over Political Leadership

Managers, whether public-minded or not, work in a political world. Organizational resources are usually scarce, and that scarcity encourages competition for resources between different interests within organizations. Often those interests take the form of factions that compete with each other (see Bolman and Deal 2017, 184–186). That competition in turn inevitably leads to the exercise of power and political skills in efforts to obtain a bigger share of the organizational pie.

Many managers balk at engaging in this politics, preferring instead to be either naïve or cynical, naïve by believing politics can be ignored or cynical by thinking that joining in politics will come to no good end (Kotter 1985). Ethics often play into their thinking as many view political involvement as likely to undermine public-minded values.

This kind of thinking could seem sensible given the poor reputation of organizational politics. As Ellen, Ferris, and Buckley (2013, 844) have observed, "politics and political behavior historically have been viewed negatively in the organizational sciences." Organizational "political behavior" is sometimes even defined simply as "self-serving acts that lead to negative organizational and interpersonal outcomes." In the military, "the term *politics* is used nearly synonymously with *careerism*," referring to "a disposition toward career advancement that emphasizes non-performance-based means" (Blass and Ferris 2007, 15; emphasis in original). This is politics in a classic Machiavellian sense of favoring expediency over morality.

That reputation clearly extends to the public realm. In his book on leadership in public administration, Van Wart (2012, 130–132) argued that "excessive attraction to the acquisition of power," which is the currency of a political approach, "can be corrupting." Moreover, "extreme and excessive use of a source of power" supposedly "leads to common leadership pathologies" whereby "power becomes corruption and influence becomes manipulation so effortlessly."

Popular perceptions mostly square with those academic perspectives. As Ammeter et al. (2002, 753) have observed, "To the average person, the term *organizational politics* is likely to conjure a host of reprehensible images that include (but are not limited to) backroom manipulation, behind-the-scenes maneuvering, and self-serving posturing" (emphasis in original). These images prompt many people, in whatever sector they work, to want to avoid organizational politics.

Yet, there may be nothing wrong with politics *per se*, that is, with using power and political skills to achieve desired organizational outcomes. While those activities can be pursued selfishly and unethically (e.g., Beu and Buckley 2004), they can also be pursued ethically and with a focus on achieving publicly valued goals and enhancing organizational performance.

A growing scholarly literature in management starts from that premise to argue for politics as a potentially positive force in organizations. As Ahearn et al. (2004, 314) have argued, politics as embodied in "leader political skill" can provide "the social astuteness and behavioral flexibility and adaptability necessary to effectively address the needs and aspirations of followers in ways that favorably influence their work reactions and behavior, and indeed, affect the climate of the work unit." Indeed, "by behaving politically, leaders can do much to address the needs of followers" (Ellen, Ferris, and Buckley 2013, 843).

This perspective recommends that public-minded managerial leaders should think politically and attempt to become effective as *political* leaders. Consistent with the Ahearn et al. (2004) and the Ellen, Ferris, and Buckley (2013) perspectives on politics, the first step in that direction involves the building of power, focusing especially—for those who are preparing to lead and do not yet hold formal power—on informal personal power. Informal power refers to the authority and potential for influencing others that leaders gain based on their personal characteristics and behaviors. Indeed, given the inevitable limitations of formal authority, public-minded managerial leaders who already hold formal power will need to draw on informal power and should continue to build that power. The second step entails the development of political skills that can be used in applying power, both formal and informal, to obtain desired outcomes. These skills can convert latent power to manifest influence.

Both steps can be illustrated through the story of Bill Bolling and the Atlanta Community Food Bank (ACFB). Bolling built the ACFB from scratch, largely by building extensive informal personal power and developing and exercising a range of political skills. How he did that suggests a political strategy that aspiring public-minded managerial leaders might follow, a strategy that does not require surrendering the moral high ground.

Bill Bolling and the Atlanta Community Food Bank

After completing a master's degree at West Georgia College, Bill and his wife moved to the Atlanta area and bought "a rambling old house" in the inner city where he could begin to pursue his personal vision of starting a community that could be a "safe place for different faith groups" and "people of different capacities" (also see Chapter 3). Bill and his wife converted the house into an "interfaith community" that Bolling has described as "attracting the least and lost—folks with mental-health issues, folks with no money, folks with no place to sleep." They came for religious ceremonies, for company, and, on occasion, for food.

Bolling's first foray into feeding the hungry came at St. Luke's Episcopal Church. Atlanta at the time had only a few programs providing food to the hungry, and one of those was a free sandwich program at St. Luke's. Bolling began helping out at the church each morning, and soon was hired as the church's Director of Street Ministries. From that experience, he concluded that he "liked serving people" (Davis 2015, D4).

Bolling soon recognized the need to expand efforts to feed the hungry, and thus began a new chapter in pursuit of his personal vision. In 1978 he started to visit congregations around the city, making the same plea to each: "Provide space to feed area hungry, and I'll get the food to you." He made the plea although, as he has confessed, "I didn't have any food, or a warehouse, or a truck" (Davis 2015, D4). Still, by 1979, he found enough takers to create the Atlanta Community Food Bank, *if* he could find sufficient food to distribute.

Bolling started small in search of that food, recalling recently: "My first grocery store was Kroger; I was going behind there to the dumpster." With "a bigger vision" that required "truckloads, not the back of my car," he approached Big Star, then the biggest grocery store chain in Atlanta. After a series of discussions, he struck a deal, gaining access to Big Star's food in exchange for assisting the chain with inventory control. The Atlanta Community Food Bank was in business.

In subsequent decades, Bolling steadily expanded the volume and sources of food being collected and distributed. Where grocery stores initially donated packaged foods only, withholding fruit and vegetables for fear of spoilage, Bolling made a "moral case" for sharing produce, too, and the stores eventually agreed. In the 1980s Bolling launched Atlanta's Table, an initiative to recycle restaurant food through a partnership with ACFB. ACFB "picks up prepared, ready-to-eat food for quick turnaround from local restaurants, caterers and hotels"; Atlanta's Table then sees that the food gets to the needy (Grillo 2012, 21). Bolling was also pivotal in getting state legislation passed to protect food donors from possible liability for old food.

Consistent with his initial vision, Bolling always saw the Food Bank as about much more than food, at its heart about giving people a "safe place to tell your story. That's the way we think about it [the Food Bank] today." Or, in other words, as a reporter summarized Bolling's thinking, "Give people food, and you open the lines to communication. It is difficult, he thinks, not to share your experiences with others while eating" (Davis 2015, D4).

That philosophy has taken ACFB into numerous other areas. A Community Gardens Project catalyzed the development of almost 200 gardens in North Georgia that grow more than 100,000 pounds of food per year to feed the needy. Kids In Need collects donations of school supplies, which are then made available to teachers in the state's more than 300 Title I schools. The Atlanta Prosperity Campaign "connects working families and individuals to money-saving programs and existing benefits, such as Earned Income Tax Credits," putting money in the hands of the low-income (Davis 2015, D4).

Bolling also played a leading role in the national food bank movement, in part by working to spread his ACFB innovations around the country and world. After starting Atlanta's Table, for example, Bolling obtained a $3 million UPS grant to help start similar programs elsewhere. That program, now under the rubric of Feeding America, can be found in more than one hundred cities. Bolling was also responsible for creating Hunger 101, an ACFB education project designed "to increase awareness about hunger and poverty on the local, state and national levels." That program, too, has spread to many other food banks (Atlanta Community Food Bank 2017).

Bolling stepped down as CEO of the ACFB—by his choice—in June 2015. Expressing an interest in reducing his workload, he took a position as Board Chairman and Senior Advisor to Atlanta's new Food Well Alliance, a partner organization to the ACFB. The Alliance describes itself as part of the "local food movement," designed to put more local food on Atlanta's tables through a combination of local agriculture, grants, training, and collaboration.

Sources of Informal Power

The idea of power usually brings to mind formal power, the authority that comes with holding an official position, such as city manager, chief financial officer, department head, or even head of a committee. Formal power reflects the popular view of power; people tend to think of public officials as powerful based on the positions they hold. Depending on the position, formal power may include: (1) the authority to hire or appoint, (2) the authority to discipline and/or terminate employees, (3) control of rewards (e.g., salary increases), and (4) agenda setting authority (i.e., the ability to prioritize the issues an organization will address).

Bill Bolling began his food bank career with no formal power. He had no organization, much less an official position with any formal authority. He had little more than a desire to serve, initially without even a clear sense of where to focus that service. To move from that desire to the iconic reality of the contemporary ACFB, Bolling had to develop and rely on extensive informal personal power.

Informal power reflects "personal qualities that build power," to use Jeffrey Pfeffer's (2010, 42-43) terminology. Pfeffer's book, *Power: Why Some People Have It—and Others Don't*, provides a good place to start in thinking about the different types of informal power that people, perhaps especially aspiring public-minded managerial leaders, can develop in organizations.

Energy. Pfeffer (2010, 45) proposes a list of the personal qualities that can translate to informal power. Energy ranks high on that list, with Pfeffer asserting that he knows "of almost no powerful person who does not have boundless energy" and is not willing to work "prodigious hours." According to Yukl (2013, 143), a high energy level is necessary for managers to "cope with the hectic pace, long hours, and unrelenting demands of most managerial jobs."

Bill Bolling clearly fits that description. As a colleague commented, "He has a strong work ethic. He doesn't get outworked." His energy level represents a first source of his informal political power.

Ambition. Ambition also ranks high on Pfeffer's (2010, 44-45) list. As he has explained, "Ambition—a focus on achieving influence—can help people overcome the temptation to give up or to give in to the irritations" of organizational life. In addition, a willingness "to make the necessary sacrifices . . . requires some driving ambition." Ambition may well be the equivalent of the motivation component of Goleman's (2003) emotional intelligence.

Bill Bolling clearly had ambition, but of a kind that suggests how the concept can play out differently in the public realm. His ambition did not fit Pfeffer's sense of a driving need to succeed. He had no interest in pursuing success as a businessman, though he believes he could have succeeded there: "I have a business degree, I'm an entrepreneur, I could have gotten very rich." Nor did he want to become a minister, despite obvious reasons for doing so. In his words again: "I'm ordained, my mother wanted me to have a big Baptist church in Greensboro. That's fine, Mom, but that isn't what God called me to do."

Bolling's ambition, as a former ACFB board member observed in an interview, "was more focused on the broader community than it was on him, realizing that if he does this for the broader community, he's going to do just fine." It is an ambition that reflects Bolling's strong desire to serve community needs (e.g., Perry and Wise 1990; Wise 2004). As such, his ambition is like that of other public-minded managerial leaders.

Focus. Focus can be another source of informal power; the individual who is clearly focused on a goal gains power from that focus. For Pfeffer (2010, 46-47), focus has several dimensions: (1) "specialization in a particular industry or company," (2) "concentration on a limited set of activities or functional skills," and (3) a more specific emphasis "on those activities within your particular job or position that are the most critical."

Perhaps so, but Bolling's example implies that a sharp focus may not always come quickly—he describes his effort as "a good ten-year process"— yet did not prevent eventual success. Knowing that he wanted to start a community, the next question for Bolling was how. The former ACFB board member suspects that Bolling's eventual focus on feeding the hungry may have been an accident of history and circumstance: "I think he could have taken a service tool in lots of different directions. . . . He got engaged at St. Luke's in the soup kitchen, and figured out, wait a minute, there's a bigger need, and just kind of built on that. All of a sudden, he had a food bank in the back of St. Luke's that needed more space."

Bolling himself has characterized the St. Luke's experience as showing him how food, relationships, and religion can combine synergistically: "I started in a church, I started on the streets, I started with seeing people around a table and sharing a meal together. So, I knew the power of relationships. Food is just a commodity; the relationship is what will bring about change." Bringing it all back to the church, he has concluded, "The food is there, and the people come, and you start that relationship over again."

Bolling's eventual focus on feeding the hungry—and the broader interest in relationships linked to food—likely became part of his informal power and a resource for building the ACFB. In his earlier years, however, the more important elements were probably his energy (the indefatigable work ethic) and ambition (the strong desire to serve). The same likely holds for many public-minded managerial leaders who need time to chart their path in life.

Empathy. Empathy, the "ability to put yourself in another's place," is another personal characteristic that Pfeffer sees as potentially "useful for acquiring power" (Pfeffer 2010, 51–52). To succeed in working with others, he has argued, "you need to understand where the other is coming from." The resulting feeling of being understood can translate to informal power in working with those others.

Bolling's approach to his work incorporates empathy prominently, as illustrated by his story about a young homeless mother who came to see him in his pre-Food-Bank days. At the time, Bolling worked in the soup kitchen in the morning and counseled troubled people in a church office in the afternoon. Assessing the young woman's situation quickly, Bolling recalls that he "got her a hotel room, told her where to go get clothes, got her some meal vouchers." Her response was unexpected, as Bolling has recounted:

> "Reverend Bill, you don't really want to help me, do you? You don't really trust me, do you? You don't really respect me?" I'm like, did I say something, did I do something? No, I'm treating you with the greatest dignity. I'm trying to help you. And she says to me, "I know where all that stuff is. You know, I've been out here for several months. I just need somebody to be with. I just need somebody who won't judge me.

I just need someone who will listen to me and my story because I'm not a bad person."

The lesson of that experience for Bolling was eye opening: "Wow, two years of graduate school and I never learned that. I realized that taking time to be with was a lot more important than what I put in the soup. And that's true through my whole career." From the perspective of Pfeffer's arguments, "taking time to be with" exemplifies empathy.

Colleagues' descriptions of Bolling also emphasize his empathy. Consider this comment from the former ACFB board member: "His ability to understand what an individual's verbal and non-verbal communication skills are saying and communication patterns are indicating is pretty spectacular. When he hears words that aren't consistent with the body language, he probes, and he wants to understand fully." While Bolling does not think of his empathy in terms of power, it undoubtedly translates to informal power in working with others.

Listening ability. That description suggests another source of informal power, one Pfeffer does not mention—the ability and willingness to listen and listen closely. Popular stereotypes often depict leaders barking orders rather than asking and listening. In reality, rather than mostly directing others, the best contemporary leaders are likely to be excellent listeners. As Stivers (1994, 368) has observed, "Listening is important because it helps administrators glean important information, define situations more carefully, hear neglected aspects and interests, and facilitate just and prudent action in often turbulent environments."

Listening has arguably become even more important in contemporary organizations where knowledge can be widely dispersed. Absent a willingness to ask questions and listen to the answers, leaders risk issuing orders that will fail because they are poorly informed. As well, people are more inclined to follow directions when they have had an opportunity for input. Both factors make listening an important source of informal power.

Bill Bolling regularly cites being "a good listener" as one of his strengths. His ability is suggested by the systematic approach he takes to the task of listening: "It's not like you just hear the words; you have to hear who's saying it, you have to look in the context of when they're saying it. When people feel heard, you can keep the conversation going." The former ACFB board member is one of those who has been impressed by Bolling's listening abilities, describing them as "spectacular. You talk to Bill, you are his and his attention is one hundred percent on you."

What Bolling sees himself gaining from listening illustrates its value as a source of informal power. In looking for sources of donated food, for example, Bolling notes how he "had to learn the business of the person I wanted to work with—the language, what drives them, how to save the guy money." Indeed, "You have to figure out what they think—their language, their motivations, their fears." That understanding and the resulting informal power require careful listening.

Knowledge and expertise. As those observations imply, effective listening can build one's knowledge and expertise, which then serve as an additional basis for informal power. As Rainey (2014, 204) has argued, "greater influence" tends to accrue to those who "have excellent substantive knowledge of government and its operations and institutions (for example, the legislative and administrative lawmaking processes) and of the policies and programs of the agencies in which they work."

A willingness to develop knowledge and expertise about the food industry served Bolling well when, after recognizing that starting a food bank would require a lot more food than could be found in a Kroger dumpster, he decided to approach the Big Star grocery chain. The initial visit did not go well, as he has recalled: "I went over there with a charity request, and they just kind of laughed me out, saying, 'Our margin is so low, if we make any money, we'll give it to United Way.'" Bolling persisted and, across a series of meetings over the course of a year, gradually made inroads. "They kept saying no, and I kept saying, well, let's figure it out. What's the problem we're trying to solve?" In other words, he sought to build his understanding—through more knowledge and expertise—of how the chain worked, before using that understanding to gain access to the chain's surplus groceries.

Bolling eventually learned that Big Star could not easily track inventory at its various stores. Acting on that knowledge, he began to fashion a solution that would help both sides:

> We ended up being able to say, look, we can measure that, we can inventory every single item that you get to us. We got so sophisticated that we could inventory by store. Now, I'm giving you [Big Star] a printout of which store is giving us what item. I had to build that capacity, and we had to build software and scan and so forth. When you can do that, all of a sudden Big Star is helping by giving us stuff that they can't sell.

Bolling would eventually help Big Star in other ways, too, as reported in an *Atlanta Journal-Constitution* profile: "He'd give the chain tax breaks [for charitable deductions]; help train employees in improved inventory methods; and make sure to give the grocery chain credit whenever anyone asked the source of its [the Food Bank's] food" (Davis 2015, D4).

The Big Star case is just one example of how Bolling built informal power by growing his knowledge and expertise. Ask Bolling a question about any aspect of food-related industries, and his answer immediately demonstrates the depth and breadth of his knowledge and understanding of the food industry and related industries.

Tolerance for conflict. Pushing for change can invite conflict since those advantaged by the status quo may resist. For Pfeffer (2010, 53), a willingness to face that conflict can provide another source of informal power. As he makes the case:

> Because most people are conflict-averse, they avoid difficult situations and difficult people, frequently acceding to requests or changing their positions rather than paying the emotional price of standing up for themselves and their views. If you can handle difficult conflict- and stress-filled situations effectively, you have an advantage over most people.

Bolling again provides a good example. Like many or most people, he characterizes himself as conflict-averse: "I'm a conflict avoider. I know that about myself." But he also recognized early in his career the need to change that, recalling saying to himself: "Eventually, I want to be effective, so I'm just going to have to learn it [how to deal with conflict]." As a starting place, Bolling realized that he could draw on his other personal qualities, especially his empathy and listening abilities: "I had to develop the other side—to stay in conflict or to learn how to listen and reframe, to learn how to empathize so that people really feel heard." His success is suggested by this assessment from the former ACFB board member: "He's not afraid of tough conversations . . . . If there's a controversial point, he doesn't avoid it. He raises it and he talks about it."

Trustworthiness. Being trustworthy can be another source of informal power. As is commonly observed, people are unlikely to follow someone they do not trust. Trustworthiness is accordingly a common characteristic of effective leaders. Summarizing her collection of profiles of exemplary public-minded managerial leaders, Riccucci singled out trustworthiness as one of a handful of personal characteristics "shared by all" and a contributing factor "to their efficacy in their respective policy areas." Similarly, as Van Wart has observed, "when asking followers what is the most basic element [of leadership], no matter whether they are inside or outside the organization, it is generally that the leader is *trustworthy*" (emphasis in original).

Bill Bolling is well aware of the importance of trustworthiness for leadership and, additionally, of the roots of trustworthiness in the leader being perceived as principled. As he has observed, "Leaders are only as good as their moral authority." In Bolling's case, the roots of moral authority grow from his religious background. As a former colleague observed, "He has an inner core that is really solidly built around his faith." Bolling's trustworthiness is also evident in his reputation for protecting what others confide. As the former ACFB board member commented, "He's a vault. You tell him something, and you say, this is for us, it stays for us." Those characteristics add to Bolling's informal power.

Persistence. Success often requires persistence, the ability to persevere in the face of obstacles and resistance. One marketing expert argues that "there's one consistent trend among successful individuals, and that trend is the ability to persevere" (Sachs 2016). That ability appears to be "a learned trait" and thus "most often a choice."

That ability can add to an individual's informal power, as Bill Bolling's story again illustrates. Bolling might understandably have accepted "no" as a final answer in his interactions with the Big Star grocery chain, but he chose instead to return to the table on numerous occasions over a year's time. He admits to taking advantage of the chain's sympathies for charitable causes, until his persistence finally resulted in the chain agreeing to share groceries with the fledging Food Bank.

Persistence carries risks. In particular, there is the need, as captured in the lyrics of the popular song "The Gambler," to "know when to hold them and know when to fold them," when, in other words, to abandon persistence in the face of what appears to be an impossible task. Bolling's experience suggests two responses to that risk. First, accumulated knowledge and expertise may frequently combine with strong listening abilities to nurture a feel for when a cause may be lost and persistence would be futile. Second, even the most effective leaders will sometimes persist but also fail; a case can be made that a track record of no failures likely reflects an unwillingness to take enough risks. Bolling himself will readily admit to numerous failures when his persistence did not yield success. His overall record, though, shows those failures paling in comparison to his successes.

Self-knowledge and self-reflection. Informal power also comes from self-knowledge, such as the self-awareness discussed in the last chapter, which in turn requires self-reflection. Self-reflection, as Bennis (1994, 56–57) has explained, can be "a means of having a Socratic dialogue with yourself, asking the right questions at the right time, in order to discover the truth of yourself and your life. What really happened? What did it do to me? What did it mean to me?" That does not necessarily come easily. According to Pfeffer (2010, 4), "Structured reflection takes time. It also requires the discipline to concentrate, make notes, and think about what you are doing. But," to return to the question of power, "it is very useful in building a path to power."

That is a path that Bill Bolling seeks to follow. In speaking to students, Bolling almost always remarks on the importance of doing the "inner work," of reflecting on and learning from his experience on an ongoing basis (see also Bennis 1994, 56–58).

Other sources of informal power. This listing of sources of informal power could continue indefinitely, for people in general as well as for Bill Bolling specifically, but the lesson for aspiring public-minded managerial leaders should by now be clear. Those who so aspire to lead should assess their own sources of informal power and seek to continue to develop that informal power in anticipation of future leadership roles.

Political Skills for Exercising Power

Power, formal or informal or both, has limited value unless complemented by political skills. Informal sources of power equate to political capital or currency; political skills provide the means to use that capital—in Yukl's terms (2000, 248), to "exercise power"—to influence others. Public-minded managerial leaders may draw on a wide range of skills in attempting to convert their informal power to action. Here, too, the story of Bill Bolling provides many illustrations.

Political mapping. A first political skill of interest is political mapping, the idea of scoping out the political environment in which one works. Political mapping entails defining, for an organization or a specific issue, (1) who the important actors are, (2) where those actors stand, and (3) how much power the various actors have (see Bolman and Deal 2017, 206–208; Bryson 2004). The resulting map can be used in strategizing for how to approach an organization's environment or a specific issue in that environment.

Bill Bolling became aware of the value of mapping early on as he contemplated how to establish the ACFB's place in the community. As he has recalled, "The community is the broad community, so you've got to map that community. There you're mapping the different sectors, the political, the business, the faith, academe, the nonprofit, and then individuals. That mapping is really important."

Networking. To be effective, mapping must link with another political skill, networking, which entails reaching out to and engaging actors identified through mapping. The ability to network is crucial in the public realm where success frequently requires partnering with other organizations. As Mendel and Brudney (2018, 173) have observed, "The act of forming a partnership builds networks of problem-solving actors and strengthens civil society by bonding people of different interests together."

Colleagues praise Bolling's networking skills, with one commenting: "He's an amazing networker. He doesn't do it in a glad-handing way. He is a connector; he really wants to connect people." Bolling himself recalls recognizing the importance of networking almost from the outset of the ACFB's development: "I learned very quickly that I could not be successful without strategic partners. In the case of the Food Bank, a strategic partner would be anyone who is growing, packaging, distributing, or selling food, but also anyone who is eating food." His networking included approaching congregations about serving as food distribution centers, grocery stores about obtaining their surplus food, eventually restaurants for their unused and unspoiled food, plus many other entities.

Networking can also be useful in looking beyond immediate needs by identifying potential future partners. Bolling illustrated this value for networking when he wanted to improve the quality of ACFB's customer service. Who in the Atlanta area, he asked himself, could help? The obvious example was the Ritz-Carlton Hotel, given its corporate reputation and frequent awards for exemplary customer service. Having earlier had the foresight to appoint a Ritz-Carlton executive to the ACFB governing board, Bolling was well positioned to ask the company to provide customer service training to ACFB staff. Ritz-Carlton agreed, and ACFB staff soon received the same training Ritz-Carlton staff receive.

Judging from some recent research, being more central in a network can further enhance the value of networking (Ammeter et al. 2002, 758). That proposition makes sense since centrality should mean more connections, potentially more and better information, and the likelihood of having more channels through which to exert influence (Cullen, Gerbasi, and Mason 2018).

Bolling personifies that centrality in his diverse community connections. As a senior ACFB staffer once observed, "One of Bill's key talents is his remarkable ability to engage the entire community, to relate to all segments of the community. . . . One minute he'll be talking and interacting with someone on the street, a homeless person, and the next he'll be meeting with a senator or a CEO" (Grillo 2012, 21).

The value of that centrality is evident in how Bolling confronted a major challenge when Walmart agreed to give the ACFB food from its many Atlanta-area stores. The challenge was daunting: With Walmart's stores spread across the sprawling Atlanta region, how could the Food Bank's trucks collect the food in an efficient manner? Bolling's centrality in the city suggested three possibilities for who might be able to help: United

Parcel Service, Sysco Foods, and Coca-Cola, all of which regularly move a high volume of goods around the Atlanta metropolitan area. Bolling approached each to ask how it scheduled the movement of trucks, before eventually persuading UPS to share its software for the ACFB to adapt to programming the movement of its trucks.

Consultation. An inclination toward and talents for consultation represent another political skill. Consulting entails asking others, including at least subordinates and external stakeholders, for input on possible actions or decisions a leader may be considering. Done effectively such that those who are consulted feel *heard*, consultation promises two principal benefits: (1) better information, contributed by those who are consulted, and (2) more support for possible eventual action, gained from listening to the consulted.

Bolling's talents for consulting proved useful in both the customer service and Walmart cases. With each, knowing who to ask—based on his networking and network centrality—was necessary to his success, but probably insufficient had he not also been able to consult, knowing both what counsel to request and how to incorporate that counsel in his decision making.

Facilitation and negotiation skills. The task often does not end with knowing who to tap in a network and what to ask. If different parties involved in an issue disagree on what to do, leaders must also know how to facilitate and negotiate. Neither is a particularly easy skill to develop.

Bolling has characterized as a "core competency" the ability "to take a conflict, or a group of people, or an idea, and facilitate progress," but he views the skill as one that can only be learned through practice: "It's just like a muscle—you might know it conceptually, but you've got to go out and practice it. You've got to move the muscle around to get it strong." Bolling traces the origins of his facilitation skills to the pre-Food Bank days when he and his wife presided over their quasi-commune, the house they owned where they gave needy people temporary housing. He views the challenges of managing the house as forcing to learn to facilitate:

> When you live in a community, you all agree to clean up after yourself;
> we agree to share the bathroom, we agree to do our chores. You live in
> a community; everybody has to come through. So, every Sunday night,
> we have a community meeting, and we'd just have to go over what got
> done, what didn't, who didn't honor what they said they were going to
> do, how it'll work if we're coming up short on money. Man, I learned
> with a very interesting group of folks. It wasn't easy. I was the leader of
> the community. I had to collect the money, pay the rent; the house was

in my name. I just look back to that as great training, not even knowing I was being trained, but you had to get things done.

Fast forwarding to more recent years, Bolling displayed his negotiation abilities in 2016 when asked to assist with a conflict between
the CEO of a non-ACFB food bank and that food bank's principal
donor. At the negotiation table were Bolling, the food bank CEO, the
donor, and the former ACFB board member who was interviewed for
this book. According to that individual's account, Bolling began the
negotiation by alternately asking the CEO and the donor to explain
their perspectives: "The conversation is occurring, but it's directional.
It's not a robust conversation [in the sense of the two sides talking to
each other], but by the end of the meeting it's a robust conversation."
In the board member's perception, "There was a bridge that had to be
built, and he [Bolling] was building it." Ultimately, "Bill bridged the
gap, and the relationship now is healing. It's better than what it was,
and there's a dialogue." That outcome serves as additional testimony to
Bolling's negotiation skills.

An ability to frame and reframe ideas. Another important political
skill is the ability to frame and re-frame ideas as a means of persuasion.
This ability can be useful in phrasing ideas and proposals in a manner that
will be more appealing to the target audience, potentially increasing the
likelihood of winning that audience's support.

Bolling takes special pride in his ability to frame and reframe ideas "in
ways people understand," but which also increase their sympathy for the
causes that matter to him. Consider, for example, how he can reframe the
work of the Food Bank to justify its role to skeptics:

> I'll ask, do you support better education? And they say, yes. Then
> [Bolling goes on to say] provide children with good food to eat and
> they'll be better prepared to learn. The same fundamental is true for
> health care. Better nutrition equals better health—and a reduced bill
> for governmental health care. National security? A better-fed pool of
> potential sailors and soldiers is good for the nation's military.

Bolling enjoys recounting another example of reframing from his work
with former Georgia Senator Saxby Chambliss, a conservative Republican
(which Bolling is not). As Bolling has recalled:

> He chaired the Agriculture Committee, so I go to him; he's my sena-
> tor. Lo and behold, he and I don't agree on much, but I found some-

thing we agreed on. He believed in nutrition programs. The reason he believed was not because there were poor people out here who needed nutrition. It was good for the farmer. . . . Both of us believed we needed to have strong ag, we needed to have strong farms, we need to not waste food, we need to feed people. Now what's a good way to do that? The public sector. So, he was a great champion for where . . . the USDA buys commodities from farmers, usually distressed product, and that product would come to us. My goodness, I testified before the Senate several times. I became an ally for him and we got more people fed.

Bolling's talents at reframing have enabled him to work successfully with a range of actors, reflecting how, as he has observed, "Being able to move between diverse communities gives you an advantage."

Bolling's skills in this regard fit how Chris Argyris and Donald Schön (1996) recommend leaders attempt to integrate inquiry and advocacy in resolving conflict. In their optimal model, the leader first asks the other parties in a conflict how they feel about the issue and what they think should be done. That initial inquiry is followed by advocacy, where the leader develops, proposes, and advocates a possible solution that combines what the leader heard from the other parties with what the leader feels the organization needs. In theory, by listening to and incorporating ideas from other parties, the leader can produce a compromise that all parties will embrace and that will also serve the organization's purposes (for a more detailed explanation, see Chapter 7).

The former ACFB board member suggested just this kind of process in how Bolling explores issues in one-on-one relationships. After listening to the other person's perspective, Bolling might say, "Can we probe on that one a little bit?" Or, "Other folks were troubled by this. Did that cause you any trouble? It doesn't make them defensive at all." In the board member's assessment, "He's so warm that you relax, your armor comes off, and you have a more real conversation."

Inspirational appeals. The ability to inspire, to make inspirational appeals, represents another important political skill (Yukl and Tracey 1992, 526). As defined by Yukl (2000, 209),

> This tactic involves an emotional or value-based appeal, in contrast to the logical arguments used in rational persuasion . . . . An inspirational appeal is an attempt to develop enthusiasm and commitment by arousing strong emotions and linking a request or proposal to a person's needs, values, and ideals.

These appeals can be useful in place of or in addition to rational persuasion and other techniques for gaining support.

Bolling's abilities to persuade clearly extend to inspirational appeals. He recognizes that the ability to motivate often begins with an inspirational vision, such as the Food Bank's mission statement (which Bolling helped to develop): "to fight hunger by engaging, educating and empowering our community." With that mission as a resource and in the spirit of "being able to move between diverse communities," Bolling has described himself as targeting inspirational appeals to specific audiences: "If you're working, say, with social work students or . . . working with a seminary, there you're touching something very different. You're not talking about common self-interest; you're talking about honoring what you feel like you want to serve people. Well, how are we going to do that?" Inspirational appeals are Bolling's answer and another of his political skills.

Exchange and pressure tactics. Not to be forgotten in the realm of political skills are the traditional political tools of exchange and pressure tactics. As defined by Yukl and Tracey (1992, 526), an exchange approach entails "an exchange of favors" that includes a "willingness to reciprocate"; or, as the cliché goes, you scratch my back and I'll scratch yours. Though sometimes perceived as socially less desirable than other approaches described here (Yukl and Tracey 1992), these tactics likely remain important tools for most public-minded managerial leaders.

That is certainly true for Bill Bolling. His openness to exchange politics is obvious, for example, in the work with Sen. Chambliss, where Bolling gained food for the Food Bank and the senator gained Bolling's support for agricultural legislation. Bolling is also unapologetic about the need to use pressure tactics on occasion:

> It kind of comes back to offering a deal you can't refuse. You're either offering a carrot or a stick. I prefer the incentive side [the carrot], but there's also the side of you don't do this, your business is not going to do as well [the stick]. . . . We have a lot of food, you need the food, we're going to be fair, we're going to be transparent, we're going to figure it out, but if you can't do that, then we don't have a deal.

Although exchange and pressure politics can carry a negative connotation as akin to bullying or manipulation, Bolling sees his use of the tactics as fair and above board:

> It's just being clear on a mutual expectation. You can be the greatest person in the world, but if you're not handling the food safely, you're

not getting food from us. That may feel like pressure because, in my contract, I can come over and visit any time I want, without an appointment. I can show up and ask to inspect everything you're doing. I can follow your truck around town. And that feels like pressure tactics—to them. I'm just saying I want to ensure the food is judiciously handled because it doesn't take but one story in the paper to hurt all of us. So, we're all in it together. Oftentimes you start out with pressure, or what feels like a negative, or a requirement and we're not going to compromise, what you want to get is to understand why we're requiring that and that you agree at the end of the day that was a good thing.

Viewed from that perspective, all manner of negotiations may require exchange and occasional pressure without necessarily compromising ethical principles.

Practicing a Virtuous Politics

Managers work in a political world. Resources are scarce and their allocation subject to intense competition. A broad range of factors, including the application of power and the exercise of political skills, can shape the results of that competition. It can be a messy, murky, and often frustrating process. It is certainly a highly political process.

Many actual and would-be public-minded managerial leaders balk at joining in this politics. Some do so in the belief that formal power will suffice for achieving their goals, and certainly formal authority may translate to more ability to accomplish desired goals. But, as Kotter (1985) has observed, managerial positions almost always come with a built-in "power gap," that is, insufficient formal authority to achieve much. Managers who rely principally on their formal authority are unlikely to get far in advancing their agendas.

Many of these leaders may also balk due to their feelings about organizational politics—confusion about how the political game is played, distaste for the unpredictability of political competition, and, possibly, fear of sacrificing their personal ethics. In making the choice to absent themselves, though, they risk undermining their effectiveness by abdicating from the competition for essential resources.

The story of Bill Bolling demonstrates how managers can both engage in this competition *and* address those concerns about organizational politics. To begin with, his story speaks volumes about how the game is played. It begins with informal power which public-minded managerial leaders can develop by attending to their own emotional development, sharpening their focus, growing their knowledge and expertise, learning to listen more effectively, developing a tolerance for conflict, remaining trustworthy, as well as reflecting regularly on their successes and failures. These personal capacities are sources of power that anyone can nurture, if to varying degrees depending on the individual, just as Bolling nurtured in himself to build the ACFB.

The manager who understands the various sources of informal personal power and develops a range of political skills will also understand better how the organizational political game is played—the unwritten rules, effective strategies, as well as different ways to compete when any specific strategy might fail. Managers who also develop their informal power and political skills should be capable of making the unpredictable more predictable—and predictable in the direction of the organizational outcomes they seek. Indeed, research suggests that political skills can bring all manner of benefits. One meta-analysis (Munyon et al. 2015, 143), for example, concluded that political skill is "positively related to self-efficacy, job satisfaction, organizational commitment, work productivity. . . , career success, and personal reputation, and negatively related to physiological strain."

Finally, Bolling's accomplishments also demonstrate that pursuing a political strategy need not require the compromising of ethical principles. To the contrary, Bolling's story shows the potential for practicing a virtuous politics, a benevolent yet effective political leadership style. Bolling has practiced that virtuous political style by combining his political power and skills with a strong religious and ethical foundation, including his sense of being called to serve. Tracing the elements of his virtuous style makes a persuasive case that politically astute leaders can enhance organizational performance, employee job satisfaction, and service to the public, while hewing to a high ethical standard. The same strategy awaits other aspiring and practicing public-minded managerial leaders who want to be both effective and ethical.

Personal Leadership Exercise 4.1

How Do You Rate Your Power and Political Skills?

Dimension	Low	Medium	High
Formal power			
Authority to hire			
Authority to discipline			
Control of rewards			
Agenda-setting authority			
Informal power			
Energy			
Ambition			
Focus			
Empathy			
Listening ability			
Knowledge & expertise			
Tolerance for conflict			
Trustworthiness			
Self-knowledge & self-reflection			
Other?			
Political skills			
Political mapping			
Networking			
Consultation			
Facilitation & negotiation			
Ability to frame & re-frame			
Inspirational appeals			
Exchange & pressure tactics			
Other?			

Which elements of informal power would you like to develop? How might you do that?

Which political skills would you like to develop? How might you do that?

Chapter 5

Becoming a Manager

For many, what the previous chapters are designed to prepare them for, will eventually become a reality as they officially achieve managerial status. The questions then turn to: What to do now? How should I behave as manager? Or, for those in the public realm on which this book focuses, how do I perform as a public-minded managerial leader? This chapter provides a brief introduction to that transition, the transition from employee to manager and potentially to public-minded managerial leader, before successive chapters examine how to approach the various elements of that role.

A Different World

As suggested in Chapter 1, managerial work typically feels much different from how work previously felt. Managerial work tends to be "hectic and fragmented," requiring "the ability to shift continually from person to person, from one subject to another" (Sayles 1979, 11–12). In addition, "The typical manager's day seldom includes a break in the workload. Managers receive almost continuous requests for information, assistance, direction, and authorization from a large number of people, such as subordinates, peers, superiors, and people outside the organization" (Yukl 2013, 24).

"Doing More Than Reflecting"

That description differs markedly from the nature of work for the typical professional who has yet to become a manager. Sayles (1979, 17) described managerial work as "almost the diametric opposite of the studied, analytical, persisting work pattern of the professional who expects and demands closure: the time to do a careful and complete job that will provide pride of authorship." Managerial work tends to be "hectic and unrelenting," "varied and fragmented," and reactive, with most interactions initiated by others, in contrast to the slow-paced, deliberate style of much professional work. Finally, where professional work typically involves extensive reflection, managerial work "is about doing much more than reflecting" (Sayles 1979, 17).

The transition from the one to the other can be difficult and challenging. As Linda Hill (2007, 2), author of *Becoming a Manager* (2003), has written: "Ask any new manager about the early days of being a boss. . . . If you get an honest answer, you'll hear a tale of disorientation and, for some, overwhelming confusion. The new role didn't feel anything like it was supposed to." One manager compared the transition to becoming a parent: "On day X minus 1, you still don't have a child. On day X, all of a sudden you're a mother or a father and you're supposed to know everything there is to know about taking care of a kid." As with new parents, new managers face a fast-paced, chaotic life unlike anything previous work prepared them for.

An Illusion of Authority and Control

Part of the difficulty for new managers derives from the illusions they often have about the power their new positions will bring. New managers frequently expect that the move into management will bring substantial additional power, power they can exercise to force subordinates to follow their orders.

New managers tend to think that their new positions will mean more formal power, in particular, the power or authority that comes with a position, including things like merit salary increases and promotions. While managerial positions usually include some formal power, new managers often assume they will gain much more formal power than actually proves to be the case. "This operating assumption," as Hill (2007, 7) has written, "leads many to adopt a hands-on, autocratic approach." In essence, many new managers adopt the stereotypical view that those in positions of authority can announce orders and trust that subordinates will readily implement them.

That kind of thinking contains several errors. First, as discussed in the last chapter, most managers have relatively limited formal powers, powers that are usually too weak to force others to regularly comply. Control over once-a-year merit salary increases, as one example, is unlikely to be sufficient to force consistent compliance with orders. Second, even if managers can force compliance, "compliance does not equal commitment" (Hill 2007, 9). Managers may obtain compliance in the sense of consistency with the letter of the law without obtaining commitment, wherein a subordinate's actions also meet the spirit of what the manager has asked. Third, many of the people whose cooperation managers need fall outside their formal authority, as with the heads of other departments in a public or nonprofit agency. Formal managerial authority will be of little value in gaining the cooperation of these peers.

Into a Fish Bowl

With the ascension to a managerial role, an individual immediately becomes more visible to and likely more scrutinized by subordinates. The professional who ascends to a managerial position moves out from the shadows, where no one took much interest, into a kind of fishbowl, where many—subordinates, in particular—may be watching. This fishbowl is akin to what work can feel like in the public realm (see Chapter 2).

The individual whose behavior was previously of only incidental interest to peers may now be the object of intense interest to those former peers who have now become subordinates. They observe, interpret, and sometimes judge, often analyzing "every statement and nonverbal gesture for signs of the new boss's motives" (Hill 2007, 8). An individual who might previously have felt barely visible may, as a manager, feel the target of intense, ongoing scrutiny.

Transparency of a manager's behavior can become extremely important in this context. Managers need to be sufficiently transparent and open in what they do—decisions they make, directions they announce, even their seeming small talk—that their behavior does not spark speculative interpretation by subordinates. In the absence of transparency, which is to say in the absence of information, subordinates may be tempted to create stories about why and how a manager is behaving, stories that may often attribute self-serving motives to the manager. Many a manager, including the most public-minded managerial leader, can recall hearing through the grapevine a nefarious interpretation of what, in reality, was an innocent, well-intended, but probably poorly explained managerial choice.

In a related manner, subordinates often view their managers as potential role models. Like it or not, employees look to their managers as models for how to behave. As a consequence, new managers who may previously have given little thought to how their behavior appeared to others must now recognize that any ill-considered behavior might be imitated by subordinates. They also do not want to behave in a manner that leads employees to think more cynically about them and the organization. Employees who see a leader as self-serving are less likely to be willing to sacrifice for the good of the organization.

On the positive side, this potential gives public-minded managerial leaders a lever to encourage through their behavior what they would like to see from subordinates. As Rainey (2014, 362) has suggested, "Leaders can show, tell, and encourage values and behaviors they want employees to adopt."

The Insider versus the Outsider

The challenges a new public-minded managerial leader will face often vary depending on whether the leader comes from inside or outside the organization.

The variability may be greatest in the areas of (1) developing organizational intelligence, meaning an understanding of how the organization works, and (2) gaining legitimacy, meaning respect and trust in the eyes of subordinates.

The leader who comes from the outside, hired from elsewhere to take a managerial position, likely faces a greater need in the area of organizational intelligence than does a leader promoted from inside the organization. While much can be learned during a hiring process, leaders new to an organization often face a steep learning curve about the organization's informal workings. Much of this knowledge falls in the realm of organizational culture, sometimes colloquially defined as "how we do things around here" (e.g., Hartmann and Khademian 2010). Every manager needs this understanding in order to lead effectively, but the need will likely be more acute for those who come from outside an organization.

An inside hire, by contrast, should already know a great deal about how an organization works by virtue of time spent there. True, there will likely be gaps in that understanding as a consequence of the limited purview of the individual's previous role. An individual who has worked only as, say, a professional in an organization may have limited their focus to the concerns of professionals, remaining mostly oblivious to larger institutional issues and intelligence. That choice can result in a substantial need to build organizational intelligence relevant to new managerial responsibilities, but likely not as great a need as an external hire will have.

The situation is likely reversed on the issue of building legitimacy with subordinates where an internal hire is likely to confront the greater challenge. Subordinates who were until recently peers of a new leader may still regard that individual as more a peer than their leader, and so may not automatically accord the individual legitimacy as leader. The transition from yesterday's peer to today's leader may lag the change in title, perhaps resulting in resistance to taking direction from the new leader.

Subordinates may accord an outside hire more legitimacy as a leader simply because the individual joins the organization with that title from the outset. Even then, subordinates often want to test a new leader before granting full legitimacy. As Hill (2007, 8) has observed, "Many new managers are surprised by how difficult it is to earn people's respect and trust. They are shocked, and even insulted, that their expertise and track record don't speak for themselves."

Getting Started

Professionals, even those who have been elite performers, seem unlikely to succeed as managers if they attempt to maintain the contemplative, studied approach that worked for them as professionals. At a personal level, too, professionals who fail to adapt their behavior seem unlikely to gain much satisfaction from their work. Employees are unlikely to feel positively about work that falls short of what a job requires. The individual who ascends to a manager's job must adapt extensively and rapidly in order to meet these challenges. Earlier chapters suggest how to get started with that adaptation.

Drawing on the Personal Foundation

Adaptation will be easier first for those who have built a solid personal foundation, as explained in Chapter 3. That foundation includes, in particular, emotional intelligence, a desire to serve, a sense of public values to be pursued, and clear personal and organizational visions.

Emotional intelligence provides basic personal tools for working with and attempting to lead others, which will be the principal focus of successful public-minded managerial leaders. Social skills are essential for interacting with others, empathy assists in understanding others, self-awareness helps in interpreting their reactions, and self-regulation can be invaluable in calibrating how to respond to others. Motivation, the final element of emotional intelligence, provides the rationale for trying to interact effectively.

Wanting to serve, the core idea of servant-leadership theory, represents a special form of motivation that is also essential to the success of public-minded managerial leaders. Knowing that one desires to serve could represent an important first step in recognizing the different demands of managerial work. That desire can give the new public-minded managerial leader grounds to consider the needs of others, perhaps especially subordinates.

A strong sense of personal and professional values enhances a leader's sense of the goals of that service. Those values can "serve not only as guides but also as sources of inspiration," potentially inspiring both leaders and their followers (Getha-Taylor 2012, 119).

Clear personal and organizational visions should further facilitate the transition to managerial work. A clear personal vision can provide guidance in deciding whether to assume those responsibilities in the first place. Does the position appear likely to enhance the likelihood of making one's personal vision a reality? Or, if not, might the possible desirability of a position suggest a need to modify the vision? Life, after all, is not entirely about following plans; opportunities can sometimes suggest a need to change those plans.

Developing an organizational vision becomes important once one assumes a leadership position. At that point, any public-minded managerial leader will likely want to build intelligence about the organization—or at least about the leader's sphere of responsibility in the organization. As noted earlier, while some leaders will begin with extensive knowledge of their organizations, few, if any, will begin with all the organizational in-telligence they need. The necessary intelligence is likely to encompass (1) important actors, both internally and externally, (2) skills, competencies, and weaknesses of those actors, (3) challenges and opportunities facing the organization, (4) relevant internal resources, (5) possible resource needs, and (6) any ongoing conflicts, both internally and externally. Some of this intelligence gathering may resemble the classic SWOT analysis of strategic planning—strengths, weaknesses, opportunities, and threats.

Another crucial dimension of organizational intelligence speaks to the rel-ative internal versus external responsibilities of a leadership position. External responsibilities have grown in importance in recent decades for all manner of leadership roles, certainly including public-minded managerial leaders. As Sayles (1979, 38) has observed, "From the point of view of subordinates, the leaders, typically, are the link with the outside world . . . Respected, ad-mired leaders are those who can deal profitably with outsiders and bring back benefits and protection." At the same time, the internal-external mix of responsibilities will vary for different leadership positions based on both the nature of the specific position and the preferences of specific leaders. Any new public-minded managerial leaders will be wise to appraise their relative internal versus external focus early in a process of assuming a leadership role.

Well-respected public-minded managerial leaders describe a variety of techniques for gathering organizational intelligence after taking new leadership positions. As described in the last chapter, Bill Bolling under-took intelligence gathering in part through political mapping, arguing that, "The community is the broad community, so you've got to map that com-munity." Donna Shalala (Radin 2012, 44), former Secretary of the Depart-ment of Health and Human Services as well as President of the Universities of Wisconsin and Miami, has frequently conducted initial surveys of orga-nizational members and external stakeholders to help in defining priorities.

Other public-minded managerial leaders pursue the same goal through yet other means. Different leaders may prefer different techniques, and the technique that is appropriate for one organization may not work well with another. Whatever the techniques, the crucial point is to give an early pri-ority to collecting extensive organizational intelligence any time one as-sumes a major managerial leadership responsibility. As that intelligence grows, public-minded managerial leaders will eventually reach the point where they will be capable of drafting a vision for their organizations.

Building and Using Informal Power

New public-minded managerial leaders are well advised to avoid the trap of over-estimating the extent of their formal powers. As Hill (2007, 8) has observed, many new managers need time to "come to the unsettling realization that the source of their power is, according to one, 'everything but' formal authority," and those who already grasp the importance of informal power enter new leadership roles with a significant advantage.

Leaders who have that recognition are likely to be prepared to lead more on the basis of informal than formal power, and could, in fact, already have developed extensive informal power—through listening, empathy, development of knowledge and expertise, and the like—that can be deployed to influence the work of their new subordinates. They may also have developed the political skills—networking, consultation, negotiation, and the like—for effectively applying their informal power.

Earlier recognition of these realities may also increase the ability of leaders to implement change during what is sometimes termed the "honeymoon" period, a brief period after assuming a leadership role when subordinates and other stakeholders are often more accepting of changes proposed by new leaders (e.g., Caplow 1983, 12–13). The willingness to embrace a new leader's agenda often declines as the leader becomes less "new."

Managing Time

Public-minded managerial leaders will also adjust better to new managerial responsibilities if they have developed strong time-management skills. The newly-appointed leader is well-advised to develop a rough schedule of how each day might play out, including how to divide time between different responsibilities. The schedule must be open to change given the potential that, on any given day, unanticipated issues are likely to arise and demand attention. The dual tasks for the public-minded managerial leader are to address those emergent issues without neglecting other issues that were on the original plan for the day.

A recurrent managerial time conflict pits people versus reflection. How can the leader address pressing issues that arise for people, especially subordinates, yet still find time for reflection? While more about doing than reflecting, managerial work must be about reflecting to some extent to ensure that larger institutional issues are not neglected. As one manager characterized the conflict (Hill 2007, 6), "The only time I am in control is when I shut my door, and then I feel I am not doing the job I'm supposed to be doing, which is being with the people."

Public-minded managerial leaders handle this conflict in many ways. Some reserve time for reflection early in the morning before others arrive, while others favor the end of the day after everyone else has left. The choice of time matters less than whether the leader finds the necessary time for reflection. The ideal approach entails a balance between interpersonal interactions and solitary reflection, a balance where the former likely weighs more heavily but the latter is not ignored.

The actual process of reflection likely varies greatly by individual. A prerequisite may be organizational intelligence, enough intelligence to be able to analyze, understand, and address organizational issues. With that intelligence in hand, many leaders will take what Daft (2012, 129–132) terms the "STOP" approach: "Step back, Think, Organize, and then Proceed." Here the leader first attempts to gain some distance or detachment in order to be able think carefully about an issue, before organizing ideas toward action and ultimately proceeding to put the ideas into operation. Thinking carefully may benefit from careful structuring of what Newport (2016) terms "deep work," time for "focusing without distraction on a cognitively demanding task" where "without distraction" may mean shutting out entirely email, phone calls, and the like.

A Strategy for a Strong Beginning

Working as a managerial leader often bears only a faint resemblance to the work that previously occupied the newly appointed leader. That may be especially true for those new managerial leaders who were previously absorbed in the contemplative, methodical, and solitary labors characteristic of professionals and technicians. This chapter has described the challenges that can result for those who subsequently move into the world of managerial leadership and recommended strategies to ease that transition.

The first elements of those strategies come from the earlier chapters on building a personal foundation and preparing for the political world of public-minded managerial leaders. Specifically, the transition to managerial work should be smoother if leaders:

- *Develop emotional intelligence*: The adjustment to managerial work is likely to be much easier for the public-minded managerial leaders who have developed their self-awareness, self-regulation, empathy, social skills, and motivation.
- *Desire to serve*: With that desire, new leaders will be more motivated to meet the challenges of undertaking managerial work, further facilitating the transition.
- *Craft a personal vision*: A personal vision can help in deciding whether to accept new managerial responsibilities and, if accepted, how to execute the responsibilities.
- *Build informal power and political skills*: Given the likelihood of only very limited formal power, having informal power and political

skills, built preferably in a virtuous manner as Bill Bolling did, will provide essential tools for any public-minded managerial leader.

Following some additional strategies can further facilitate the transition. Newly-minted public-minded managerial leaders are well advised to also:

- *Seek to understand the often-dramatic change from working as a professional to working as a manager*: Managerial work is a different world, and the new manager who does not understand the differences at the outset will be in for a bumpy ride.
- *Adjust to the visibility that comes with a managerial title*: Subordinates scrutinize managers much more closely than they do peers, and new managers probably receive the most scrutiny. Any manager, but especially a public-minded managerial leader, needs to consider how their choices might be perceived and interpreted and calibrate those choices accordingly.
- *Gather organizational intelligence*: A crucial initial task for any public-minded managerial leader, even those with experience in an organization, is to learn about the organization, especially the part of the organization that falls in the leader's domain.
- *Assess the relative importance of internal versus external responsibilities*: Most public-minded managerial leadership positions include both kinds of responsibilities; an early and often ongoing task for a public-minded managerial leader is to estimate their relative importance of the two and allocate time accordingly.
- *Learn to manage time*: The time demands on a new public-minded managerial leader can be daunting. Leaders need to learn how to manage their time, finding a balance between time for people and time for planning and reflection.
- *Craft an organizational vision*: As a final element of a strong beginning, a new public-minded managerial leader should attempt to craft a clear and attractive vision of what the organization, or the leader's part of the organization, can become. That vision should draw from the organizational intelligence the leader has developed and reflect extensive consultation with others inside as well as outside the organization.

With the support these elements can provide, the new public-minded managerial leader should be able to get off to a good start. Success over the long term will depend on developing a range of other skills, skills that are the subjects of the coming chapters.

Personal Leadership Exercise 5.1

How Prepared Are You—or Were You—to Become a Manager?

If you are already a manager (or have previously been a manager):

- Did you understand how work as a professional differs from work as a manager?

- Did you understand that you would not gain substantial formal power?

- Did you understand that you would be working in more of a fish-bowl atmosphere?

- Did you understand how the job would differ depending on whether you come from inside or outside the organization?

- Did you understand the need to increase your organizational intelligence?

Based on your experience, what would you have done differently or do differently in the future?

If you have not yet become a manager:

- Do you understand how work as a professional differs from work as a manager?

- Do you understand a manager's position usually does not include substantial formal power?

- Do you understand a manager's position means working in more of a fishbowl atmosphere?

- Do you understand how the job differs depending on whether you come from inside or outside the organization?

- Do you understand the need to increase your organizational intelligence?

In light of your answers, how might you prepare yourself for a future managerial position?

Chapter 6

Managing and Motivating People

Leadership at its core is about people, about a leader being able to persuade others to follow in a manner likely to enhance goal achievement. To do that, leaders must find the right people, guide and support them in their work, motivate them to perform, hold them accountable for their performance, and effectively address conflicts when they arise.

The next several chapters examine how leaders can accomplish those ends. In this chapter we examine basic principles of human resource management and motivation, especially how to hire, manage, and motivate others. Chapter 7 explores how to develop the manager-employee relationship, including how to address conflicts that might arise, while Chapters 8 and 9 consider how to make decisions while involving others and how to work with teams and run small-group meetings.

While much of the discussion in this chapter focuses on tasks that ultimately fall to the human resource staff, public-minded managerial leaders need to understand at least basic human resource management principles. At a minimum, these leaders need to grasp the role that the "implementation of human resources activities, policies, and practices" play in supporting an "agency's operational and strategic objectives" (Pynes 2013, 37).

Principles of Effective Human Resource Management

To develop that understanding, public and nonprofit agencies increasingly engage in strategic human resources management (SHRM). SHRM has two principal components: (1) development of realistic information on the capabilities and talents of current staff, the staff who comprise the current human resources, and (2) the integration of human resources activities and policies in agency performance (Pynes 2013, 37). As for public-minded managerial leaders, as Pynes (2013, 37) has asserted, they "need to understand how their workplaces will be affected by impending changes and prepare accordingly for the changes."

Commit to Caring

Effective SHRM best begins with a commitment of top leadership to caring about the hiring, development, and support of employees. Such a commitment might seem to be a given, but that is not always the case in a contemporary employment climate that often constrains investing in employees. Financial constraints sometimes persuade organizations to move toward contract labor, hiring temporary workers to do much of the organization's work. Temporary workers typically receive no fringe benefits, such as health insurance, and can usually be terminated when their contributions are no longer desired. That approach can reduce organizational costs for both salaries and benefits, but it does so at the sacrifice of some caring for employees.

Those cost reductions also often prove to be of limited duration, offset eventually by higher costs over the long term. That can happen if the failure to invest in employees results in less capable and less motivated employees, employees who may retard rather than enhance organizational performance. What was gained in the short term may then be lost in the long term. Given that risk, organizations are typically better advised to commit to caring for and investing in employees from the outset.

Organizations willing to make that commitment should make their choice known to current and prospective employees. Making the choice known signals the organization's values, taking a first step toward building a foundation of trust and loyalty among employees. Taking that first step also sets the stage for an organization to take further steps to cement the foundation.

Hire the Right People

Investing in employees starts with hiring the right people, people who seem the best fit for the jobs available (see Bolman and Deal 2017, 139). As Keohane (2012, 61) has observed, choosing subordinates is one of the "most consequential and revealing activities in which leaders engage." After all, "It is people who deliver the programs and services that public and non-profit stakeholders expect; therefore, planning for and selecting qualified and competent employees must be done with strategic purposes in mind" (Pynes 2013, 176).

To hire the right person, a manager needs in advance of any hiring to review what kinds of skills and attitudes a position requires, before considering who, among a field of candidates, appears to be the best fit. This "best fit" criterion should be applied cautiously, though, lest it discourage the hiring of people who look different from an organization's current workforce. That possibility could discriminate against diversity, ruling out women or candidates of color, as well as potentially insulating the organization from new ideas that could enhance its dynamism. Any hiring process must balance the desire for a good fit with the values of promoting diversity and gaining different perspectives.

In the public realm, that balance may best be achieved by looking for people whose values comport with the organization's values. Looking across a set of viable candidates, whose credentials suggest the strongest commitment to the values the organization seeks to promote? With a nonprofit focused on protection of the environment, for example, managers might look for candidates whose background reflects a commitment to environmental values. Selection should then become not so much a matter of finding someone who fits the mold as of finding someone who identifies with the organization's goals.

Public-minded managerial leaders may want to delegate most hiring responsibilities, but there is value to retaining at least some involvement. That involvement can increase the likelihood of the leader's judgment exerting influence over who is hired and how new hires feel about the leader, perhaps cultivating loyalty to that leader. Involvement may also help to build a "density of administrative competence," that is, a larger base of competent administrators below the level of the top public-minded managerial leader. Having more competent administrators should promote stronger organizational performance (Doig and Hargrove 1990, 3).

Invest in Employees

Once hired, employees need opportunities to develop and improve their skills (Bolman and Deal 2017, 144). Some of this responsibility falls on public-minded managerial leaders. If they want capable and loyal employees, leaders must commit to their development, especially early on when new employees may have limited understanding of institutional opportunities and constraints.

Some of this development will come through training opportunities offered through the organization or by third parties. However, organizations who make use of these opportunities are wise to plan in advance for how employees can apply training once back on the job. All too often, employees receive training that they find potentially valuable, only to be disappointed by limited opportunities to apply lessons from that training in their own work. Public-minded managerial leaders must also ensure that employees who receive special training are not able to take that training immediately to a different organization. To minimize that risk, organizations often require a period of post-training time with the organization as a condition for receiving training in the first place.

Reward Good Performers

People who perform well should be rewarded for their efforts. That should mean higher merit salary increases as well as, on occasion, efforts to match better offers from competing organizations.

This principle can sometimes be difficult to implement. For one thing, many organizations experience difficulty in defining what constitutes good performance. Or, when good performance can be defined, organizations that increasingly rely on teams (see Chapter 9) may have difficulty in differentiating who on a given team deserves the credit and the rewards. However performance is assessed, it is crucial that employees *believe* a good faith effort is being made to reward the better performers (see Selden, Ingraham, and Jacobson 2001, 604). Otherwise, the incentives for employees to *try* to perform well are compromised.

Provide Job Security

Historically, job security represented one of the principal advantages public sector jobs had over private sector jobs, with civil service and merit systems often guaranteeing job security except in cases of malfeasance. Time has blurred that distinction. Accounts from the private sector tell of people who retain jobs in spite of poor or even reprehensible performance, while legislative attacks have weakened civil service protections in many places (e.g., Selden, Ingraham, and Jacobson 2001, 606)

Whatever public-private differences may persist, job security remains an important element of effective human resource management. To be sure, employees should not feel *so* secure in their jobs that they become complacent; performance measurement systems should be in place to identify and address those who do not perform well. For those who do perform well, though, feeling secure in their jobs may enhance their work focus, instead of their being distracted by the worry that the rug could be pulled out from under them.

As a consequence, when faced with budget cuts, public-minded managers usually look to laying off employees only as a last-ditch option. Preferable options include (1) attrition, where positions that come open are not filled, or (2) furloughs, where employees share the burden of budget cuts by not being paid for days they are required not to work.

Promote from Within

Another means for showing that employees are valued is to promote mostly from within, filling higher-level positions from current lower-level employees. This practice enables organizations "to recoup the investment they have made in recruiting, selecting, training, and developing their current employees" (Pynes 2013, 177). In addition, "Promoting qualified incumbent employees rewards them for their performance and signals to other employees that the agency is committed to their development and advancement." The practice can demonstrate to employees that their organization values their work enough to increase their responsibilities, showing at the same time that there is a career ladder they might hope to climb. Seeing the potential to advance may also increase the likelihood that employees will think longer-term about their work and the organization's performance. All of these factors together are also likely to increase trust in and loyalty to the organization.

Promoting from within promises benefits for the organization and the public-minded managerial leader, too. For one thing, it can capitalize on the value of institutional knowledge, knowledge of how the organization works and how to make it work better. Those who are promoted from within are likely to have developed institutional knowledge, while outside hires must start from scratch. Hiring from within may also reduce errors because those who know an organization better should be less likely to err.

The Risks of Inbreeding

If taken too far, efforts to protect jobs and to promote from within risk inbreeding where an organization becomes too insular and resistant to new ideas. Organizations need to be open to innovation and being overly supportive of current employees can compromise that openness. It can also discriminate against diversity, especially when the current workforce lacks diversity.

For that reason, organizations are usually best advised to seek a balance between nurturing current employees and remaining open to hiring new employees with new ideas. Consistent with this counsel, some evidence suggests a curvilinear relationship between employee turnover and organizational performance (Hicklin and Meier 2008): For all the reasons cited earlier, too much turnover appears to be damaging to organizations, but some turnover appears to stimulate healthy organizational development. For the public-minded managerial leader, that evidence may recommend a happy medium of seeking some, but not too much, employee turnover.

Pursue Diversity

Increasing the diversity of a workforce offers one vehicle for introducing new ideas to an organization. As Pynes (2013, 115) has explained, "Diversity can lead to more creative alternatives and higher-quality ideas, primarily from the introduction of different and opposing ideas and viewpoints." Diversity also represents an important value for any public-minded managerial leader (see also Chapter 3)—the goal of diversifying a workforce to better represent previously underrepresented segments of the population.

The track record of the public and private sectors mostly suggests more success in achieving workforce diversity in the public realm than in the private, likely reflecting the former's longer history of concerns for "representative bureaucracy" (e.g., Krislov and Rosenbloom 1981; LaPorte 1971). Yet, "the evidence also indicates that public organizations have not invested in diversity management programs as much as private businesses have" (Choi and Rainey 2014, 320). Both facts imply a persisting need for public-minded managerial leaders to give a high priority to diversity.

The logical starting place for any organization involves (1) assessing the current diversity of the organization and (2) charting a plan for increasing that diversity, as necessary. That plan will likely include targets where potentially more diverse applicant groups might be found and strategies for attracting applicants from those sources.

Planning should also extend to how to facilitate the organization's adaptation to increased diversity. Increased diversity can translate to more interpersonal differences, and those differences provide a fertile environment for conflict. Planning may be needed both for preparing existing employees for diversity and for assimilating new, more diverse employees in the organization (e.g., Choi and Rainey 2014; Pitts 2009).

Success calls for a difficult balancing act: "Management must balance two conflicting goals: get employees to accept the dominant values and encourage acceptance of differences" (Pynes 2013, 127). On the one hand, "It is important for new employees to accept the organization's culture; otherwise, they are not likely to be accepted." On the other hand, the organization "must acknowledge and demonstrate support for the differences that these employees bring to the workplace."

Achieving both goals often requires extensive workplace changes that may not sit well with some traditional employees. Possible changes include "more flexible work schedules to accommodate" family demands, adaptations for individuals with disabilities, and even English as a Second Language programs for employees from immigrant populations (Pynes 2013, 27).

While research offers mixed evidence on the effects of diversity initiatives on such organizational outcomes as employee turnover and organizational performance (e.g., Choi 2008; Ely 2004), positive results appear more likely when those initiatives are well managed. Choi and Rainey (2014, 160), for example, found higher perceived organizational effectiveness where diversity initiatives produced more diversity *and* were "effectively managed." Pitts (2009, 328) similarly concluded from his research that effective "diversity management is strongly linked to both work group performance and job satisfaction." In addition, "people of color see benefits from diversity management above and beyond those experienced by white employees" (Pitts 2009, 328). The keys thus appear to lie in both pursuing greater diversity *and* effectively managing that diversity.

Empower Employees

Finally, effective human resource management also seeks to empower employees through a variety of means, including nurturing employee autonomy, sharing more information, involving employees in decision making, and sometimes redesigning work. These strategies are discussed in more detail later in this chapter and in Chapter 7 (see also Bolman and Deal 2017, 144).

Motivation

How can a public-minded managerial leader motivate employees? Following the principles of effective human resource management represents an important first step. Feeling wanted, feeling secure in one's job, having a career ladder in sight, and being rewarded for quality work can motivate employees to perform well. But employee motivation is a complex phenomenon that extends well beyond those factors to, more broadly, what drives people's choices in how they lead their lives. An effective approach to motivating employees requires an understanding of this complexity, including how motivation may play out differently in the public realm than in the private realm.

While there are many theories of what motivates employees (for a comprehensive review, see Pynes 2013, 306–311), attention here will focus on only four, the four that may be most relevant for public-minded managerial leaders and their employees.

Public Service Motivation

Many people in the public realm—and elsewhere—are driven in good part by what has become known as public service motivation (PSM), that is, the desire to serve and to do good for others and for society. People with PSM seek "to perform acts that contribute to the public good as a way of satisfying their personal needs" (Wise 2004, 674). They gain satisfaction from their work at least in part through unselfish or altruistic service. As developed in the work of people like Hal Rainey (1979) and Jim Perry and Lois Wise (1990), PSM represents a motivation intrinsic to work in the sense that people gain satisfaction from the inherent nature of the work. That contrasts to extrinsic motivations, such as desiring higher pay or more recognition for one's work.

PSM in the public realm. Public service motivation is thought to figure more prominently in the public realm than in the private realm. Anyone who wants first to make money, so the thinking goes, will likely head to the private sector where the earning potential is greater. Those who choose the public or nonprofit sector will do so for reasons other than financial gain, and high among those reasons may the anticipated satisfaction of serving (Rainey and Bozeman 2000; for a case illustration, see Maciag 2013).

The motivation to serve may take a number of forms, with one study (Brewer, Selden, and Facer 2000) suggesting an initial four:

- *Samaritans*: those who desire to assist the needy, while likely expecting them to work on their behalf, too. Samaritans might work in anti-poverty programs or food banks; for example, Bill Bolling.
- *Communitarians*: those who want to give back to community but have no special interest in the indigent. Communitarians may find satisfaction working, for example, for civic groups that attempt to address community-wide needs.
- *Humanitarians*: those who are motivated by a strong sense of social justice. Humanitarians might focus their efforts on civil rights or civil liberties organizations and agencies.
- *Patriots*: those who are willing to risk personal loss in the name of personal duty and the public good. Patriots include members of the military as well as police and firefighters.

That list might be extended to include a few other types, such as:

- *Environmentalists:* those who desire to protect the environment, as through conservation or wildlife preservation. Environmentalists might work for public or nonprofit sector environmental agencies or groups.
- *Egalitarians:* wanting to promote the interests of a disadvantaged group to which the individual belongs and/or believes has suffered injustices. Egalitarians might focus their efforts on, for example, making the public bureaucracy more representative of the public it serves.
- *Aesthetes:* lovers of art and/or culture who want to promote the arts through their work. Aesthetes might work for museums, symphonies, and the like.

Using PSM to motivate. The importance of PSM in the public realm suggests its potential as "a low-cost driver of job satisfaction" (Homberg, McCarthy, and Tabvuma 2015). In that spirit, Christensen, Paarlberg, and Perry (2017) recommend a number of PSM-related strategies that public-minded managerial leaders might employ to motivate employees:

1. *Select employees in part on the basis of their PSM*: Emphasize the agency's public service focus in job advertisements, and then look for applicants who already value the kinds of service the organization performs. "Value congruence enhances prospects for employees to be driven by higher-order extrinsic or intrinsic motivations" (Christensen, Paarlberg, and Perry 2017, 532), especially those motivations central to what an agency is about. (At the same time, there may be value in recruiting for other motivations, too, such as the potential for challenging work, since "individuals who have high levels of PSM and are interested in" specific public service positions may already be applying [Linos 2017].)

2. *Socialize employees to the agency's public service contributions*: Orientation efforts might emphasize the value of those contributions and their importance to the agency, as perhaps by holding "formal induction ceremonies" to "impress on newcomers the importance of entering the fold" (Goodsell 2011, 492). Mentoring might be structured to link committed senior staff with new employees, recognizing that "having a supervisor or coworker with strong public service values" is "associated with higher levels of public service motivation" (Christensen, Paarlberg, and Perry 2017, 535).

3. *"Leverage relationships between employees and beneficiaries"* (Christensen, Paarlberg, and Perry 2017, 536): Design work in a manner that facilitates direct contact between employees and agency beneficiaries, thereby reinforcing the employee sense of serving a deserving population (see also Jensen 2018, 54). Or, if direct contact is not feasible, encourage employees to think and write about the value of the service they are providing.

4. *Emphasize internally an organization's specific PSM*: Make the organization's public service contributions a central component of its organizational culture. Public-minded managerial leaders might regularly reiterate those contributions as central to what the organization is about.

5. *"Develop leaders who communicate and model public service values"* (Christensen, Paarlberg, and Perry 2017, 537): Work to see that other agency leaders identify with the agency's values and encourage them to communicate those values and to embody them in practice.

In general, many or most people who work in the public and nonprofit sectors do so in part from a desire to serve; any managerial efforts that help to meet those desires seem likely to enhance employee motivation. Those efforts should also contribute to greater job satisfaction, given substantial evidence of a strong relationship between PSM and job satisfaction in the public realm (Homberg, McCarthy, and Tabvuma 2015).

Public-minded managerial leaders face a variety of challenges in trying to motivate through the public service values of their agencies. For one thing, frequent criticism from elected officials and pundits could undermine employee beliefs that they are serving a good cause. In addition, extensive use of performance measurement and management systems sometimes distracts employees from the public goods they value because, ironically, they must attend to performance reporting requirements (see Heinrich and Marschke 2010). Effective public-minded managerial leaders must figure out how to maintain a focus on broader public goals—and the belief of their employees in those goals—in the face of these threats.

Responsible Professionalism

Many employees, regardless of the sector in which they work, are motivated in part by the opportunity to exercise their professional competence in an effective manner. In the typical bureaucratic context of specialization and division of labor, these employees can be motivated by the opportunity to apply their specialized skills proficiently to organizational tasks, looking for the satisfaction of "a job done well."

In the public sector, that motivation may include the additional element of being a "responsible bureaucrat," being, that is, an administrator who is responsible and accountable to the elected officials to whom one reports. The task of employees in this context is to implement political decisions with "neutral competence," competence with respect to their professional or other specialized skills, neutrality in terms of a lack of partisan or ideological bias in what they do. That neutrality traces to the traditional idea of a "separation of politics from administration" in the public sector, with elected officials supposedly addressing politics and public policy while administrators handle the implementation and administration of that public policy (for additional explanation, see Thomas 2012, 15–16). While widely disputed as an accurate characterization of the policy process, that perspective holds meaning for many public employees who seek to follow orders from elected officials in applying their technical competence, upholding laws as they apply their professional skills.

Using responsible professionalism to motivate. The salience of responsible professionalism implies several possible strategies for use by public-minded managers in leading and motivating employees. Most generally, this perspective implies the need to encourage employees in developing and exercising their own responsible professionalism. That approach might include these specific elements:

1. *Coach new employees on their responsibilities in the organization*: Most professionals will benefit from initial counsel on how to perform their work effectively in a specific agency context. They are likely to welcome assistance from superiors in assimilating to the organization and to their role within it.

2. *Transition employees from dependence to independence*: One goal of that coaching should be to move employees from dependence to independence. Most employees will hope to gain increased autonomy in their work over time, although the accountability of responsible professionalism will always place a ceiling on how much autonomy is possible (e.g., Argyris 1964).

3. *Share information*: Sharing of information can give employees a greater sense of investment in an organization, at the same time likely improving their ability to do their jobs. With technology having made information an increasingly leaky resource anyway, it often makes sense to provide more information directly to employees rather than taking the chance that they will find it elsewhere, but perhaps not in as accurate a form.

4. *Involve employees in organizational decision making*: Autonomy should also be balanced with some involvement of employees in the making of important decisions. While it must be carefully calibrated (see Chapter 7), this involvement can give employees a sense of expanding the value of their specialized skills for larger organizational decisions.

All of these strategies support the goal of empowering employees, as recommended earlier in this chapter.

Economic Self-Interest

Almost everyone works to some extent to promote personal economic self-interest. This is the traditional perspective on employee motivation, the idea that employees are motivated principally by the compensation and benefits they receive. That truth holds for the public realm as well as for the private, with some political economists even arguing that economic self-interest dominates other motives in driving employee choices about public-sector work. Developed by economists and political economists (e.g., Buchanan and Tulloch 1962; Niskanen 1971) several decades ago, public choice theory holds that those who work in the public realm are concerned primarily about promoting their own self-interest, though often not in the same manner as with private sector work. For example, economic self-interest for some public-sector employees may focus on fringe benefits and job security, both of which have traditionally been relatively more generous in the public sector. Or, some employees may seek those benefits in combination with less demanding work.

Beyond those purely self-interested motivations, even those employees who are driven principally by PSM or responsible professionalism are also likely to want to be rewarded appropriately for their work. Wanting to serve the public interest need not entail a vow of poverty or indifference to material rewards.

Using economic self-interest to motivate. Options in the public realm are more limited for using economic self-interest to motivate employees. Public-minded managerial leaders should seek to reward good performers to the extent possible, to invest in those good performers, and to protect their jobs, but limits on discretionary economic rewards in the public realm point to the need for some alternative strategies. As a few options, public-minded managerial leaders might:

1. *Correct flawed performance appraisal systems*: Performance appraisal systems, the usual mechanism for allocating merit salary increases, are frequent targets of criticism. They are sometimes characterized as essentially "meaningless because most employees receive an above average rating" (Selden, Ingraham, and Jacobson 2001, 604). In the City of Atlanta in 2001, for example, only 33 of more than 8,000 employees were rated "less than effective" in their municipal jobs (Edwards and Thomas 2005, 370). In other cases, employees complain that "objective performance measures are lacking and supervisors are biased in their rating" (Selden, Ingraham, and Jacobson 2001, 604). Where these problems exist, the savvy public-minded managerial leader should prioritize seeing that they are addressed, seeking to build employee confidence in the credibility of the systems as mechanisms for merit salary allocations.

2. *Emphasize transparency and fairness in allocating discretionary salary increases*: Where potential salary increases are modest, employees may be even more sensitive to possible unfairness in their allocation. It is all the more important then to be transparent in explaining how the increases are allocated. Transparency can often answer questions about fairness, increasing the likelihood of the answers being in the affirmative.

3. *Nurture other motivations*: When potential financial incentives are limited, they often cannot be employed as principal motivators. A

better option may be to emphasize and attempt to encourage interest in the other available motivations, such as public service motivation and responsible professionalism. Doing so could either cultivate more interest in those motivations among the economically self-interested or help to persuade them to look for alternative employment in more lucrative settings.

Work-Life Balance

Work-life balance has gained increasing attention in recent years as yet another important motivating factor in the work world. More and more employees appear to be making choices about work and jobs based at least in part on achieving a balance between the demands of their work and desires for the rest of their lives, including family, job flexibility, work location, and the like.

These choices can make good sense for both employees and employers since perceptions of a better work-life balance appears to increase satisfaction with both sides of the equation, work and life. In one study of employees from seven cultures (Malaysian, Chinese, New Zealand Maori, New Zealand European, Spanish, French, and Italian), perceived work-life balance "was positively related to job and life satisfaction and negatively related to anxiety and depression" (Haar et al. 2014, 361). These relationships proved strongest in more individualistic cultures, suggesting a potentially greater importance of work-life balance is likely in the highly individualistic United States.

Public-minded managerial leaders might address this motivation by offering more work options conducive to a better work-life balance. Those options could include:

1. *More ability to telework*: Having the opportunity to telework, performing some or all of one's work from home, can enhance the work-life balance. The State of Tennessee, for example, recently gave many of its employees the option to work remotely. Of the 6,000 who initially chose to do so, 80 percent "say they have a better work-life balance." The state government benefited, too, with productivity said to have increased and sick leave reduced by 37 percent (Barrett and Greene 2019, 55).

2. *More flexible hours*: A more flexible work schedule can also contribute to work-life balance. Where feasible, employees might be given more flexibility in when they put in their hours. Some employees, such as parents of minor children, might also welcome the option to work reduced hours, as perhaps on a half- or three-quarter time basis.

A challenge can arise if more flexibility devolves to a kind of "gig-economy" arrangement, where both employee hours and benefits are reduced. Resource constraints can sometimes force such arrangements, but they should not be confused with providing a better work-life balance.

The Poorly Motivated

Finally, many or most work settings will include some employees who might most accurately be characterized as poorly motivated. These employees may not care much about PSM, responsible professionalism, economic self-interest, or work-life balance. Some may have reached the latter stages of their careers and are only counting the days until retirement; others may see their jobs as transitional until they find something preferable; still others may work simply to receive a paycheck (and thus are motivated to some extent by economic self-interest), caring little about the quality of the work they perform.

Public-minded managerial leaders will likely find these the most difficult employees to motivate since, after all, nothing appears to motivate them much. Still, some options might be explored, such as:

1. *Redesigning jobs*: Some employees might have lost motivation due to the dreary nature of their work, as often happened historically with assembly-line workers in factories. Leaders might at least investigate the possibility of redesigning jobs to increase their interest for the job-holders.
2. *Dialogue with the employee*: Given the likely uncertainty about how to work with a seemingly unmotivated employee, a leader might seek a conversation with the employee, perhaps exploring whether the employee has interest in any of the motivations described earlier. The next chapter suggests how the leader might pursue such a dialogue.
3. *Reprimand or terminate*: In extreme cases, the leader might want to consider a formal reprimand or perhaps movement toward termination of the employee. The next chapter also discusses how these options might be pursued.

Multiple Motivations as Typical

All four types of motivation, excluding a lack of motivation, seem likely to hold salience to some extent for most employees in the public realm. Consider, for example, the motivations of directors of master of public administration (MPA) and public policy (MPP) programs, as revealed in a recent survey (Killian and Wenning 2017). Asked about the reasons they took their jobs, respondents cited factors reflective of three of the four principal motivations.

Table 6.1

Motivations for Taking Director's Positions in Master of Public Administration and Public Policy Programs

% saying reason was
"very or extremely important"

Public service motivations:
- Promote the program's mission   56.9%
- Promote the program's core values   56.9%

Responsible professional motivations:
- Increased responsibility   26.9%
- Sufficient administrative support   26.9%
- Increased autonomy   23.5%
- Professional growth   42.3%

Economic self-interest:
- Financial stipend   30.8%
- Course release or reduction   26.9%
- Greater job security   17.6%

Responsible professionalism or self-interest?
- Increase professional status   36.5%
- Increased authority   25.5%
- To grow professional network   19.2%

Source: Killian and Wenning (2017).

As shown in Table 6.1, these directors showed the most interest in PSM-like motivations, with 56.9 percent majorities mentioning promoting the program's mission and promoting the program's core values as important reasons for taking their jobs. But significant proportions of respondents, ranging from 17.6–42.3 percent, reported also being motivated by factors reflective of responsible professionalism, economic self-interest, or a combination of the two.

The composite picture likely approximates what public-minded managerial leaders would hope to see in their employees. Public service motivation weighs most heavily, as one might desire for work in the public realm, but the directors are also motivated to be responsible professionals—and to have the resources they require (e.g., administrative support, autonomy)—as well as to succeed personally (e.g., a financial stipend, professional growth). Although the survey questions did not ask, these leaders could also have been motivated to strike a healthy work-life balance, too. With such a workforce, a public-minded managerial leader might see a ready path for motivating employees by emphasizing the opportunity to pursue an agency's public service values through the exercise of responsible professionalism in the context of reasonable pay and benefits.

As that study also illustrates, it would likely be a mistake to assume that any given employee is driven by only one type of motivation. Even the most zealous champions of an agency's public service goals may also be influenced by their professional identities, a desire to be well compensated, and a need to balance work with other parts of life. Organizational strategies need to recognize this reality by being attentive to multiple factors likely motivating any given employee.

The importance of different motivations is also likely to vary across agencies, between individuals, and within specific individuals over time. Agencies will vary, in particular, in the strength of their commitment to public service values, with that variability likely to influence the motivations of agency employees (see Goodsell 2011). Within any given agency, some employees will probably identify more with public service values, others more with their professional identities, and still others with personal self-interest. The motivations of employees may also vary over time as a function of personal development, leadership changes, or other factors. The difficult task for the public-minded manager and leader is to discern and know how to respond to these different motivations.

Working with People

Leadership by definition requires followers, and people can no longer be expected to follow simply because they are told to do so. Gaining followers requires that leaders know how to win others over. Those efforts can begin by respecting basic principles of an effective human resource management strategy and being attentive to what motivates workers in the public realm.

Research strongly suggests that this kind of strategy will bear fruit. Most notably, Liu et al. (2007, 510) concluded from an "examination of 92 studies encompassing over 19,000 organizations" that "human resource management has significant value for organizational performance." Specifically:

skilled investments in: (1) HR planning, (2) compensation level, (3) incentive compensation, (4) training, (5) internal promotion, (6) employment security, (7) participation, (8) selectivity, (9) grievance procedures, or (10) flextime (in that order) will yield benefits in terms of increased productivity, decreased employee turnover, and greater financial returns.

These benefits also appear to increase substantially when "multiple practices are implemented systematically and reinforce each other."

Following these HRM strategies and being responsive to varying employee motivations provide the foundation for building positive relationships between public-minded managerial leaders and their employees, relationships presumably crucial for organizational performance. As Hassan and Hatmaker (2015, 1146) have documented, "the relationship between a manager and an employee" is an important "general factor in influencing performance of public employees." That linkage will be even stronger if, as Hassan and Hatmaker also found, managers build on that foundation by "supporting, recognizing, consulting, [and] delegating," strategies discussed in coming chapters.

But will most public-minded managerial leaders be able to implement those strategies given how, in the public sector in particular, they are often hamstrung by personnel rules and regulations (see Chapter 2)? While those constraints are real, they may also sometimes be exaggerated and used as excuses for the failure to act. Ample evidence suggests that motivated public-minded managerial leaders will typically be able to find enough flexibility in personnel rules to pursue the kinds of initiatives discussed here (see, for example, Wright and Pandey 2010).

That flexibility may even be on the rise given the trend toward loosening the shackles of many supposedly rule-bound personnel systems. As Selden, Ingraham, and Jacobson (2001, 606) observed of state governments at the start of the new millennium, "the notion of a state civil service with a uniform system of employment, recruitment, classification, and compensation is giving way to a more flexible and varied structure. The emerging strategy to decentralize authority for personnel functions is increasing the autonomy of state agencies and managers." The persistence of that trend since then—and its spread to other levels of government and the nonprofit sector—offer hope for public-minded managerial leaders who might want to experiment with innovative human resource practices.

Personal Leadership Exercise 6.1

How Would You Rate Your Agency/Organization's Adherence to the Principles of Effective Human Resource Management?

Principle	Poor	Fair	Good
Committing to caring for employees			
Hiring the right people			
Investing in employees			
Rewarding good performers			
Providing job security			
Promoting from within			
Avoiding inbreeding			
Pursuing diversity			
Empowering employees			

In light of your answers, what might you recommend you or your agency/organization do to improve its human resource management?

Personal Leadership Exercise 6.2

How Do You Rate the Motivations of Personnel in Your Agency (or the Motivations of Specific Employees)?

Motivation	Low	Medium	High
Public service motivation			
Responsible professionalism			
Economic self-interest			
Work-life balance			
Low motivation			

What might you recommend you or your agency/organization do to better motivate employees?

Chapter 7

Developing Relationships with Subordinates

The effectiveness of public-minded managerial leaders depends substantially on the quality of the relationships they can build with subordinates and other coworkers. For those relationships to be of high quality, leaders must succeed at two principal tasks. First, they must develop and employ an interactive communication style capable of nurturing productive relationships where they work effectively with others in pursuing organizational goals. Second, they must be able to address the conflicts that inevitably arise between managers and employees. This chapter examines managerial strategies for accomplishing both tasks.

Building Relationships Through Interactive Communication

The work of building productive relationships begins with public-minded managerial leaders establishing effective communication with their subordinates, including communication both to and from those subordinates, as supportive evidence from both scholars and practitioners attests. Evidence on the value of communication *to* subordinates comes, for example, from the research of scholars Jim Pedersen and Justin Stritch (2018, 67), who found that employee trust of managers derives principally from those managers "communicating clearly and fully following through on commitments" and "providing frequent feedback to employees on their job performance." On the other side of the coin, evidence on the value of communication *from* subordinates comes from the examples of public-minded managerial leaders such as Lillian Borrone, the well-respected former Director of the Port Commerce Department of New York and New Jersey. Borrone observed that "departments that encourage staff participation are often likely to spawn a greater number of innovative ideas than units in which the manager makes all decisions unilaterally" (Schachter 2012, 64).

When public-minded managerial leaders talk with subordinates, the communication can serve important functions for both sides (see Sayles 1979, 110–112). On the managerial side, leaders (1) need information to know what's occurring around the organization, (2) want to motivate subordinates toward better performance, (3) seek to assert authority, to the extent necessary, such that subordinates follow directions and, as a result, (4) expect the parts of the organization to work together more smoothly. On the other side, subordinates may (1) need information, as, for example, on management's preferences, (2) want at least some direction or guidance, (3) hope to share information and exert some influence, and (4) would like to receive some affirmation along the way.

Interactive communication along these lines can contribute to the effectiveness of public-minded managerial leaders in a number of ways (see Sayles 1979, 37–44). First, it can build their credibility by providing opportunities to both increase and demonstrate their understanding of the organization. They can increase their understanding by soliciting and listening to employee input; as Mary Parker Follett observed almost a century ago, "good ideas percolate from many points in an organization, not merely from the top of the hierarchy" (Schachter 2012, 64). They can demonstrate their understanding by combining employee input with their own knowledge and goals to fashion solutions that employees are likely to embrace because leaders have shown their willingness to "share power with anyone who has competence and is relevant to deciding about the action in question" (Argyris and Schon 1996, 117).

Second, public-minded managerial leaders can provide both representation and buffering for subordinates, representing their ideas to higher levels while also buffering the subordinates to some extent from demands from above. Both functions promise to enhance managerial credibility with subordinates.

Third, this interactive communication can provide practice in getting subordinates to follow directions, in part because they joined in developing the directions. Ironically, by listening to and thereby empowering subordinates, public-minded managerial leaders may actually increase their influence with those subordinates. The practice of subordinates following directions may build momentum for more of the same in the future.

Finally, this kind of communication can assist leaders in showing employees how their work contributes to the achievement of the important public values at the heart of an agency's work (e.g., Moynihan, Pandey, and Wright 2012). In a kind of virtuous cycle, the clearer sense of the importance of their work can, in turn, increase the ability of those employees to contribute to agency performance (e.g., Moynihan, Pandey, and Wright 2012). (See Chapter 11 for a more detailed discussion of this process.)

A Three-Step Evolution

Development of the manager-subordinate relationship often follows a three-step process, as suggested by leader-member exchange (LMX) theory (see especially Graen and Uhl-Bien 1995). At the outset, a new employee may start in a "stranger" phase relative to the manager, assuming a role that is largely scripted, probably based on the job description, where influence flows mostly one way from manager downward to subordinate. As the two sides interact over time, they may transition to an "acquaintance" phase where they test possible changes in their roles and influence begins to flow upward as well as downward. Finally, if the testing proves successful, the relationship may mature into a "partner" phase where roles are negotiated and influence operates reciprocally. "Partners," as defined by Rosenbach, Pittman, and Potter (2012, 80), "are those who have the competence and energy to do the job that they are assigned but who are also attentive to the purpose of the organization."

LMX theory proposes that the manager-subordinate relationship builds through exchanges of both tangible items, such as financial rewards, and intangibles, such as trust, respect, empowerment, and influence. The public-minded managerial leader typically assumes the role of facilitator in this process, leading but not controlling a process characterized by extensive give and take. Without that give and take, leaders are unlikely to gain the information they need, and subordinates are unlikely to feel either heard or influential.

Relative to the three-step evolution, employees may expedite the transition from one phase to the next by seeking extra roles, while the leader in return offers more benefits for the follower—sharing more information and influence as well as showing more confidence in and concern for the employee. Along the way, the leader and the subordinate are likely to build the kind of interactive communication style recommended at the outset of this chapter.

Not all subordinates will want this kind of relationship with their superiors. Some may be content in the initial scripted stranger role, especially if they do not envision themselves in an organization for the long term. Even some who anticipate longer tenure may prefer the more limited expectations implied by the stranger as opposed to the partner role. That might be the case, for example, for some who do not identify strongly with an organization's vision and consequently lack the public service motivation necessary to desire partner status (see Chapter 6).

Subordinate interest in interactive communication and a partnership relationship will vary for other reasons, too. Well-educated professionals may be especially likely to prefer the partner option as supportive of their usual desires for autonomy, empowerment, and influence, while some semi-skilled and unskilled employees may be content with more limited relationships with their superiors. On the other hand, judging from experience with team-based reforms of factories, many semi- or unskilled laborers may also prefer partner relationships, especially as an alternative to the alienating drudgery of the traditional assembly line (e.g., Bolman and Deal 2017, 146–147).

Preferences will also vary by context with extensive interactive communication likely a better fit for some organizations than for others. One study suggests that a "team-oriented organization" may embrace interactive communication more readily than will "an organization in which individuals worked [mostly] alone on technical tasks" (Anderson, Spataro, and Flynn 2008). Consistent with that notion, "extraverts attained more influence" in the team-oriented organizations.

LMX theory recognizes these possibilities by asserting that organizations typically include "in-groups" and "out-groups," the latter comprised of employees who for whatever reason have not moved into partner or perhaps even acquaintance roles. For public-minded managerial leaders, that reality counsels not to expect all subordinates to buy into extensive interactive communication and the desirability of cultivating partner status. At the same time, a goal of fairness implies that leaders should offer everyone the opportunity to advance to partner status even as they accept that some will decline the offer.

The Challenge of "Feedback-Avoiding Behavior"

Organizations often face a challenge from feedback-avoiding behavior, where employees resist providing or receiving feedback, typically from a fear that feedback could result in supervisors perceiving poor performance, even sometimes when employees are performing at high levels (Moss and Sanchez 2004, 33–34). Employees may fear that those perceptions could lead to managerial threats to employee reputations, self-esteem, and perhaps even job security. Better to avoid feedback entirely, many employees may think, than to risk those negative consequences.

The commitment to strong interactive communication can help to address this problem by encouraging feedback and thereby discouraging feedback-avoiding behavior. As a first step in that direction, managers can explicitly emphasize that communication from lower to higher levels is welcome and will not be punished. Former Georgia Governor Joe Frank Harris, for example, asked his staff to implement a policy of "no surprises." If a potential issue arose somewhere in state government, the governor wanted to be alerted by his staff, rather than risk being surprised by hearing first about the issue through a question at a public press conference (personal communication to author).

As a second tactic, the public-minded managerial leader might engage in active listening and adopt "a learning mind-set" when interacting with subordinates (Moss and Sanchez 2004, 41–42). Active listening, as characterized by Cloke and Goldsmith (2011, 35), "does not actually *start* with listening, rather it begins when the listener clears the decks and focuses his or her *undivided* attention on the person who is about the speak." It is the kind of listening at which Bill Bolling appears to excel, as described in Chapter 4. This approach also entails occasionally restating what is heard, both to demonstrate having listened and to test the accuracy of what was heard. Developing a learning mind-set, in turn, means trying to learn from what subordinates report to build understanding of the organization.

Public-minded managerial leaders can sometimes enhance the quality of communication by showing compassion for subordinates. Compassion refers to "expressed feelings of affection, caring, and tenderness toward subordinates or colleagues without the expectation for specific organizational benefits." At least some evidence (Eldor 2018, 86) suggests that "compassion in the public service workplace may . . . be salient in effecting public service work performance."

In addition to welcoming what comes through their doors, managers are also well-advised to actively pursue feedback, as, for example, by occasionally visiting employees where they are working, an approach known as "distance management" or "management by wandering around" (MBWA). As described in the management classic *In Search of Excellence* (Peters and Waterman 1982, 289), Walt Disney was famous for practicing MBWA at Disneyland, walking the grounds to gain a feel for how the entertainment park was functioning, a feel that he did not find attainable by any other means. Or, in an example from the world of public-minded managerial leaders, former IRS Commissioner Charles Rossotti (2005, 91–92) was another believer in MBWA, saying: "One way I could gain a better feel for the work, and encourage upper managers to do the same, was occasionally to go to work with some employees who were dealing with taxpayers. . . . I have no doubt that I learned more than I could have learned any other way about how the IRS really worked."

By practicing these various techniques, public-minded managerial leaders are more likely to be able persuade their subordinates to communicate information that needs to rise up the chain of command. Success in that effort will likely improve manager-subordinate relationships while also making for better-informed public-minded managerial leaders with greater understanding of organizational functioning.

Other Benefits of Interactive Communication

Effective interactive communication can bring other benefits, too. Two notable examples are (1) communication can improve an organization's ethical sensitivity and (2) assist leaders and organizations with the problem of succession planning.

On the former, the transparency that underlies better communication seems likely to increase ethical sensitivity. Whether leaders or subordinates, people are likely to feel less latitude to engage in unethical behavior where there is open communication. Open communication, after all, means that less that happens in an organization can go without observation or comment. Anyone who engages in unethical behavior in that kind of context risks being identified and possibly disciplined (see also Hassan, Wright, and Yukl 2014).

On the latter, as Crosby and Bryson (2005, 100) have explained the problem, "Among the changes that organizational leaders should expect is the likelihood of people in leadership roles moving on to other assignments, retiring, becoming disabled, or dying. Replacement leaders must be mentored and developed if they are to assume additional responsibilities." Strong patterns of interactive communication, including the development of partnership relationships between leaders and subordinates, could serve as an important first step in succession planning. The more leaders interact with subordinates about organizational issues, the better prepared those subordinates may be to assume additional responsibilities when succession becomes necessary. The same processes should also enhance the ability of subordinates to succeed each other. Along the way, leaders build the "density of administrative competence" which March (1981) envisions as "what makes organizations function well."

Addressing Conflict

No matter how diligently a public-minded managerial leader encourages and responds to communication from subordinates, conflicts will arise. People will disagree on what direction or strategy offers the best route to organizational success; they will compete over scarce resources that must be divided among different parts of an organization; and, sometimes, different personalities will simply clash. For these and other reasons, conflict is inevitable in manager-subordinate relationships and organizational life more generally. That reality makes an ability to address conflict with subordinates—and others—a crucial competency for public-minded managerial leaders.

When to Duck

Faced with the possibility of conflict, many people do their best to duck, manifesting the common preference for conflict avoidance (see also Chapter 4). As Cloke and Goldsmith (2011, xvi) suggest, "our first response is often to avoid or suppress conflict, or try to make it go away." That preference is so deeply ingrained that people will sometimes duck conflict at significant personal cost, including ceding scarce resources to other parties to a conflict.

Choosing to duck will sometimes be the best choice (as many long-married couples might attest). Some conflicts may be fleeting, reflecting personal tensions that will quickly dissipate after a brief blow-up. Another type of conflict people may decide they can work around arises when the opposing parties interact only infrequently ("maybe we can forget this ever happened if we never speak of it again"). In situations like these, one might reasonably decide that there is too little to be gained—and perhaps too much hostility to endure—to warrant trying to address the conflict.

The place to start when a conflict arises typically will be by deciding whether to duck. For the public-minded managerial leader, that decision may come down to whether the likely benefit of attempting to resolve a conflict exceeds the cost of letting the conflict go unaddressed. Only when a conflict interferes significantly with daily responsibilities will the need to take it on be clear. That would likely be the case, for example, if failing to address the conflict:

- Allows continuation of a work behavior that, in the assessment of the manager, unnecessarily impairs the organization's functioning, or
- Creates the impression with others that the manager is hesitant or unwilling to face conflicts.

In both cases, the effectiveness of the public-minded managerial leader and perhaps that of the organization stand to suffer if the conflict is not addressed, providing strong reasons not to duck.

The Inquiry and Advocacy Approach

When conflict must be addressed, Chris Argyris and Donald Schön (1996) describe several approaches to its possible resolution; approaches that, as adapted by Lee Bolman and Terrence Deal (2017, 160–166), involve different combinations of inquiry and advocacy. Inquiry refers to asking questions, where one party asks questions of another party, as a manager might ask a subordinate. With true inquiry, the questions are informational, designed to elicit the perspectives of the other party. For example, confronted with a tardy subordinate, a leader might ask, "I saw you arrived late today. What happened?" Or, where a subordinate submits a problematic proposal, the question might be, "You went over budget on the project proposal. How did that happen?"

At the other side of these approaches, advocacy entails the first party, again presumably a managerial leader, proposing and making the case to the other party, presumably a subordinate, for a possible solution to the conflict. Dichotomizing inquiry and advocacy as high or low, Bolman and Deal (2107, 164) produce four approaches to resolving conflict, as summarized in Table 7.1.

Table 7.1

Combining Inquiry and Advocacy in Addressing Conflict

		Inquiry	
		Low	High
Advocacy	Low	Passive	Accommodating
	High	Assertive	Integrative

The passive approach. Looking at the cells in the table, a passive approach falls low on both inquiry and advocacy, with the leader neither asking questions nor proposing solutions. Ducking would qualify as a passive approach if the leader asked no questions in addition to not advocating a solution. Ducking where the manager does not advocate a solution but did ask questions qualifies as an accommodating approach, high on inquiry and low on advocacy. Here, after asking questions, the leader accepts and accommodates the subordinate's preference. In neither the passive nor the accommodating approach does the leader take an active role in attempting to craft a compromise.

The assertive approach. The assertive approach, low on inquiry but high on advocacy, is what Argyris and Schon refer to as Model I. In classic command-and-control style, this approach finds the leader moving immediately to push for a preferred solution, seeking no information before doing so. A leader who takes this approach usually follows a sequence along these lines:

- First, define the goals and the resolution for achieving them.
- Seek to "maximize winning and minimize losing," where winning entails achieving those goals.
- Engage the issue unilaterally, offering no opportunity for input from the subordinate (i.e., no inquiry).
- Attempt to force the subordinate to accept the preferred solution, applying pressure as necessary (Argyris and Schon 1996, 92–94).

Returning to the earlier examples, a leader taking the Model I approach might say to the tardy subordinate: "I saw you arrived late today. That's not okay and I won't tolerate it. Is that clear?" Or, with the subordinate who produced an over-budget proposal: "I saw your proposal exceeds our budget. That's unacceptable. Find a way to reduce costs." In theory, the leader could listen to feedback from the subordinate after announcing the solution, but, philosophically, the leader who takes the assertive approach does not believe the subordinate has valid input to offer. As both of those examples illustrate, leaders who choose the Model I approach attempt to use authority to force subordinates to comply.

The assertive approach holds little promise for successfully resolving conflicts. For one thing, by avoiding any inquiry, the approach circumscribes the information on which any solution will be based. Less information increases the chances of a poorly informed solution, a solution that may not actually solve the conflict. This approach can also result in winning the battle but losing the war. The leader may prevail in the short term, coercing a subordinate into compliance, but, in the long term, those tactics could cause resentment, perhaps engendering resistance and further conflict. People do not like being coerced, and, even if they succumb, they may remember and could welcome an opportunity to exact revenge, even if revenge only means offering lukewarm support for the manager on a future issue. Leaders who prefer the Model I approach should anticipate eventual pushback.

The integrative approach. By contrast, the integrative approach, which Argyris and Schon term Model II, entails trying to work with the other person in a mutual effort to resolve conflict. This approach gives priority to maximizing useful information and to sharing influence in order to obtain that information. At the core of this approach, the leader—and, with this approach, we can speak again of the public-minded managerial leader—will:

- Seek to "generate valid and useful information."
- "Share the problem in a way that leads to productive inquiry."

- Share "power with anyone who has competence and is relevant to deciding about implementing the action in question," such as a resolution to a conflict.
- "Reject the unilateral control that usually accompanies advocacy," as with Model I, but do "not reject the skill or competence to advocate one's purposes."
- At the point of advocacy, "construct positions to which people involved can become internally committed" (Argyris and Schon 1996, 117–121).
- In sum, treat conflicts as opportunities (Cloke and Goldsmith 2011, 15), opportunities to create better-informed decisions that will meet with broader acceptance.

The integrative approach rests on the premise that problems seldom result from one person alone, typically deriving instead from the different parties who are in conflict. As a result, this approach envisions effective solutions as more likely to result from processes where both sides are heard and their knowledge and preferences are reflected in the solution.

When pursuing the integrative approach, public-minded managerial leaders may want to keep a few additional guidelines in mind, including:

- Ask first for the subordinate's perceptions of what's going on with the issue as well as what help the subordinate might offer for resolving the issue. As Cloke and Goldsmith (2011, 11) have observed, "Clearly, finding a solution to your conflicts depends on your ability to understand what caused them."
- In asking questions, minimize emotions to reduce possible tension that result from conflict. As Yukl (2013, 235) counsels, "Stay calm and professional."
- After asking a question, "allow the other person enough time to answer. Don't be afraid of silence" (Headlee 2017, 166).
- Engage in active listening by being attentive to employee concerns as well as occasionally restating what the employee has said.
- Offer the managerial or organizational perspective second, after the subordinate finishes speaking, including what that perspective implies might be needed in any resolution of the issue.
- Be open to employee questions about the organizational perspective.

On occasion, issues issue can be resolved by taking the accommodating route, accepting what the subordinate proposes and prefers because that meets organizational and managerial needs. Anyone who has served as a public-minded managerial leader will recognize this scenario. The actions of a subordinate appear from a distance to be undesirable or unacceptable, but, given the opportunity to explain, the subordinate can show the wisdom of those actions.

In most cases, the public-minded managerial leader will eventually need to transition to advocacy, attempting to craft and explain a possible resolution to the subordinate. The leader's task is to integrate information from the employee with the leader's needs and those of the organization, looking for a possible solution that will meet everyone's needs. That proposed solution will likely involve some reframing of the issue in order to incorporate both managerial and subordinate perspectives. In building the Atlanta Community Food Bank, for example, Bill Bolling reframed his interest in getting food donations from the city's major grocery chains to include the promise of inventory control and monitoring, a promise that ultimately proved persuasive to the chains (see also Chapter 4).

The integrative approach in action. Consider how the integrative approach might play out with the case of the tardy subordinate, especially if this was not the first instance of tardiness. The conversation might begin as suggested earlier with the public-minded managerial leader asking:

> Leader: "I saw you arrived late today. What happened?"
> Subordinate: "I have a six-year-old who I have to get to school in the morning, and sometimes we run late."
> Leader (still seeking information): "Is that an ongoing issue? I've seen you arrive late a few other days."
> Subordinate: "It does happen occasionally, but I haven't been late a lot."

Here the leader may need to consider what direction to take. Is the tardiness so minor relative to the quality of the subordinate's overall work that it does not warrant trying to change? If that were the case, the leader might take the accommodating approach, saying something like, "Okay, thanks for the explanation. Try not to be tardy, and in the future let me know if the problem worsens."

Or, if the leader instead views the problem as sufficient to warrant asking for a change, the dialogue might continue as follows:

> Leader: "I understand, but the tardiness has become enough of a problem that we need to figure out a solution. Do you have any ideas?"

With this question, the leader offers an opening for the subordinate to propose a solution, which should give the subordinate a greater sense of empowerment, without obligating the leader to accept whatever the individual might propose. That strategy might prove very effective if the subordinate were to respond: "What if I worked late on the days that happens?" The leader might then weigh if the proposal meets the needs of the organization, or if instead there is an early-morning organizational need that requires the subordinate's presence. Absent the latter, the leader might move toward concluding the negotiation by saying, "Sure, that's okay with me. One other thing, though: On days when that's the case, stop by and let me know. Okay?"

While a relatively simple problem with a similarly simple solution, this exchange illustrates how, by asking questions and listening carefully to the answers, a public-minded managerial leader can craft an integrative solution—the employee's preferred solution, in fact—that meets the needs of the organization, too. Adding the final request for the subordinate to report any tardy days retains an element of ongoing monitoring. This approach also avoids any disciplinary action, at least for the moment, without foreclosing that option

Conflicts Over Employee Performance

Where an issue concerns a subordinate's performance, the public-minded managerial leader might usefully incorporate some additional elements into the integrative approach. First, the leader should try to be open minded about possible causes of poor performance, engaging in additional investigation if the causes are not immediately clear. Second, if the subordinate will be asked to make changes, the leader should try to word the request as "effective, non-threatening feedback" (Moss and Sanchez 2004, 40). Third, whatever solution the leader might eventually propose should avoid personal elements, such as references to their "personal flaws" (Headlee 2017, 132). Drawing an example from professional sports, Brad Stevens, head coach of the Boston Celtics professional basketball team, illustrates how this might be done:

> In evaluating players, both during games and in film sessions, Stevens is careful with language, according to coaches, players and team higher-ups. He focuses on actions: *We didn't get this rebound. You should have made this rotation earlier.* The criticism is never about the player's character. No one is labeled lazy or stupid or selfish. Stevens simply describes what did or did not happen, and what should happen next time (Lowe 2018).

The most effective requests from a public-minded managerial leader will focus on controllable behavior, behavior the subordinate has the ability to change. Even with these requests, the leader should still test the proposed solution, leaving room for the subordinate to suggest modifications. Showing concern for subordinates in this manner can be very effective in gaining their support. In the case of Celtics' coach Stevens, his use of this approach "has gone a long way in securing buy-in, players say. They feel Stevens is *with* them, even as he holds them—and himself—to almost impossible standards" (Lowe 2018).

Tools for Advocacy

In advocating for solutions as part of the integrative approach, some techniques are more effective than others, with consultation, collaboration, rational persuasion, logic, and inspirational appeals among the most effective (Yukl and Tracey 1992, 533). The integrative approach is by nature consultative and collaborative, of course, and the public-minded managerial leader who listens well should be capable of using rational persuasion and logic in making the case for a solution that was presumably fashioned to be responsive to the subordinate's interests. The integrative approach thus makes extensive use of several of the most effective techniques for advocacy.

A leader might also utilize inspirational appeals as part of an integrative approach, especially if the subordinate is known to be strongly motivated by specific public service values (as explored in the last chapter). The manager might then consider if and how to link those values to the issue at hand to encourage cooperation and possible compromise. That might entail saying, "This is an issue where our reaching a resolution could make a big difference for the people we serve." Or, for someone who places a premium on responsible professionalism: "I know how strongly you feel about this [professional value]. We could promote that much more effectively if we can find a compromise."

Flattery, ingratiation (trying to please), personal exchanges ("I'll scratch your back if you'll scratch mine"), and pressure tactics typically represent less effective tools of persuasion because people tend to view these tactics as socially undesirable. As Yukl and Tracey (1992, 533) have explained, the targets of these tactics "may become resentful or angry with the agent for trying to coerce or manipulate" them. The resulting risk of alienating subordinates should make public-minded managerial leaders wary of using these tactics.

Still, some of these tactics can occasionally be used in a manner that is both effective and ethical. That appeared to be the case, for example, with Bill Bolling's use of pressure and exchange tactics, as described in Chapter 4. Bolling freely admitted to sometimes using the ACFB's food as a bargaining chip when needing to negotiate better distribution by an ACFB partner; if the distribution could not be improved, Bolling might threaten to terminate the relationship with that partner. That was not his preferred approach, but he felt it sometimes necessary and it appears entirely ethical.

Pro's and con's to the integrative approach. The Model II approach offers many potential advantages to public-minded managerial leaders. First, since the perspectives of both parties to a conflict should be reflected in any resolution, the likelihood is higher for shaping a solution that both will buy into. Second, the greater potential of buy-in increases the chances of being able to implement the decision successfully (see Chapter 8 for more on this point); people who agree with a decision are likely to support its implementation. Third, leaders who listen well will likely enhance the self-esteem and comfort of their subordinates, which could also improve their performance. Fourth, these gains for subordinates can build the credibility of the leaders, potentially increasing their ability to count on those employees in the future.

Given those advantages, why wouldn't all public-minded managerial leaders use the integrative approach routinely? There may be several reasons. First, starting by asking questions can feel like relinquishing control, which could seem counterintuitive when the goal is to change a subordinate's behavior. In reality, though, beginning by asking questions only surrenders "the floor," not control. The leader gives the employee the opportunity to speak to the issue, not to dictate a solution. Moreover, careful crafting of questions can limit the risk of subordinates misperceiving their power in the situation.

Second, public-minded managerial leaders could also be wary of the integrative approach because the advocacy component requires thinking on one's feet, not necessarily an easy task. The leader must take the subordinate's answers to the initial questions and try to integrate them into a solution that meets everyone's needs, those of the employee, the manager, and the organization. This kind of on-the-spot reframing of an issue can be challenging, especially since conflict can bring tension and tension can constrain creative thinking.

This problem need not limit use of the integrative approach. For one thing, in most situations, the leader need not respond immediately. Often the leader might instead acknowledge the need to consider the subordinate's ideas before discussing a solution, asking for time to consider before meeting again to seek a resolution. In addition, practice with the approach can develop the ability to think on one's feet, making the approach easier to use with repetition. The process should also become easier with the continued development of a leader's emotional intelligence, especially the attributes of self-awareness, self-regulation, and empathy (Goleman 1998). Empathy can help in understanding the perspectives of others, as revealed through inquiry, while self-awareness and self-regulation can facilitate coping with the emotional stress of a conflict situation.

The challenge in the end is to build sufficient confidence to follow the integrative approach when desirable. Anyone who might hesitate should keep in mind that the approach seeks cooperation, not obedience, and most people respond more positively to the former than to the latter. Indeed, in the midst of a conflict where one might anticipate confrontation, being asked instead for one's opinion can be disarming. Finally, if the other side does not respond positively, does not welcome an invitation to cooperate in resolving a conflict, public-minded managerial leaders have other options.

When Cooperation Fails

Persisting in seeking cooperation once the other side has clearly rebuffed good-faith overtures is likely to be futile and can prove counterproductive. Any time one side to a conflict persists in seeking cooperation in the face of the other side's intransigence, a risk arises of the noncooperating party taking advantage of the cooperating party, as, for example, if the latter continues to make concessions and the former does not reciprocate. Public-minded managerial leaders should be careful not to fall into that trap.

Responding to Defection

In his classic book, *The Evolution of Cooperation* (1984), Robert Axelrod drew from his research to propose a set of principles for how best to nurture cooperation and to respond to "defection," that is, the choice by another party in a conflict not to cooperate. Axelrod's principles provide a framework for strategizing how to respond when another party rejects offers to negotiate a solution to a conflict.

As his first principle, Axelrod's (1984, 117) recommended: "Don't be the first to defect." That is, do not be the first party to decline to cooperate in attempting to address a conflict. As he has explained, "The reason is that your own initial defection is likely to set off a retaliation by the other player. This will put the two of you in the difficult position of trying to extricate yourselves from an initial pattern of exploitation or mutual defection." Any public-minded managerial leader who wants to resolve a conflict should consequently not be the first to exit a possible negotiation.

A second Axelrod (1984, 118) principle begins to address how to respond to a resistant party: "Reciprocate both cooperation and defection." In other words, if the other party cooperates, the public-minded managerial leader should also cooperate, but, if the other party defects, that leader should defect, too. As the basis for that counsel, Axelrod's research has strongly suggested "that something approaching a one-for-one response to defection is likely to be quite effective in a wide range of settings." On a few occasions, the leader might make a second attempt at cooperation in the hope of avoiding "unending mutual recriminations," but only if the other party cannot readily exploit "an excess of forgiveness" (Axelrod 1984, 120).

In practice, many well-intentioned managerial leaders ignore this advice, preferring to forgive resistant subordinates and try again—perhaps even again and again. They may do so from a discomfort with drawing hard lines, preferring what may seem a kinder approach of offering additional opportunities to cooperate and negotiate. That is a risky strategy, though, because the uncooperative subordinate who is repeatedly "forgiven" could take advantage, "exploiting easy-going rules" for personal gain (Axelrod 1984, 120).

Making matters worse, the risk for the leader extends beyond the specific subordinate to future interactions with others who observed the initial interaction. As Axelrod (1984, 151) has explained, "when third parties are watching, the stakes of the current situation expand from those immediately at hand to encompass the influence of the current choice on the reputation of players." Giving ground when the other side holds firm could foster a perception among those third parties of the leader being a pushover, perhaps encouraging them to test the leader's resolve themselves. Ironically, that risk could be greatest for managers who otherwise favor policies to support and empower subordinates since supportive leaders may be more reluctant to draw lines and set limits (Bolman and Deal 2017, 346).

The public-minded managerial leader is better advised to respond in kind, reciprocating any defection by a subordinate. That might entail threatening to place a formal reprimand in the employee's personnel file, an option that falls within the prerogatives of most public-minded managerial leaders. A threat rather than an actual reprimand might give the subordinate a last opportunity to change behavior, thereby avoiding the official rebuke, yet still leave the leader the option to issue a reprimand if the subordinate remains intransigent.

The threat of a reprimand might be paired with a directive to the subordinate to develop a proposed solution, as in the earlier dialogue for the integrative approach in action. The leader might say, "You don't like my approach. Okay, come up with your own and let me know when you're ready to discuss." This tactic borrows the firmness of the Model I unilateral approach, but without its coercion. The request reopens the possibility of returning to the integrative approach, but with the onus for moving in that direction now squarely on the subordinate. By making no commitment to accept the subordinate's proposal, the leader shows no weakness, only a willingness to engage in additional discussion if the subordinate so chooses.

Public-minded managerial leaders might also heed two more Axelrod principles in interacting with resistant subordinates. First, instead of being "slow to anger," the better choice is "to respond quickly to a provocation" (Axelrod 1984, 184–185). A rapid response reduces the risk of misinterpretation because, "The longer defections are allowed to go unchallenged, the more likely it is that the other player will draw the conclusion that defection can pay." Second, respond proportionately, attempting to match the level of resistance. As Axelrod (1984, 119) has explained, "extracting more than one defection for each defection of the other risks escalation. On the other hand, extracting less than one-for-one risks exploitation."

To assist in these efforts, the savvy public-minded managerial leader will recognize the availability of a variety of persuasive techniques for bringing subordinates—and others—to the table. These could include appeals to public service values or to a subordinate's sense of responsible professionalism as well as other sources of motivation discussed in the last chapter. They might also employ rational persuasion, logic, or inspirational appeals, each of which can be effective in the right situation. A leader might even approach a resistant subordinate's peers to see if they have ideas for how to persuade the individual to cooperate.

If efforts to rekindle a negotiation still fail, the leader will at least have started a process toward resolving the issue through disciplinary action, likely first by threat of a reprimand, followed by an actual reprimand, followed potentially by gradual—proportionate—escalation of further disciplinary action, to the extent additional steps prove necessary. That kind of sequence can build the paper trail that, in a worst-case scenario, could eventually be required to terminate an employee (the incriminating paper trail that often seems to be missing when employers otherwise see cause for termination).

When the Resistant Party Is a Peer

The dynamic necessarily changes when the resistant party is a peer, not a subordinate, someone with whom the leader interacts at an equivalent level in the same organization or a different organization. The fact that a peer does not report to the manager immediately removes the possibility of disciplinary action, narrowing the range of options available to the public-minded managerial leader.

Assuming an issue where a peer has rebuffed overtures to engage in integrative negotiation, the leader might begin by following the same Axelrod guidelines recommended for working with resistant subordinates. That is, (1) don't be the first to defect, (2) reciprocate both cooperation and defection, (3) respond quickly, and (4) respond proportionately. Since none of those guidelines presumes a reporting relationship between the parties, the guidelines should apply as much to working with peers as to working with subordinates.

The question in dealing with peers arises at the point when disciplinary action might have been taken with a resistant subordinate. Lacking that tactic, how might a manager reciprocate defection? A first option might be a final appeal to public service values, similar to the appeal that could be made to a subordinate, perhaps saying: "This is an issue where our reaching a resolution could make a big difference for the public we serve." Where appropriate, a similar appeal might be made to responsible professionalism.

If that approach fails, the public-minded managerial leader will likely want to move to more of a hard-bargaining approach (e.g., Schelling 1958). Here the leader approaches the conflict with the goal of gaining as much value as possible, taking a "win-lose" approach in contrast to the "win-win" integrative approach. At this point, open communication no longer remains a value and the leader may instead attempt to conceal information in order to create uncertainty on the other side. Threats may also hold value, but only if they are credible. Threats are still preferable to sanctions, if sanctions are even possible, since they leave open the option to resume a negotiation if the other party wishes. One specific possible threat might be to take issues to a higher level, as perhaps to the other party's superior. That might function much like the threat of a reprimand to a subordinate, with the obvious qualification that the threat will not work if the other side is following directions from a superior.

Finally, following political principles, a public-minded managerial leader might attempt to build an alliance in opposition to the resistant party. That alliance might include other employees or managers in the same organization as well as peers in other organizations, people who might be recruited through the integrative approach that the opposing party has rebuffed. A leader who is adroit at networking might be able to assemble a group of sympathetic peers whose collective capacity could overpower the resistant party.

Meshing Relationship Development with Different Leadership Styles

Scholarship on leadership has documented a range of styles that different leaders follow in working with subordinates and peers (e.g., Rainey 2014, 293–294). Here are a few of the most prominent examples:

- *Laissez-faire:* This style allows employees to pursue their work mostly as they see fit with the leader providing relatively little supervision or assistance.
- *Directive or task-oriented:* This style focuses on completing tasks and emphasizes providing direction to subordinates on which tasks to complete and how.

- *Supportive or relationship-oriented:* This style focuses more on encouraging than directing employees, trying to build positive relationships with subordinates and others.
- *Coaching:* This style represents a combination of directive and supportive approaches, providing both direction on what to do and support in meeting the challenges of work.
- *Participative:* This style emphasizes involving subordinates in jointly making decisions about their work and the work of the organization more generally.
- *Delegating:* This style is a variation on the directive approach wherein the manager assigns tasks to subordinates, monitoring occasionally to assess compliance and performance.

Each of these styles will prove effective in some situations. As two examples, the directive style may be effective where tasks have some ambiguity and complexity and group members are comfortable with authoritarian leadership, as likely in parts of the military; and the participative style appears to be effective where tasks are more ambiguous and unstructured, and employees prefer autonomy and a high level of personal control, as perhaps in university academic departments (see House 1996, 326–327).

On the whole, though, no single style is likely to work all of the time because each suffers from blind spots: a directive manager is unlikely to listen well; a supportive manager may not provide enough direction; a coaching style may prove exhausting as the manager attempts to do too much with too many; a participative manager may involve others too often, distracting from their core responsibilities (see also Chapter 8); and so on.

The principal lesson from this chapter's strategies for developing relationships with subordinates is that different approaches will be required for different employees and even for different situations with the same employee. To some extent, that need can be addressed by the leader hiring assistants whose talents fill gaps in the manager's skills. For the most part, though, the most effective public-minded managerial leader will be able to move between leadership styles depending on the situation.

To do so effectively, these leaders will need the strong communication skills outlined here, including an ability to ask good questions, a capacity to listen closely, a talent for crafting integrative solutions to meet the needs of multiple parties, and a willingness to confront rather than shrink from conflict. The public-minded managerial leader who cultivates these skills should be able to develop productive relationships with a broad range of employees and peers.

Personal Leadership Exercise 7.1

Rate the Quality of Your Communication with Subordinates (or, If You Are not a Manager, the Quality of Your Superior's Communication with You).

Communication element	Poor	Fair	Excellent
Communicating clearly			
Providing feedback			
Encouraging feedback			
Engaging in active listening			
Developing partnership relationships			
Providing representation & buffering			

In light of your answers, how do you rate the overall quality of this communication?

What changes might you recommend to improve the quality of this communication?

Personal Leadership Exercise 7.2

Rate Your Ability to Address Conflict.

Dimension of conflict	Poor	Fair	Excellent
Knowing when to duck conflict			
Not ducking conflict that should be addressed			
Asking informational questions first			
Making appropriate use of the accommodating approach			
Re-framing to propose integrative solutions			
Successfully resolving conflicts			

In light of your answers, how would you rate your overall ability to address conflict?

What, if anything, might you change to improve your ability to address conflict?

Personal Leadership Exercise 7.3

Rate Your Ability to Address Conflict When the Other Side Resists Negotiation.

Tactic	Poor	Fair	Excellent
Not being the first to defect			
Reciprocating both cooperation & defection			
Maintaining a one-for-one response to defection			
Being wary of messages that might be communicated to third-party observers			
Using threats before sanctions			
Drawing on a variety of persuasive techniques			
Escalating disciplinary action as necessary			
Building supportive alliances where appropriate			

In light of your answers, how would you rate your overall ability to address conflict when the other side resists?

What, if anything, might you change to improve your ability to address this kind of conflict?

Chapter 8

Making Decisions—
With and Without Others

Public-minded managerial leaders carry as one of their principal responsibilities the need to make decisions, many of which will hold substantial implications for their organizations. As former university president Nannerl Keohane (2012, 101) has observed, "Making decisions is one of the characteristic activities in which leaders engage." That reality can regularly raise questions of whether others should be invited to join in making decisions and, when invited, to what extent they should share authority over those decisions.

A traditional view of leadership sees these questions as nonissues. In the words of Cloke and Goldsmith (2011, 175):

> In most hierarchical organizational cultures, there is an unspoken understanding that the role of managers is to solve problems, leading to solutions that are unilateral, hierarchical, and bureaucratic, in ways that conform with existing rules and regulations. It is often assumed that any manager who cannot do so without help from below is incompetent.

From that view, it is the leader's responsibility to make decisions and issue orders; followers should comply in implementing those orders.

That perspective, if ever accurate, is increasingly unrealistic and, where honored, potentially counterproductive. As explained in earlier chapters, people have become increasingly resistant to being told to follow orders without any explanation of why. Leaders for their part frequently need information and support from others if they are to make informed decisions that can be effectively implemented. At the same time, achieving those goals does not require that everyone be involved in making every decision; too much involvement can actually undermine organizational effectiveness. Substantial evidence suggests that "the middle ground between directive and participative styles is typically more effective" (Eagly 2013, 5), but how can leaders find that middle ground?

As that question implies, determining when, to what extent, and how to involve others in making decisions are important concerns for public-minded managerial leaders. The abilities necessary to make these determinations represent important political skills in the sense, as defined in Chapter 4, of "activities taken within an organization to acquire, develop, and use power and other resources to obtain one's preferred outcomes" (Ferris and Treadway 2012, 11). The political skills lie in (1) knowing when and to what extent to involve—or not involve—others and, when working with others, (2) knowing how to facilitate discussion both to encourage free expression of opinions and to move toward a decision the group will support. This chapter addresses the first of those skills; the next chapter considers the second.

The Cases For and Against Involving Others

There are good reasons both to involve and *not* to involve others in making decisions. On the positive side, the potential benefits of involvement include:

- *More and better information:* More information can make for a more informed decision. Leaders can access that information by involving others in decision making and listening to what they have to say.
- *More commitment to decisions:* If those who are involved in decision-making feel they were listened to, they are more likely to support the eventual decision. That support should enhance the likelihood of successfully implementing the decision.
- *A stronger group identity:* Being involved with others in making a decision can increase participants' sense of identity as a group, which in turn can improve a group's functioning.
- *More knowledge and understanding shared by the group:* Group members can learn from each other when they interact in a decision-making process. Their greater shared knowledge can then enhance future individual and group performance.
- *A more comfortable culture for well-educated workers:* Being involved in decision making typically better fits the wishes of an educated workforce, adding to the comfort employees feel in their jobs.

- *Increased respect for the group's leader:* Leaders who oversee effective decision-making processes where others are involved usually build respect for themselves as leaders.

If involving others in making decisions were only about those benefits, more involvement would be the obvious choice. Reality, though, brings a number of possible costs, including:

- *More time to reach a decision:* The more people who are involved in decision making, the more time may be required to reach a decision. More people want to have a say and more perspectives must be considered, both of which can lengthen the process.
- *A loss of control:* The change from deciding by oneself to deciding with others likely requires the surrender of some control. Some leaders will not want to relinquish that control.
- *Increased conflict:* With the voicing of different opinions, group members may recognize differences of opinion among themselves. Those differences will sometimes lead to conflict and unpleasantness.
- *Deterioration into chaos:* Decision-making processes can sometimes spin out of control in the face of many opinions and no obvious compromise.
- *Decreased respect for the group's leader:* Just as effective involvement can build respect for a leader, a flawed effort to involve others in decision making can undermine that respect. That could happen if any of the above risks materializes or if the leader is perceived as asking for others' opinions too often, perhaps appearing indecisive or weak.

With so much potential for both benefits and costs, when and how to involve others in decision making can be difficult questions to answer. Public-minded managerial leaders want the benefits that involving others can bring, but do not want to incur the possible costs. What to do?

Involving Others as a Sometimes Thing

The short answer to these questions is that involvement of others in decision making should be a sometime thing. The participation of subordinates and other stakeholders in making decisions is only sometimes needed and, when needed, is not desirable to the same extent on all occasions. Adapting a model from the work of management scholars Victor Vroom with Philip Yetton (1973) and later with Arthur Jago (1988), this chapter presents a contingent approach to determining if and how to involve others in decision making. This approach views the degree of involvement desirable as depending on the nature of the issue being decided, with some issues calling for more involvement and others for less.

The core of the approach boils down to two competing guidelines. On the one hand, more involvement of others in decision making will usually be desirable when (1) leaders lack significant information that they could obtain from others and/or (2) successful implementation depends on others accepting the decision. On the other hand, involvement of others may need to be limited if the issue carries quality constraints that any decision must respect. Those constraints could be technical or scientific (e.g., a scientific standard that must be respected), financial (e.g., a budget ceiling that cannot be exceeded), or some other kind of constraint (e.g., a legislative mandate).

These guidelines play out in terms of a number of specific characteristics of any issue that may be up for a decision. To determine how much to involve others, leaders need to answer a sequence of questions about these characteristics (see Vroom and Jago 1988, 55–65). Specifically:

1. How important is decision quality? That is, what quality constraints should the eventual decision respect? In the public realm, most decisions bring some quality constraints, likely including budget limitations, technical criteria (e.g., engineering standards), and mission consistency (i.e., the decision must be consistent with the agency's mission).

Quality constraints provide grounds for limiting others' involvement in decision making, but they do not necessarily recommend zero involvement. Other characteristics of an issue may recommend involvement, at which point the question becomes how to involve others while still protecting quality constraints.

2. Do I have the information necessary to make a good decision? Leaders may lack information on what employees or other stakeholders prefer, how well earlier programs worked, as well as other aspects of an issue. Leaders who see themselves lacking necessary information are well advised to consider involving those who may have that information.

3. Is the decision structured? Structure refers to whether a possible decision is limited to two or a few options—in other words, a "forced-choice" decision—instead of being open to a broad range of options. It is a structured choice, for example, if a local planning agency is considering whether to purchase a particular Geographical Information System (GIS) software program. By contrast, the choice would be unstructured if the agency were considering more broadly how to improve its GIS capabilities.

Structured choices usually recommend less involvement of others in decision making. After all, a forced-choice offers less latitude for others to exert influence than do open-ended issues where discussion could help to shape the choices themselves. Involving others extensively in structured choices risks irritating those who participate since they may wonder why their choice is so constrained. Where extensive involvement appears desirable, it is usually better invited *before* the decision becomes structured.

4. *Is acceptance of the decision by others important for effective implementation, and, if so, is that acceptance reasonably certain if those others are not involved in the decision making?* The need for acceptance in order to successfully implement a decision represents a principal reason for involving others in decision making. Involvement in that scenario could result in more support for the decision by those who are involved.

The importance of that principle becomes evident when leaders do not heed its counsel, as when Sean O'Keefe, administrator of the National Aeronautics and Space Administration (NASA) decided in 2004 to terminate the popular Hubble Space Telescope: "He knew the decision would be controversial. He reached it personally and gradually, in conversations with NASA officials, often indirectly, without much open discussion and debate. It came across as a one-man decision." When his decision leaked, it was seen "as arbitrary and capricious. The political backlash was immediate, loud, and harshly personal" (Lambright 2012, 77–78). In short, by ignoring the need for public acceptance of a controversial decision, O'Keefe undermined the decision, forcing him later to backtrack.

Involvement of others in decision making should not be necessary—and could be undesirable—if those others are likely to accept the decision regardless of whether they are involved. At the same time, many a leader has erred by assuming the outcomes of a decision would be so positive that those whose acceptance is needed will readily embrace the leader's unilateral decision. Those errors may be especially common with issues where a decision will impact a broader public, with history documenting many examples of leaders whose optimism about public acceptance of their unilateral decisions proved naïve when public opposition eventually mobilized (for a case example, see Thomas 1995, 81–83).

5. *Do the others who might be involved in decision making respect the issue's quality constraints?* Leaders need to ask how those who might be involved in decision making feel about the issue's quality constraints. If they might be skeptical or even opposed to the constraints, that expectation provides additional grounds for limiting involvement in making the decision.

Again, though, a likelihood of opposition does not necessarily recommend avoiding involvement entirely. If there are other reasons for broadening involvement, such as needs for information or for acceptance of the eventual decision, the decision-making process should be designed to balance the competing needs, providing voice for the contrary opinions, protection for quality constraints, and, in the end, a means to reach a better decision than could have been reached without that involvement.

6. Is conflict among subordinates likely on the preferred solution? Where the answer to the last question is negative, that is, where resistance to quality constraints is anticipated from those who might be involved in decision making, another question arises, the question of whether there may be disagreement *among* those who might be invited to join in the decision making. That is, are they likely to disagree among themselves?

Any anticipated disagreement will usually recommend *more* involvement in decision making. More involvement in this situation promises to make the disagreement more obvious to group members, thereby making more evident the difficulty of finding a resolution that can satisfy everyone. That recognition might either provide a starting place for finding a compromise acceptable to the group or, if not, build understanding and sympathy for the plight of the leader who must make a decision.

7. Is there a desire to develop the group as a group? Finally, there is the question of whether the leader wants to develop the group, cultivating members' identity with the group, their shared knowledge, and the group's ability to deliberate and make decisions. Unlike the earlier questions, this one speaks to a goal of the leader who is in charge, not to characteristics of the issue.

A desire to develop a group provides grounds for leaders to involve the group more than they might otherwise have been inclined on the premise that participation in an effective decision-making process can enhance members' sense of bonding with the group. One risk in such efforts lies in the potential for group members to see their time together as wasted unless they feel they are addressing real issues.

Does a time constraint recommend less involvement? One might suspect that a time constraint on a decision would recommend *less* involvement in decision making than might otherwise appear desirable. Although that logic may occasionally hold, it appears likely to mislead most of the time. A possible time constraint should consequently not be a factor in determining how much to involve others.

For one thing, the time constraints on decisions that leaders mention mostly do not hold up to close scrutiny. In their original research on involvement in decision making, Vroom and Jago (1988, 87) found that managers usually cited "a severe time constraint simply to justify or rationalize their preferred autocratic style."

The argument for the importance of time constraints also fails to recognize that decisions typically come with two kinds of time constraints. The obvious constraint focuses on the time available to make a decision, supporting the argument that less time availability recommends less involvement of others in decision making. Looking farther down the road, though, there will also often be a time constraint on the time required to *implement* a decision, and this second constraint may be inversely related to the first. That is, accelerating initial decision making may produce an earlier decision, but the resulting lack of involvement could result in more resistance to implementation from those who were excluded from decision making. By contrast, spending more time making a decision may result in greater decision acceptance, which could expedite implementation. Public-minded managerial leaders are consequently well-advised to consider the potential implementation costs in excluding interested others from decision making before letting an apparent time constraint rush a decision.

Choosing a Decision-Making Approach

Far from being an either-or choice, there are at least six options for how to involve others in decision making (see Vroom and Jago 1988, 32–37). Moving from least involvement to most, these are the decision-making options:

- *Unilateral decision-making*: Leaders decide on their own, choosing not to involve anyone else.
- *Modified unilateral*: Leaders seek information from others, but still decide alone, never suggesting that decision-making authority will be shared.
- *Individual consultation*: Leaders consult with others individually, sharing the issue with one person at a time, before deciding alone. As the crucial difference from the modified unilateral approach, the sharing of the issue implies that the opinions of others will be considered in the eventual decision.
- *Group consultation*: This approach takes consultation a step further to where the leader shares the issue with others as a group, not as individuals, although still deciding alone. This approach can be useful for getting a sense of the opinion of the group *as a group,* but it runs the risk that the group could recognize its opposition to the perspective of the group leader, complicating that individual's ability to make a decision contrary to the group's perspective.
- *Group decision*: The leader shares the issue with others as a group, and then attempts to reach agreement as a group on a solution. This approach obviously increases the power of the group in that the leader has surrendered the power to decide alone.
- *Delegated decision*: The leader delegates authority to others, withdrawing fully from decision making. This does not necessarily mean that the leader exerts no power over the decision making. The leader could still assert parameters to the group, stipulating specific scien-

tific and/or legal principles or a budget limitation that the eventual decision must respect.

The choice between these approaches depends on the characteristics of the specific issue, as best explained by considering each in turn.

Unilateral

The unilateral approach makes best sense for issues where, in answer to the earlier questions about issue characteristics, the leader perceives:

- A need to respect quality considerations,
- No need for additional information, and
- Either no need for acceptance of the decision by others or, if there is such a need, a belief that others will accept the decision without being involved in its development.

This approach would also fit if the issue included this additional characteristic:

- A structured choice between two or a few options.

With a concern for quality combined with no clear value to involving others, these issues make obvious candidates for leaders to decide on their own. These are the kinds of decisions where, if others were involved, they might wonder, "Why take my time when you could have decided on your own?"

The risk to taking this approach lies in the leader misjudging needs for information or acceptance. If a need for either or both becomes evident, having taken this approach can result in a decision that is ill-informed (for lack of necessary information) or that others will resist (for lack of the involvement necessary to gain their acceptance) or both. A belated recognition of either need would recommend changing to a more participatory decision-making approach.

Modified Unilateral

This approach becomes desirable with only one change from the first scenario. The leader still perceives:

- A need to respect quality considerations,
- No need for acceptance of the decision by others or, if there is such a need, a belief that others will accept the decision without having been involved, and
- Either a structured or unstructured choice.

With the one change from the first scenario, the leader now sees:

- A need for additional information.

That need serves as grounds to involve others, but only to obtain the necessary information, not to nurture acceptance.

The modified unilateral approach might be appropriate, for example, for some types of hiring. Consider a hypothetical case of a manager of a small governmental department who needs to hire an assistant administrator to serve as his top aide. The manager perceives important quality considerations (e.g., proficiency with specific software programs, people skills for interacting with other departmental employees and other parts of the organization), but, since the individual would work mostly for the manager, there may be no need for acceptance of the new hire by others in the department. At the same time, the manager sees value in having another perspective—a form of additional information—in choosing among the applicants. Since history suggests that most of the candidates for this type of position will be female, he decides to ask a senior female professional in the department to assist in the hiring. In the end, the two agree on a pool of three candidates to interview and, subsequently, on which candidate to hire. If working as intended, the additional perspective of the senior female professional gives the leader more information and ultimately more confidence in the hiring choice.

The choice of a modified unilateral approach over the unilateral approach often depends on the specific leader. In the hiring of the administrative assistant, a different leader might have perceived no need for additional information, feeling confident in her ability to reach an effective decision unilaterally. Different leaders could choose different decision-making approaches, with the different approaches effective for both.

On the other hand, a choice for broader consultation or even a group decision would probably not be an effective means for making this hire, regardless of a leader's preferences. A broader consultation with other departmental employees could waste the time of others who have little or no information to provide and whose acceptance of the new hire is not crucial. That choice would likely amount to inviting *more* involvement than is necessary.

Individual Consultation

As issues become more complex, more extensive involvement becomes desirable. The least extensive approach finds the leader engaging in individual consultation, consulting separately with different individuals before making a decision. In contrast to the modified unilateral approach, individual consultation implies some sharing of influence, but the leader still ultimately makes the decision.

This approach may be desirable when the leader perceives a relatively uncomplicated issue, one featuring:

- A need to respect quality considerations,
- A possible need for additional information, and
- An unstructured choice.

That description could fit the hiring of the administrative assistant profiled earlier. The leader would in fact have engaged an individual consultation if decision-making authority was shared with the senior female professional who assisted in the hiring.

An individual consultation will usually be appropriate, too, where an issue includes these additional characteristics:

- A need for acceptance of the decision as a condition for its effective implementation, and a low likelihood of obtaining that acceptance without involvement in making the decision, and
- Possible or likely disagreement with organizational goals among those who might be involved in making the decision.

Issues with these characteristics pose difficult challenges for leaders. As the crux of the problem, there are quality constraints that must be protected, but acceptance is needed from others who likely disagree with at least some of the constraints. An individual consultation offers the highest likelihood of success by (1) permitting the stipulation of quality constraints as parameters, (2) engaging others in decision making in a manner likely to nurture decision acceptance, while (3) avoiding convening those others as a single group that might recognize its shared opposition to core quality constraints. That recognition could risk mobilizing the group in opposition to the core goals for the issue.

Issues along these lines may pit leaders against their employees, an unpleasant and unpromising prospect that can make these the most difficult issues to resolve. Such issues can arise, for example, when agencies undertake large-scale organizational change that might entail reorganizing departments, revising core programs, and reformulating job descriptions. The scope of those changes can threaten employees, perhaps leading to questioning of organizational goals.

Public-minded managerial leaders facing such issues may be tempted to withdraw to a unilateral or modified unilateral approach, hoping to avoid or minimize conflict. Doing so amounts to abandoning hope of obtaining the acceptance necessary for effective implementation of the decision. In addition, conflict may not be avoided but only postponed; the conflict that is sidestepped by deciding unilaterally could erupt as heated and destructive during implementation.

As a consequence, the better choice usually involves consulting with others individually, looking for ways to tweak a decision in a manner that will enhance the potential for acceptance. For example, the broad organizational change that can produce dogged resistance might be adapted in ways that will win over at least some of the opposition. Consultation might even reveal areas of agreement with goals that were not initially evident, perhaps leading to strategies that can facilitate the change initiative.

On the other hand, any manager who faces many decisions along these lines could be pardoned for polishing the résumé and seeking a different workplace. No matter how important these decisions might be, a steady diet of them and of the corrosive conflict with fellow workers they may bring will inevitably take a toll on most managers. Some might decide there are better ways to make a living.

Group Consultation

Other complex, but less difficult issues call for group consultation, where the leader consults with the group as a whole, while reserving the prerogative to decide away from the group. This approach can be desirable if the leader perceives:

- A need to respect quality considerations,
- A possible need for additional information,
- A need for acceptance of the decision as a condition for its effective implementation, and a low likelihood of obtaining that acceptance without involvement in decision making,
- Possible or likely disagreement with organizational goals among those who might be involved in making the decision, and
- Likely disagreement among those who might be involved over the organization's goals.

That last characteristic represents the one change from the previous scenario, with the leader anticipating disagreement over goals among those who would be involved in any deliberations.

That difference recommends a group consultation instead of the individual consultation recommended for the last scenario. The likely disagreement among those who would be involved implies that a group consultation will not risk mobilization against organizational goals. To the contrary, consulting with the group should make the disagreement more evident to those who participate, perhaps taking the first steps toward resolving or ameliorating the disagreement. If not, those who are involved should understand better why the decision cannot easily be made by the group and so perhaps must be made by the leader. In other words, a group consultation in this situation could build sympathy for the need for a leader to make the decision in the face of the group's inability to do so.

A group consultation might be attempted, for example, by a public-minded managerial leader whose department has been asked to make a significant budget cut in the face of an organizational financial crisis. Departmental employees might initially disagree on where to apply cuts, perhaps feeling that their areas should be spared with other areas subjected to most of the cuts. With a group consultation, those employees might either agree to a compromise strategy, possibly by everyone sharing the pain, or concede the need for the department head to decide. In either case, that leader will likely be viewed more positively than if the decision had been made unilaterally.

Importantly, the leader in a group consultation retains the authority to make the decision after hearing from the group. That fact provides protection for the issue's quality constraints; the leader will presumably be sure to incorporate those constraints in the eventual decision. Those constraints should be further protected by the leader stipulating them earlier at the outset of any deliberations.

Group Decision

Multiple scenarios lend themselves to a group decision process where the leader shares the issue and then makes the decision collaboratively with other group members. In the most obvious case, the leader would perceive an issue as having these characteristics:

- A need to respect quality considerations,
- A possible need for additional information,
- A need for acceptance of the decision as a condition for its effective implementation and a low likelihood of obtaining that acceptance without involvement in decision making, and
- Agreement with organizational goals among those who might be involved in making the decision.

Here the leader must involve others in deliberations in order to obtain their acceptance of the decision, but can do so with less concern about threats to quality constraints given the group's agreement with organizational goals. Asserting the quality constraints up front can again provide additional protection for those constraints.

A group decision will sometimes also prove possible in the previous scenario, where there is:

- Disagreement on organizational goals among those who might be involved, but also
- Disagreement *among* group members on those goals.

The leader might initially approach decision making here as a group consultation, but retain the option of moving to a group decision approach if deliberations suggest the likelihood of compromises that do not threaten quality constraints.

Finally, the group decision approach may also be desirable for some issues where the same characteristics hold as described above and, in addition, the choice is structured. Here, though, the decision-making process might be limited to a discussion of the choices, followed by a vote, assuming no consensus emerges. The risk in these situations is that participants may question why they are given only a limited choice and perhaps push for opening the discussion to a broader range of options.

Delegated Decision

Public-minded managerial leaders will find that some issues are best delegated to others. Yukl (2013 96–97) suggests that delegation to a subordinate makes sense when the subordinate "has more expertise . . . , is closer to the problem and can obtain more timely information about it. . . , or because the manager simply does not have the time necessary to do the task properly." With that context, delegation of decision making may make the most sense if the leader perceives an issue having these characteristics:

- No quality requirements,
- A need for acceptance of the decision as a condition for its effective implementation,
- A low likelihood of obtaining that acceptance without involvement in making the decision, and
- Agreement with organizational goals among those who might be involved in making the decision.

Those characteristics in combination suggest an issue where the manager might be able to delegate authority without fear of repercussions. After all, there are no quality requirements that a decision must respect, group acceptance is needed, and the group is expected to agree with organizational goals.

The manager might even consider delegating the decision if, with the other characteristics unchanged, the issue includes quality requirements. Those quality requirements could be protected by the manager stipulating them as parameters in the charge of the decision-making group. Here, though, delegation might be a sensible option only if the manager has a strong sense of a well-developed group with a strong commitment to organizational goals.

When Group Development Is a Goal

If group development is a goal, managers will usually want to err on the side of more involvement in decision making. More involvement should contribute to the group's development, with the group decision approach offering the most promise toward that end.

Whether group development is a goal will sometimes drive the choice between disparate approaches to decision making. Consider, for example, the scenario where a modified unilateral approach was recommended earlier:

- A need to respect quality considerations,
- No need for acceptance of the decision by others or, if there is such a need, a belief that others will accept the decision without needing to be involved in its development, and
- A need for additional information.

A public-minded manager who is new to the role and interested in developing a unit's employees as a group might choose a group consultation instead of the modified unilateral approach, seeing consultation as more likely to develop the group's identity and deliberative capacity. That choice should be made cautiously, however, given the risk of group members perceiving their involvement as more ritualistic than substantive.

Ironically, efforts at a group's development through the group consultation or group decision approaches can increase the latitude of the public-minded managerial leader to utilize the unilateral or modified unilateral decision-making approaches on other occasions. A group that feels empowered by its leader to influence many decisions may reciprocate by trusting the leader to make some decisions *without* its input. Sharing authority and empowering employees can thus potentially lead to those employees in essence empowering their leader to act without their involvement.

If Uncertain About Issue Characteristics?

Uncertainty about specific issue characteristics poses a principal challenge to following these guidelines. What if the leader does not know if others will accept a decision without being involved in decision making? What if the leader has a poor sense of group members' attitudes toward organizational goals? Or, what if events demonstrate that the leader erred in initial perceptions of an issue's characteristics? Any of those possibilities could undermine the ability to follow the earlier guidelines in choosing a decision-making approach.

Uncertainty is best addressed by retaining flexibility in the choice of decision-making approaches, as the three examples below illustrate:

- A modified unilateral approach might be broadened to an individual or group consultation if the leader, in seeking information, identifies an unexpected need for group involvement in order to obtain group acceptance.
- A group decision approach might be replaced with a unilateral or modified unilateral approach if initial discussions reveal that the group will embrace a decision made without their involvement.
- Questioning by others may lead the leader to rethink a quality constraint that had been asserted as a parameter, perhaps suggesting more latitude for group involvement in making the decision (for an example, see Thomas 1995, 46–48).

These and other uncertainties recommend that public-minded managerial leaders, after choosing a decision-making approach, remain open to adopting a different approach if new information justifies.

Other Sources of Variability

Personal and organizational factors will also affect leader preferences among the different decision-making approaches. Some leaders are more comfortable with participatory approaches, while others may prefer to engage participation sparingly, yet both may be effective in decision making. The nature of an organization's work may also affect inclinations toward more or less participation. For example, organizations where work is done mostly by teams may lean more toward participatory approaches than will organizations where work is more technical and individually focused (e.g., Anderson, Spataro, & Flynn 2008).

Effective managers will also frequently employ more than one decision-making approach in deciding an issue. A process might begin with a modified unilateral or individual consultation approach where the manager seeks only to learn others' perspectives. Those perspectives might suggest the desirability of a more participatory approach to decision making, an approach such as a group consultation or a group decision.

Core Principles to Keep in Mind

Given the many permutations of issue characteristics and the many other reasons for varying decision-making approaches, no single set of guidelines can easily cover all eventualities (but see also Vroom and Jago 1988). As a result, where the earlier guidelines might confuse or not suffice, public-minded managerial leaders might try to keep a few overriding principles in mind. In brief, when contemplating possible involvement of others in decision making, the public-minded managerial leader should:

- Begin by defining any quality constraints that an eventual decision should respect.
- Consider whether additional information is needed in order to make a well-informed decision.
- Assess whether others' acceptance is required for effective implementation of a decision.
- After selecting an approach, retain flexibility in case initial steps in decision making suggest a need for course correction.
- Recognize that, while not always desirable, a more participatory managerial approach typically results in higher employee job satisfaction (e.g., Kim 2002).

Common Mistakes in Involving (and Not Involving) Others

Public-minded managerial leaders who are unfamiliar with this model and its core principles can fall victim to a number of mistakes in how they engage others in decision making. Observation of various leaders suggests the nature of the most common errors, while the model suggests how the errors can be avoided or mitigated.

Error #1: "I need to protect my quality concerns, so I can't involve others." The error here lies in believing that quality constraints will necessarily be endangered if others are involved in making a decision. In reality, the model provides two means for structuring decision making in a manner that will *both* involve others *and* protect quality. First, before decision making begins, leaders can stipulate parameters that any decision must respect, in the process implying an intent to veto any proposed decision that would compromise those parameters. Second, actual involvement can be limited, perhaps to consultation as opposed to a group decision, such that ideas from the group are considered, but not necessarily fully reflected in the eventual decision. Even with these limitations, others can still be involved in a manner likely to increase their support of any decision.

Error #2: "I'll ask for others' opinions (but I don't need to listen)." Asking and not listening, which is to say asking for opinions but not sharing authority over a decision, does more harm than good and is usually a worse choice than not asking at all. When asked for their opinions, people will want to be heard and perhaps to influence the decision. If they are not heard and their opinions are ignored, they may become cynical or resentful, likely undermining both their support for implementing the decision and their willingness to join in future decision making.

Error #3: "I should always involve others." At the other end of the spectrum, managers are often encouraged simply to involve others more in decision making, sometimes regardless of the nature of the issue at hand. The error comes in not recognizing that most employees do not need or want to be involved in most decisions. Asking them to participate more than necessary—more than the model recommends—both wastes their time and undermines the standing of the group's leader.

Errors #4+: Trying to involve, but not understanding how. When they actually try to involve others in decision making, group leaders can err in many additional ways, including:

- They may spend more time talking than asking and listening. While involving others requires guidance and thus contributions from leaders, it also requires that those leaders listen and take note of what they hear.
- They may neglect to assert quality criteria at the outset, inviting resistance if those criteria are announced only belatedly as reasons not to make a decision that already has group support.
- Or, leaders may lose control of the decision-making process entirely because they do not understand how to move from the divergent process of hearing different opinions to the convergent process of crafting a decision the group can embrace.

The good news is that many public-minded managerial leaders already appear to follow the principles of the model closely and effectively. Some probably do so from an intuitive sense of how to work with others, but most likely learned from experience, including unpleasant experience. A savvy manager will learn lessons from, on the one hand, a decision that fails for lack of involvement in its development or, on the other hand, a loss of standing with peers due to inviting excessive involvement.

Knowing when and to what extent to involve others in decision-making represents the first step in making effective decisions. There are also the questions of how, when choosing one of the highly participatory decision-making approaches (i.e., a group consultation or a group decision), to work effectively with groups to resolve issues and reach decisions. These questions are the focus of the next chapter.

Personal Leadership Exercise 8.1

Choosing an Issue That You or Your Agency Recently Decided or May Decide Soon, What Were Its Characteristics?

Issue characteristic	Yes	No
Did the decision have quality constraints?		
Did you have sufficient information?		
Was the decision structured?		
Was acceptance of the decision important for implementation, and, if so, was that acceptance likely without involving others?		
Did the others who might be involved respect the issue's quality constraints?		
Were the others who might be involved likely to disagree among themselves on the preferred solution?		
Was there a desire to develop the group as a group?		

Based on these characteristics, what do you believe would be the appropriate decision-making approach?

Which approach was actually taken to making the decision?

To the extent you can tell, how effective was the decision in terms of:
- Quality (i.e., respecting quality constraints, being well informed)
- Implementation (i.e., whether implemented, time required to implement)

To what extent and how do you believe the choice of decision-making approaches affected the quality of the decision?

Chapter 9

Leading Small-Group Teams and Meetings

Public-minded managerial leaders must devote extensive time to working with small-group teams, structuring and managing the teams, and running their meetings. These teams serve as the usual vehicles for addressing the issues that, as described in the last chapter, call for collaborative decision making through the group consultation and group decision approaches. Their meetings, in turn, function as the forums where these decisions are made.

These are not simple tasks. An extensive literature documents the frequent failures of teams (e.g., Lafair 2015), and facilitating small-group meetings may be even more challenging; witness the frequent complaints about frustrating and unproductive meetings. One recent national employee survey, for example, found employees ranking "wasteful meetings" as the most frequent problem—cited by 62 percent of the respondents—interfering with their work (Workfront 2018).

That need not be the case. Managed effectively by public-minded managerial leaders, small-group teams and their meetings offer an enormous potential for improving organizational performance. Leaders who grasp what that effective management entails gain the capacity to make these teams rewarding experiences for their members and productive tools for their organizations. This chapter offers guidelines for building that capacity.

Small-Group Teams and Meetings Defined

Small-group teams in the organizational context refer to groups typically numbering three–fifteen employees whose work focuses on a common function. Larger than fifteen—and many experts prefer a lower ceiling of twelve or thirteen—and the group is no longer small; lower than three and the entity is a one-on-one relationship, not a group as such. While the upper limit of fifteen might seem arbitrary, it is crucial for the dynamics of groups, especially for their meetings, as explained below.

Some small-group teams are created by a formal directive to attend to a specific issue, while others develop informally based on recognition of common interests by the members-to-be. They may form around the membership of a small department, a subgroup within a department, or an interdepartmental group. They may follow hierarchical lines, as with the first and perhaps the second of those examples, or, they may cross those lines, as with the third. The interdepartmental teams are likely tasked to address issues the organizational chart is perceived as unable to address. Small-group teams may also be ongoing or ad hoc, created as temporary entities (some of which become permanent). The crucial point may be that the form corresponds to the issue on which the group will focus.

All but the smallest organizations probably include some small-group teams focused on specific organizational functions or tasks, with the number of teams varying between organizations for any number of reasons. More groups are likely where an organization's work calls for more coordination, while fewer may be needed when an organization's work is more individually focused, as with much technical work (e.g., Anderson, Spataro, and Flynn 2008). Some organizational cultures also encourage more work by small groups.

These groups become relevant for small-group meetings when they must coordinate their work to some extent, thereby requiring meeting and making decisions. That decision making should occur through either the group consultation or group decision approach where leadership is more facilitative than top-down in nature. Only a collaborative approach can ensure the essential sharing of information and influence.

The Growing Popularity of Small-Group Teams

Although supportive data are scarce, small-group teams as organizational tools appear to have grown substantially in popularity over recent decades. The reasons for that growth may trace first to the evolution from a manufacturing to a service economy, with the latter usually calling for more collaboration than does the former (e.g., Osborne, Radnor, and Nasi 2013). Collaboration is the stuff of small-group teams, making those entities more likely to be found where organizations focus more on services, as is certainly the case with public and nonprofit organizations.

Globalization and the accelerated pace of technological change, two other facts of life for contemporary organizations, add to the momentum for using small-group teams. Where traditional organization charts may have responded to the needs of an earlier era, globalization and technological change have often transformed those needs, catalyzing the emergence of new issues for which those organization charts have no answers. Organizations must then develop new arrangements to address the new issues.

The increasing diffusion of information further encourages the use of small-group teams. Information once represented a principal basis for power and authority; those who sat at an organization's strategic apex possessed more information and held more power in part for that reason. But information has proved a leaky resource in the era of the internet, handheld devices, and the like. As information has diffused, leaders increasingly recognize that they cannot make well-informed decisions unless they can access information from elsewhere in their organizations (see also Chapter 8). That information is more easily accessed through collaborative small-group teams, where members routinely share knowledge and ideas, than from traditional superior-subordinate relationships.

Higher levels of education also contribute to preferences for a collaborative, team-oriented environment (e.g., Kim 2002). As people become more educated, they become more likely to question authority. Leaders no longer find it as easy to issue demands and expect compliance since employees increasingly want to know why—or even if—they should follow an order. The more educated will usually be more comfortable working in small-group teams where decisions are shaped collaboratively, not imposed unilaterally.

All of these factors point to the limits of traditional hierarchy and specialization and the potential for small-group teams to address contemporary organizational issues. As a result, small-group teams appear to have become an increasingly common vehicle for performing the work of organizations and *between* organizations (on the latter, see also Chapter 10).

While the management literature mostly focuses on either teams *or* small groups and not on small-group teams as such, that does not appear to reflect any difference in how the two terms are defined. The real distinction comes in what the literatures on the two terms emphasize. The literature on teams focuses mostly on what makes teams effective, while the literature on small groups mostly addresses specific practical questions around how to run the groups' meetings. This chapter will summarize the important insights from both perspectives, beginning with how to develop small-group teams before turning to how to run effective small-group meetings.

Starting a Small-Group Team

All too often, small-group teams commence their work without having a clear sense of why they were created or what they are tasked to accomplish. Starting in that manner risks disaster since, without a shared understanding, team members may head in different directions based on different views of what the team is about. For that reason, public-minded managerial leaders are wise to begin any small-group team initiative by attempting to resolve these basic questions about purpose and structure.

First Questions

The obvious first question is whether a team is needed at all. The answer should come down to a determination, made by following the last chapter's guidelines, of whether there are issues that require collaborative attention from some kind of small-group team. If so, the manager or leader needs to weigh whether an existing organizational group can assume that role or if a new team should be created.

Assuming a team appears desirable, the next questions concern the team's composition, who to include or to invite to participate. As the core principle, anyone who shares the common interest—a stake in the issue the group is charged to address—should be included or at least represented. Recalling the last chapter, if one goal is to obtain acceptance for a team's eventual decisions, its composition should represent every perspective whose acceptance will be needed. Additionally, the group's membership should bring the expertise necessary to address the team's tasks. If the membership falls short on either criterion, the group's leader should consider seeking additional members to provide the missing elements.

Leaders should also recognize the importance of diversity in a group's membership. Sunstein and Hastie (2015, 104–105) are emphatic about "the immense importance of *diversity*, not necessarily along demographic lines, but in terms of ideas and perspectives" that members can bring to a team's work. Beyond diversity in general, there is the specific importance of gender diversity: Small groups generally perform better when they include women (Sunstein and Hastie 2015).

Intelligence should not be overlooked in selecting team members either. Not surprisingly, substantial evidence suggests that "groups with smarter members perform at higher levels" (Sunstein and Hastie 2015, 202). Finally, it also helps to have members who are good team players since "good players mesh" (Sunstein and Hastie 2015, 204), increasing the potential for a team's success.

Satisfying all of the criteria can sometimes swell a group's size to where manageability becomes an issue. Small-group teams function effectively only if they remain small enough to allow for both broad participation of members and effective resolution of issues. Groups with more than fifteen members are likely to struggle to achieve one or both of those goals. Having to listen to ideas from all fifteen members could test the patience of team members, while hearing from all fifteen might not leave enough time to resolve issues.

Leaders have several options when a team's size pushes beyond that ceiling. First, they might review the membership to confirm if everyone is necessary, that is, if every participant serves an essential role. A negative answer for any given participant might provide grounds to ask that person to step aside. Second, the group's effective size might be reduced by limiting the participation of some members to specific points in the team's process, those points where their special skills or perspectives may be needed. Third, the group might be divided into two or more subgroups, with each subgroup assigned a specific part of the task. The full group might still convene occasionally, but not routinely. Or similarly, a subgroup might be selected to function as a smaller executive committee that will make or recommend decisions for the full group's review.

Questions of Purpose and Authority

Once a team is created, attention should turn to defining its purpose in more detail. This detail should clarify what the team's goal will be, including what it hopes to achieve in addressing its core issues. That detail might come from a charge given to the group from higher in the hierarchy or from a public-minded managerial leader who created the group. In either case, as Tropman (2014, 73) has argued, "All decision groups should have a written copy of their mandate, their statement of mission and position."

Even with a mandate in hand, there remains value in engaging discussion by team members of their understanding of that purpose, in the context of small-group meetings, as discussed in more detail below. The most effective small-group teams, in any event, begin with a shared sense of a common purpose, including agreement of at least what the basic issue is, if not on all of its aspects.

A related question focuses on assessment, how the team will measure success. Although the answer here may be found in the charge behind the group's creation, it will still likely be worthwhile for the team to discuss how it wants to measure success. That discussion becomes essential if there is no mandated assessment plan from higher authorities.

Small-group teams are also well-advised to seek clarity at the outset about their authority and capacity. How far is the group expected to go in addressing an issue? Is there a commitment to implement any recommendations from the group? Management, perhaps especially in the public realm, is notorious for attempting to sidestep issues by delegating them to a "study committee," often in the covert hope that concern for issues may dissipate while the committee labors, eventually eliminating any need for action. Those who are asked to lead study committee teams may want to investigate if that is the intent in their case. More generally, gaining a prior commitment from higher levels for use of a team's work can potentially energize a small-group team as it begins work.

Questions about authority and capacity should also extend to whether the group will have the resources necessary to conduct its work. Some of these resources are human, such as the membership issues addressed earlier. Others could be financial (e.g., funds for travel, for hiring experts) or temporal (e.g., adequate time to complete the group's expected work). It can be problematic if teams do not know at the outset whether they will have the resources they need.

Answering these questions successfully provides a good foundation on which to build a team. That foundation should include (1) a clearly defined purpose, (2) specific, measurable goals for assessing the team's success, (3) the necessary expertise for achieving those goals, (4) representation of all important perspectives, (5) manageable size, (6) adequate resources of time and money, and (7) a plan for implementing the team's ultimate recommendations (see also Bolman and Deal 2017, 105–106).

Still unaddressed are important questions about who will lead the group and how. Substantial evidence argues for the value of having someone who is formally in charge—a designated official team leader. At the same time, the most effective collaborative teams do not follow a strict hierarchical model where a leader runs the group in a command-and-control manner. Effective team leaders facilitate more than direct, working with groups to reach collective decisions. How they can do that becomes clearer with the next topic, facilitating small-group meetings.

Facilitating Small-Group Meetings

Much of the work of teams and of organizations must be accomplished in small-group meetings. Small-group meetings are pervasive in organizations, with managers frequently spending half or more of their working hours in these meetings. The success of a public-minded managerial leader consequently depends heavily on being able to run these meetings effectively.

Potential Benefits

Many of the potential benefits of small-group meetings are those that come with participatory decision making, as detailed in the last chapter. Those benefits start with decision making itself: The value of making decisions cannot be overstated given the difficulties organizations often have in reaching decisions. Effective small-group meetings can help to address those challenges. Decisions should also be better informed, assuming a participatory process that encourages the surfacing of relevant information. Successful small-group meetings should also lead to participants feeling more committed to eventual decisions, another of the principal benefits of participatory decision making. People are more likely to buy into decisions they helped to make, and small-group meetings provide an ideal setting for engaging the participation that can build that commitment.

Small-group meetings also offer the potential for resolving issues more creatively and effectively than is likely with other decision-making approaches. That can happen first as a result of the stronger information base that can result from an engaged small-group discussion. Small-group meetings may be especially useful in surfacing "tacit" knowledge, knowledge people have but that has not been recorded for others to know. The discussion of specific issues in small-group discussions may prompt participants to share this information that only they previously knew, adding to the group's collective knowledge. Effective meetings also sometimes encourage participants to propose creative and innovative solutions that might otherwise have been overlooked. All these positive tendencies of small-group meetings are part of the phenomenon sometimes termed "the wisdom of crowds" (Surowiecki 2005).

More generally, effective small-group meetings can contribute to the development of the group as a group. As detailed in the last chapter, components of group development begin with (1) a clear definition of the group and of the group's identity and (2) enhancement of the group's knowledge as a group, resulting in a greater shared knowledge base and group memory. Group development may also enhance these important elements of group culture:

- *A common commitment:* Team discussions may build a shared commitment of group members to the group's goals.
- *A collaborative climate:* The give-and-take essential to effective small-group meetings can increase the inclination of members to col-

laborate with each other, leading eventually to the group having a collaborative climate.

- *Collective accountability*: Collective accountability means that the team as a whole, not any individual member, feels accountable for its successes and its failures. Effective small-group deliberations can build that sense (see also Bolman and Deal 2017, 106).

All of these elements should increase the group's potential to address not just the issue at hand, but other issues that may arise in the future.

Common Malfunctions

Yet, small-group meetings typically "fail to live up to their potential" (Sunstein and Hastie 2105, 5), and no organizational process may be more reviled. One popular cartoon derisively caricaturizes small-group meetings as "the practical alternative to work" (Tropman 2014, 1). Worse yet, almost half of the respondents to a recent survey would choose going to a Department of Motor Vehicles office, a classic bureaucratic horror, over "sitting through a pointless work meeting" (Workfront 2018).

Regardless of the potential benefits, most people may be more familiar with the malfunctions that underlie the poor reputation of small-group meetings, with that familiarity likely based on personal experiences with many of the problems. Those problems include:

- *The information-only meeting*: These meetings find the group leader only informing participants, offering little or no opportunity for them to voice opinions or debate issues.
- *Preoccupation with the trivial*: Small-group meetings sometimes focus on insignificant issues to the neglect of what's important, in the process wasting everyone's time and leaving the important issues unaddressed.
- *Domination by a minority*: Domination by a minority finds a few group members monopolizing discussion while the majority remains silent, resulting in the opinions of most participants never being voiced.
- *"Group think"*: In the extreme case of domination by a minority, the group makes an unwise decision reflective of a minority perspective, with that decision carrying the authority of the group as a whole. In essence, groups here "amplify the mistakes of their members" (Sunstein and Hastie 2015, 13) in a process that has become known as "group think." Group think has been cited to explain such disastrous decisions as the U.S. choice to invade Cuba in the so-called "Bay

of Pigs" fiasco and NASA's choice to launch the ill-fated *Challenger* space shuttle despite serious objections from shuttle engineers (e.g., Bolman and Deal 2017, 181–184).

- *Meeting more than necessary:* Making matters worse, organizations tend to overuse small-group meetings. Meetings expert John Tropman (2014, 61) concluded from his research that, "for the most part, groups meet twice as often or twice as long as necessary." That may happen, according to one private-sector executive, as the consequence of "a culture that rewards collaboration for collaboration's sake, or more commonly, an organizational structure that necessitates more people being involved than should be required" (Herrera 2017).

Basic Principles for Facilitation

The horrors of small-group meetings may derive principally from the fact that few leaders are trained for the task. The initial responsibility to run a small group often falls on a leader as part of a promotion or a job reassignment, with an implied expectation that the leader will learn by immersion. Some leaders do, perhaps because they possess a natural gift for working with small groups. For most, though, running small-group meetings will be a matter of trial by fire with no firefighting equipment available when flames threaten.

The risks of small-group meetings can be minimized and the potential benefits maximized if public-minded managerial leaders know and follow a number of guidelines. Most generally, recalling the discussion of servant-leadership theory in Chapter 3, effective small-group leadership starts with group leaders thinking of themselves as "servants, not masters" (Jay 1976). That is, they view themselves as servants of the group and the group's purposes, tasked with providing the leadership necessary to assist the group in achieving its purposes. That leadership should be principally facilitative, too, helping more than directing the group.

In that spirit, public-minded managerial leaders new to running small-group meetings should take responsibility for several meeting functions:

- *Planning:* Leaders need to plan meetings, determining what their purposes are, which issues need to be on the agenda, who should attend, and the like. They should also see that all necessary materials are available to group members in a timely fashion in advance of as well as at any meeting.
- *Sequencing:* They need to strategize for how to sequence the issues

on the agenda. Some issues fit better early in a meeting, others later; some call for more of a group's energies and time, others for less.

- *Soliciting and limiting:* They should solicit opinions, sometimes attempting to draw out the uninvolved as well as perhaps limiting the time taken by the talkative.
- *Summarizing and deciding:* They should periodically propose possible areas of agreement or disagreement, attempting to assess the group's readiness to make a decision. Or, observing persisting disagreement within the group, they will sometimes want to suggest that a decision be postponed.

In exercising these responsibilities, group leaders function as (1) idea leaders, orchestrating the discussion of ideas, (2) idea managers, providing the appropriate organizational and environmental context for issues, (3) decision-group administrators, managing the agenda to see that decisions are made as necessary, and, finally, (4) meeting heads, running the actual meetings (Tropman 2014, 77). Fortunately, effective leaders need not perform all of these tasks on their own. They should instead seek and welcome assistance from other group members in almost all of the functions.

Purposes for Meetings

Those basic principles play out as more detailed guidelines for various aspects of facilitating small-group meetings, starting with setting a meeting's purpose. While that "may seem like an obvious requirement . . . , a lot of meetings start with no clear sense of purpose" (Bryant 2017). If a lack of purpose becomes clear in planning a meeting, the meeting should probably be canceled.

Any small-group meeting will have one or more of four general purposes (see Jay 1976). The first is to set the group's "legislative framework," meaning its structure and rules for operating. These are the issues that, as discussed earlier, arise at the launch of any new small-group team. That is, what's the purpose of this team or meeting? Who should be included? Even if an official charter provides initial answers to these questions, additional discussion in a group's early meetings may help to clarify those answers and increase member buy-in.

A second purpose is informative, providing information for the group to digest and discuss. A primary informative purpose seldom makes sense unless the meeting will offer members an opportunity to discuss the information. Absent that opportunity, information can usually be communicated more efficiently and effectively via email or hard copy. As that logic implies, an informational purpose may be one reason for a meeting, but seldom the primary or only reason. A group leader who runs frequent informational meetings risks alienating attendees, who could be pardoned for asking, "Why did we need to meet to hear what we could have read?"

The other two purposes for small-group meetings speak to the two distinct phases of decision making. At the front end, a so-called "originative," "divergent," or "identification" purpose focuses on generating ideas for what might be done about an issue. As Sunstein and Hastie (2015, 128–129) describe this phase, it should focus on "the problem of generating many alternative solutions, without giving any of them a time-consuming and inhibiting evaluation." The idea is to surface options, holding assessment for later.

At the same time, small-group meetings are not well utilized for simply listing ideas. As Sawyer (2007, 70) has explained, "Groups do worse at additive tasks, such as coming up with simple lists of ideas." They "work better for the complexity of the real world—where new ideas are complex combinations of prior ideas, where the task is new and unfamiliar to the group members, and where new ideas often depend on visualization and abstraction."

Assessment should occur at the back end when the intent *is* to make decisions, consistent with the final "executive," "convergent," or "selection" purpose of small-group meetings. With this purpose, the goal is to evaluate and winnow the range of ideas previously generated, culminating in a choice among the options. Depending on the issue, the originative and executive purposes can sometimes be accomplished at the same meeting, while at other times separate meetings will be needed. The crucial point is to recognize that the two processes follow very different dynamics: "The qualities of a good selection process—critical, anxious, skeptical evaluation—are antithetical to the qualities that make for a creative, open-minded, divergent process like identification" (Sunstein and Hastie 2015, 129).

There are few definitive rules on when each of the different purposes will be appropriate. As one ironclad rule, a primary purpose of an initial meeting of any new small-group team should be setting a group's legislative framework. Many small groups ignore that counsel, choosing instead to start in a vacuum, giving no more than passing attention to discussing their charge and the procedures they will follow. That choice often comes back to haunt groups when the lack of ground rules eventually results in conflict among members. Otherwise, most meetings will have multiple purposes, carrying over some issues from earlier meetings, beginning discussion of new issues, sharing organizational news, and so on.

Setting the Agenda

In setting a meeting's agenda, the public-minded managerial leader will typically ask group members for items in addition to what the leader has already identified. To ensure everyone has time to think about the issues, the final agenda should be announced well in advance of any meeting, with some experts recommending a deadline of the midway point between the date of the last meeting and the date of the next (Tropman 2014, 31).

With every agenda item, managers should plan in advance for how much decision-making authority to share with the group, using the guidelines defined in the last chapter. Most writing on small-group meetings assumes a group decision approach where all members share authority equally in making any decision, but leaders will sometimes prefer a group consultation, consulting with the group at the meeting, but retaining ultimate authority for making the decision. (Any less sharing of decision-making authority, such as an individual consultation, does not call for a group meeting.) An effective public-minded managerial leader should have a clear sense entering a meeting of the extent to which authority might be shared on specific issues.

Group leaders should also know and make explicit any parameters or constraints on specific decisions that might be made at a meeting. These parameters are the quality requirements discussed in the last chapter, including budget constraints, scientific and technical standards, and relevant legislative mandates.

As another part of their planning, public-minded managerial leaders will often want to talk in advance with some group members about their participation in the meeting. One private sector executive has even suggested that "the real meetings happen before the meeting. You need to have conversations with the key players before you ever get in the room" (Herrera 2017). Those conversations might include encouraging members who feel strongly about an issue to be sure to attend and speak up. A leader might even indicate an intent to call on specific members at the meeting, thus ensuring that their perspectives are heard. While such a request may sometimes be designed to build support at the meeting for the leader's perspective, the goal of public-minded managerial leaders will more often be to see that all sides of an issue are heard before a decision is made.

Finally, the group leader should plan in advance for someone to serve as recorder at the meeting. Every group needs a "group memory," a record of its deliberations and decisions, and it is too much for the group leader to perform this function in addition to leading the group. Another member of the group or a staff support person needs to be designated in advance to take this role, ultimately providing minutes or another kind of summary of the group's work.

Sequencing Topics

Small-group meetings will be more effective if topics are sequenced strategically. For one thing, as already suggested, the generation of ideas should precede and be separated from the assessment of ideas, whether as different parts of one meeting or divided between two or more meetings. A manager can best keep the two processes distinct by, at the outset, asserting the principle and then ensuring that the group does not succumb to any temptation to mix the two.

Experts suggest a number of other principles for how best to sequence topics at small-group meetings (see especially Tropman 2014, 39–40), including:

1. Begin with relatively easy items, to warm up the group.
2. Slot the most difficult item(s) in approximately the middle third of the meeting, when the group should be the most focused and alert.
3. Limit the number of difficult items to one or two at any given meeting. Groups seldom have the individual or collective energy to address multiple difficult issues at the same meeting.
4. It is "always a good idea to end the meeting on a positive note, one of agreement and accomplishment" (Tropman 2014, 45). In that spirit, the final topics might be (a) nondecision items, such as new items for initial discussion only, or (b) planning of next steps, including "who is responsible for what and what the deadlines are" (Bryant 2017).
5. Plan out how much time each item will require and stick to the plan.
6. Set a maximum meeting length of ninety minutes, perhaps two hours in rare cases, recognizing that the energy of participants will flag by then.

Soliciting and Limiting

A leader's facilitator role during a meeting involves two competing tasks: soliciting information and ideas on the one hand and limiting participation on the other. In the ideal case, as Google learned from "its quest to build the perfect team," members will speak "in roughly the same proportion" (Duhigg 2016). The leader wants to encourage members to speak, thereby maximizing the information base for any eventual decision, but may also need to restrain talkative members from monopolizing discussion.

In performing the first role, leaders may best start "by indicating their willingness and their desire to hear uniquely held information" (Sunstein and Hastie 2015, 107). They can further encourage the sharing of information by announcing, "before deliberation begins, that different members have different, and relevant, information to contribute" (Sunstein and Hastie 2015, 112). There may be value, too, in setting an expectation that group deliberations could surface conflict. As one private sector executive has observed, "People bumping up against each other is what helps us not just improve our work product but also ourselves as human beings" (Herrera 2017).

With any given issue, leaders will usually initiate the discussion by introducing the issue, describing any relevant context, and explaining necessary parameters—and then shutting up. Leaders need to provide all necessary background information for an issue in advance of a meeting, being sure also to bring copies of relevant materials to the meeting. After that, silence becomes golden. As another private sector executive has explained (Bryant 2017), "if you're running a meeting, be crystal clear on the agenda and what you want to accomplish, but then it's time to *be quiet and let others* speak" (emphasis in original). Leaders can set the tone at meetings, and talkative leaders imply both a lack of interest in what others have to say and a risk that offering a contrasting view could be perceived as challenging the leader. Another means to achieve that same goal is for the leader to ask another member to introduce the issue.

Sharing of information can be encouraged in other ways, too. As already suggested, leaders may want in advance of a meeting to encourage specific group members to share their perspectives. Encouragement at the meeting itself might focus especially on "timid or more junior employees" for whom "speaking up can be at best nerve-wracking and at worst a terrifying experience" (Herrera 2017) and on women, given substantial evidence that men tend to out-talk women in group settings, typically by a two-to-one ratio (Sunstein and Hastie 2015, 106).

As the second part of the competing roles, leaders will at times need to limit the speaking time of some in order to ensure that everyone can be heard. This can require a difficult balancing act since visibly limiting the time for some could lead to self-silencing by others who were already less inclined to talk. A reasonable balance might be struck by asking a talkative member who is holding the floor to complete a thought, then seeking opinions from others who have yet to speak. If the problem persists, the leader might arrange a private conversation with an overly talkative group member.

Leaders will want to contribute their own perspectives at times, but they need to walk a fine line in doing so. Leaders who too readily express their opinions risk discouraging others from voicing opposing views for fear of appearing to challenge managerial authority. As a good rule of thumb, leaders might refrain from offering their opinions until everyone else has had a chance to speak. For the same reason, managers need to be cautious about correcting misunderstandings or factual errors. Corrections should be offered only if essential and then in a manner least likely to discourage member participation.

Summarizing and Deciding

Small groups eventually need to move toward closure, a task that calls for melding diverse opinions into decisions group members will embrace. That can be difficult given what Tropman (2014, 39) characterizes as the "fundamental tension between maintaining group cohesion on the one hand and taking action on the other." As he has explained, "Decision making tears at the cohesion of the group" because "decisions usually have winners and losers."

To set the groundwork for an eventual decision, the group leader might ask members early on in the process to discuss the criteria against which various options will be judged. If agreement can be reached on those criteria, subsequent assessment of alternatives might proceed more systematically.

As discussion progresses, it is the leader's task to watch for when agreement may be emerging, perhaps suggesting the moment when the leader might reasonably propose a decision. Here the leader plays the role of "decision manager," someone who "listens to the various contributions and then helps to develop a synthesis" (Tropman 2014, 155). It is hardly a simple task since it "requires in-process conceptualization," not just thinking on one's feet, but combining and recombining ideas in pursuit of a consensus decision. This is the same kind of thinking required in the integrative approach to conflict discussed in the last chapter.

Alternatively, if no consensus emerges, the leader needs at some point to decide what to do next. An obvious option is to hold a vote. However, as Cloke and Goldsmith (2011, 196) have explained, while "widely considered the best form of decision making in a democracy," voting "can also be highly competitive, contentious, and unnecessarily adversarial." As a result, "voting is *less* preferable than consensus, which is grounded in interests, does not result in anyone winning or losing, invites participants to modify their ideas to meet everyone's needs, includes the useful ideas of dissenters and resisters, and encourages participants to own their decisions" (emphasis in original).

Still, decision making with small groups will sometimes require a vote, especially as a group's size approaches the upper limits of twelve to fifteen. Reaching consensus among so many participants can frequently prove impossible, leaving a vote as the only option. When that is the case, though, leaders should seek first to craft a proposal that accommodates as many of the different perspectives as possible, only then holding a vote.

Another option when no clear consensus emerges in the time allotted is to suggest closing the discussion for the moment. A recommendation for closure without a decision could include suggestions for—and perhaps brief additional discussion of—next steps, such as collecting more information, delegating the issue for review by a committee, and/or resuming deliberations at a future meeting. A vote might still be necessary, but only after making another attempt to reach a consensus.

As groups move toward decisions, their leaders will sometimes need to protect against some counterproductive group tendencies (see especially Sunstein and Hastie 2015, 67). As one example, groups can be swayed by the initial opinions expressed, with those opinions often leading prematurely to a group decision. For another, groups can tend toward polarization given a common tendency for discussions to move members from an initial moderate stance to an eventual more extreme stance.

Group leaders have a number of strategies available to combat these tendencies. Facing a premature rush toward a decision, a group leader might call on members who are known to hold different opinions. A leader who anticipates that risk in advance of a meeting might seek out a group member to play devil's advocate, "deliberately advocating a position that is contrary to the group's inclination" (Sunstein and Hastie 2015, 114). If all else fails, the leader might personally adopt the devil's advocate role.

Finally, moving effectively toward closure requires that small-group leaders keep an eye on the clock. At the front end, according to Macy's chairman Terry Lundgren, "If the meeting is at 8, you're not here at 8:01, because the meeting's going to start at 8" (Bryant 2017). At the back end, "Just as important as starting on time is ending on time," permitting participants to return to their other work on schedule. In between, the leader should see that individual topics do not take more time than allotted.

The "Boss" as Facilitator

As this discussion implies, there is frequent tension between being the boss, the superior to whom group members report, and also serving as facilitator of the group's meetings. Even if that boss is a public-minded managerial leader who really wants to hear the candid opinions of group members, members may hesitate to voice their sentiments when the person in charge of the meeting may also be the person who conducts their performance evaluations.

That tension leads many students of small-group meetings to recommend separating the functions of boss and group facilitator. As Doyle and

Straus (1982, 33–34) observed decades ago, "the big trouble is that the manager attempts to play too many roles at one time. It is like trying to be the referee and scorekeeper as well as captain of the team." Recognizing this issue, some organizations employ outside facilitators while others share the facilitator function, following a "distributed leadership" model where multiple or all members rotate in and out of leading groups (e.g., Spillane 2006).

While those may be attractive options, most public-minded managerial leaders still choose to serve as their own small-group facilitators. To do so effectively, they are wise to recognize the tension between their roles as superiors and as group facilitators, and, reflecting that recognition, limit their assertiveness in meetings. As already suggested, that could entail their (1) saying little at the beginning, (2) encouraging others to speak, (3) listening to what others say, (4) offering their own opinions only after everyone else has, and (5) looking for solutions that include others' perspectives.

The Challenge of Virtual Meetings

Many organizations now hold at least some of their meetings by virtual means, where participants join meetings online from different locations. That choice offers as its principal advantage the ability for people to participate from almost any location, eliminating the need for travel to a common site. That offers an enormous advantage where possible participants are geographically dispersed, likely saving both time and money.

The same guidelines suggested for in-person meetings apply to virtual meetings, but some new concerns arise. Most obviously, virtual meetings depend on all participants having reliable internet connections. That criterion is not always satisfied, especially as meetings extend in length. Virtual meetings also often allow participants to tune out occasionally without being noticed, potentially detracting from the full group focusing on an issue. That problem can be exacerbated by the fact that virtual meetings are more subject to the distractions that may intrude on participants when they participate from somewhere off-site (e.g., a home office).

The greatest concern, though, may arise from the likely reduced face-to-face interactions with virtual meetings. Ample evidence shows that face-to-face interactions are crucial for building understanding and trust. As summarized by Nobel Laureate Elinor Ostrom (1998, 6–7), "consistent, strong, and replicable findings are that substantial increases in the levels of cooperation are achieved when individuals are allowed to communicate face to face." Face-to-face interactions appear to enhance the ability to read the emotional subtext and nuance in what others say, increasing the likelihood of cooperation and trust.

Given these risks, virtual meetings likely work best as supplements to in-person on-site meetings. Beginning with the latter might help a group develop understanding and trust of each other, providing a social foundation for subsequent virtual meetings. Additional in-person meetings might be alternated with virtual meetings to reinforce and maintain trust and understanding. Of course, all of these recommendations could become moot if the technology for virtual meetings were to progress to more closely resemble in-person meetings.

Leading as a Small-Group Member

Most people serve as group members more than as group leaders. The small groups on which they serve stand to function more effectively if members have a sense of how to lead *as* group members, not only as leaders. The ability to lead as a member might best begin with an understanding of the various guidelines offered earlier for small-group leaders, with group members attempting to support the leader in adhering to the guidelines. As a few examples, group members could:

- Join in discussions, but be careful not to monopolize the floor. Support the balanced participation that is a hallmark of effective groups (Duhigg 2016).
- Seek out differences of opinion by encouraging others to speak.
- Avoid changing their own minds simply to avoid conflict. Embrace the potential for conflict to produce a creative solution.
- Not assume someone must win and someone must lose: Help to search for solutions where, to the extent possible, everyone wins.

Meeting the Challenges of Small-Group Teams

These guidelines do not provide a foolproof approach for building successful teams or running effective small-group meetings. Anyone who has become an effective small-group leader can attest to the struggles that typically come with the job. The guidelines should help, but leading teams and small-group meetings requires an openness to experimentation and trial and error.

To become effective in those roles, public-minded managerial leaders will learn from their errors, develop a tolerance for the occasional sting of criticism after those errors, and return to the work of small-group teams and meetings to try again—and likely again and again after that. Consistent with the counsel offered throughout this book, they will assess the sources of those errors, plan for how to avoid repeating them, and then resume the work of leading the groups.

Starting a Team Process

The process begins with building the appropriate structure for any small-group team. Following the planning process outlined early in this chapter should address some of the common pitfalls of teams, including (1) a lack of explanation of the team's charge, (2) a lack of clarity on the eventual goals, (3) exclusion of key actors, and (4) inadequate resources (Lafair 2015). Doing so should also help to establish five of what Bolman and Deal (2017, 105–106) term the "distinguishing characteristics of high-quality teams:"

- *A clearly-defined purpose in response to a demand or opportunity.*
- *Specific, measurable goals defined by the group.*
- *The right mix of expertise.*
- *Manageable size.*
- *Adequate resources of time and money.*

Addressing Small-Group Meeting Malfunctions

In turn, following the recommendations for small-group meetings should help to correct how they commonly go awry. Consider how the recommendations speak to each of the possible malfunctions enumerated earlier:

- *The information-only meeting:* This kind of meeting should be a thing of the past if the guidelines are followed. As they stipulate, information sharing should be no more than a secondary purpose for most meetings. Even a minimally effective group leader should be able to see that this guideline is observed in both agenda planning and actual meetings.
- *Preoccupation with the trivial:* The guidelines address this problem first by recommending limiting agendas to significant group issues; if the only issues are trivial, following the guidelines should result in canceling the meeting. As an additional protection, the guidelines charge the group's leader with monitoring discussion in meetings to ensure a consistent focus on important issues, curbing any temptation to be sidetracked to the trivial.
- *Domination by a minority:* It is part of a group leader's charge of to see that a minority does not dominate, sometimes by asking long-winded participants to abbreviate, other times by encouraging nonparticipants to contribute, and occasionally by having private conversations between meetings to counter any specific individual's tendency toward monopolizing discussion.

- *Group think*: A group leader's commitment to everyone having their say offers a first safeguard against this potentially worst potential malfunction of small-group meetings. That commitment should include setting a tone to ensure that fear does not result in divergent opinions being self-silenced, as well as occasionally encouraging some group members to play devil's advocate or by the leader taking that role.
- *Meeting more than necessary:* Following the guidelines outlined here should minimize the risks of meeting either too long or too often. Meeting too long can be avoided if the group leader, consistent with the guidelines, (1) plans in advance for how much time to give to each agenda issue and (2) holds the meeting to those time limits. Adhering to the basic guideline of not meeting in the absence of a significant agenda should curb any tendency toward too frequent meetings.

Building Effective Teams

Effective facilitation of small-group meetings can also continue the process of building the teams that the small-group meetings are designed to serve. As suggested earlier, effective small-group meetings should produce benefits for the team such as more, faster, better informed, and more creative decisions that are easier to implement.

Along the way, successful meetings are also likely to nurture three other crucial "distinguishing characteristics of high-quality teams" (Bolman and Deal [2017, 105–106]):

- *A common commitment*: Open discussions that result in group decisions should nurture member commitment to common goals.
- *A collaborative climate:* Collaboration in small-group meetings should contribute to an overall collaborative climate.
- *Collective accountability*: The sense of a common group identity that can come from effective small-group meetings will likely translate to a sense of collective accountability.

Benefits for the Leader

All those benefits depend, though, on having a public-minded managerial leader who understands how to build a successful small-group team. The task will likely be challenging and difficult, especially for the first-time team leader, and may well spark occasional criticism of that leader.

For the committed public-minded managerial leader, though, the eventual benefits will likely outweigh the difficulties the process may have brought. Beyond the many organizational benefits, facilitating effective small-group meetings and teams can prove personally fulfilling. Anyone who has been part of effective small-group meetings and teams knows the professional and personal satisfaction that they can bring.

Effective leadership of small-group meetings and teams also promises to enhance the leader's standing in the eyes of group members. Given the frequent failings of small-group team initiatives, participants typically respond very positively to the leader who oversees an effective effort. Those positive feelings may, in turn, make the leader's job easier as group members become more inclined to support the leader in the future. A classic virtuous cycle may ensue where positive feedback enhances the work experience of group members and the group's leader in a mutually reinforcing manner. It is a scenario that any public-minded managerial leader would welcome and that most should be able to achieve by following the guidelines detailed here.

Personal Leadership Exercise 9.1

How Do You Assess a Team in Which You Participated Recently?

Criteria	Yes	No
Was a team actually needed?		
Were all of the necessary people included on the team?		
Was the team sufficiently diverse?		
Did the team have 3–15 members?		
Was the team's goal defined clearly at the outset?		
Was the team's authority defined clearly at the outset?		
Did the team have adequate resources of time and money?		
Was a team leader defined clearly?		

In light of your answers, how would you assess the team's initial preparation?

What might you have done differently about the team's initial preparation?

Personal Leadership Exercise 9.2

Rate a Small-Group Meeting That You Recently Attended, Preferably for the Team Assessed Earlier, for Adherence to the Criteria for Effective Small-Group Meetings.

Criteria	Yes	No
Participants numbered 3-15		
The purpose was clear and not an informative purpose only		
An agenda & all necessary information were provided in advance		
The leader was clear how much influence would be shared on any decisions to be made at the meeting		
Parameters and constraints on decisions were defined before discussion		
Someone was assigned to be the recorder		
The meeting's leader encouraged others to speak before voicing any opinions		
Most or all attendees participated in discussions		
Discussion was not dominated by one or a few attendees		
Generation of ideas was separated from their assessment		
Time was not wasted on trivial issues		
The meeting's leader moved effectively from discussion to resolution and decision-making		
Decisions were made by consensus, not by votes		
Meeting length did not exceed 1 ½ hours		

In light of your answers, how effective do rate the meeting overall? How does your assessment relate to the criteria?

What, if anything, do you think should be done differently to make the next meeting more effective?

Chapter 10

Looking Upward and Outward

The need to work upward to superiors and outward to the external environment presents enormous challenges for public-minded managerial leaders. To be effective, these leaders need to develop productive relationships with those superiors and with a broad, often ill-defined array of external actors who interact in a variety of roles with the agencies these leaders direct. The enormity of the challenges derives from both the number of actors and the diversity of tasks that leaders see when they look upward and outward.

Unlike with their subordinates, public-minded managerial leaders cannot presume to lead peers who are external to their organization, much less the superiors to whom they report. Yet, some of the same strategies recommended for work with subordinates can be useful with these relationships, too, and, where that is not the case, other strategies are available. This chapter examines the various strategies available to public-minded managerial leaders for building effective relationships with their superiors and with several principal types of external actors.

Looking Upward: The Boss[1]

In superior-subordinate relationships, it is usually the prerogative of the superior to set the initial framework, even if the subordinate is also a manager. The best course of action for the public-minded managerial leader as subordinate may consequently be to wait for the superior to make the first move, then following that individual's lead in developing their relationship.

The Goal: A Partnership Relationship

At the same time, subordinate status need not mean that a subordinate leader comes to a relationship with a new superior without goals or ex-

---

1. This chapter mostly uses the term "superior" as the more accurate formal description than "boss," which could imply a highly control-oriented relationship.

pectations. Following the logic of leader-management exchange (LMX) theory (see Chapter 7), the leader as subordinate might have as a principal goal to develop a partnership relationship with superiors (Graen and Uhl-Bien 1995). To recall, LMX theory proposes a desirable progression in the superior-subordinate relationship from (1) a stranger phase, where the subordinate's role is largely scripted, to (2) an acquaintance phase, where superior and subordinate test possible expansion beyond scripted roles, before ideally culminating in (3) the partner phase, where roles are negotiated and influence operates reciprocally. That progression supposedly evolves through exchanges—the leader-member exchanges—of both tangibles (e.g., financial rewards) and intangibles (e.g., trust, respect, empowerment, influence), with the quality of the exchanges determining how far the evolution proceeds.

Just as public-minded managerial leaders may want to develop partnership relationships with subordinates, they will likely hope for the same status with their superiors. After all, a partnership relationship can bring substantial benefits, including more trust and more respect from the superior as well as possibly more support of initiatives proposed by the subordinate leader.

As the idea of a progression implies, that kind of relationship takes time to develop. Public-minded managerial leaders as subordinates might attempt to expedite the progression by seeking to provide more in their part of the exchange, perhaps including more information, a willingness to assume more responsibilities, and the like. As part of this effort, leaders as subordinates will also likely work to facilitate the kind of productive interactive communication pattern with their superiors suggested as desirable for relationships with subordinates in Chapter 7.

The public-minded managerial leader as a subordinate manager might seek, as one specific goal, to schedule regular meetings with the superior, if the superior does not suggest that first. The meaning of "regular" will vary for any number of reasons. For one thing, more frequent meetings may be desirable in organizations that are more interactive, less frequent meetings in organizations that are less so. The point for the subordinate leader and the superior is to find a meeting frequency that fits their needs.

Typically, superiors will lead these conversations, asking questions and providing other opportunities for the subordinate manager to offer input. The subordinate leader may sometimes take the initiative by, for example, reporting problems, raising questions, and asking for direction or guidance on specific issues. Ideally, the superior will act more as a facilitator than a boss, leading a process that entails extensive give and take, but the choice of that approach obviously lies with the superior. The public-minded managerial leader as subordinate should seek in these meetings to meet the needs of the superior, which might include feedback on what's occurring around the organization, progress reports on previous directives from the superior, and proposals for possible new initiatives.

The leader as subordinate may also encourage movement toward a partnership relationship through occasional use of a combination of inquiry and advocacy as part of the Argyris and Schon integrative approach to issues. Recalling from Chapter 7, the party who initiates discussion of an issue begins by asking for the other party's perceptions and feelings about the issue (inquiry), before possibly proposing a solution crafted to integrate both parties' perspectives and preferences (advocacy). The public-minded managerial leader as subordinate might find occasional opportunities to pursue this approach with a superior. If, for example, the superior mentions a problem in need of a solution, the subordinate leader might ask the superior informational questions about the issue, before perhaps eventually suggesting a solution—if that can be done without seeming to overstep the limits of subordinate status. On other occasions, the leader as subordinate might even attempt this approach in addressing conflict with a superior.

If successful, efforts of this kind could bring at least two benefits. Most immediately, the superior in cooperation with the subordinate public-minded managerial leader might find solutions or at least amelioration of pressing problems. In the longer term, successful interactions of this kind could nurture the interactive partnership relationship that the leader as subordinate likely desires.

Implications of Mutual Dependence

Gabarro and Kotter (1993) offer another potentially useful perspective in describing the superior-subordinate relationship as one of "mutual dependence between two fallible human beings." Mutual dependence means that each party depends on the other: The superior depends on subordinates for feedback on how lower levels of the organization are functioning and for support in implementing decisions; the public-minded managerial leader as subordinate may want direction as well as a receptive ear for complaints that have arisen from below. Fallibility means that neither party knows all or understands everything, with both parties being fully capable of mistakes.

This perspective holds several implications for public-minded managerial leaders as subordinates. Most obviously, mutual dependence underscores the value of subordinates to their superiors; leaders who want to build strong relationships with those superiors should prioritize meeting their superiors' needs. As the other side of the coin, leaders as subordinates should recognize their dependence on those superiors, and seek to cultivate relationships that will meet both sides' needs. Finally, recognition of their fallibility could nurture even more mutual dependence if each side sees the value in helping the other side avoid the mistakes that fallibility brings.

Managers as subordinates can also improve these relationships by developing a better understanding of their superiors—their leadership styles, preferences, weaknesses, and the like. As one example, some superiors will process information better by listening, while others prefer reading. Working with the former, the leader as subordinate might plan for more oral presentations; working with the latter, more written presentations make sense. As another example, superiors vary in how much information they want, some wanting to be kept very well informed, others less so. Leaders as subordinates might again attempt to gauge their superiors' preferences and respond accordingly.

Leaders as subordinates might also look for their superiors' blind spots and try to help in addressing them. In some cases, superiors know their blind spots and hire assistants who can help there (e.g., Doig and Hargrove 1990, 3), likely explaining that need to those assistants. Much of the time, though, it may fall to the subordinate leader to discern those blind spots and figure out how to help. For example, where a superior might be too sparing in affirming quality work, leaving productive employees feeling unappreciated, a perceptive subordinate leader might either step in to provide that praise or diplomatically suggest that superior do so.

There are other strategies, too, that leaders as subordinates might use to build productive relationships with their superiors, including:

- Where possible, resolve issues so they do not land on the boss's desk, minimizing the frequent governmental tendency to elevate issues to higher levels in order to avoid the risk of mistakes (e.g., Hartmann and Khademian 2010, 850).
- Keep superiors out of trouble, as by addressing issues before they blow up.
- Be cognizant of the various forces competing for a superior's time, tempering requests accordingly.

In short, public-minded managerial leaders as subordinates may be best advised to be cautiously proactive in developing relationships with superiors. Proactive might mean seeking more frequent meetings to enhance mutual understanding of important issues, while caution recommends limiting those requests, especially if the relationship has not yet reached the partnership stage. Proactive could also mean experimenting with inquiry and advocacy and the integrative problem-solving approach, while caution recommends being sparing in that experimentation and assessing initial results before experimenting further.

When Difficulties Arise

Almost everyone at some point faces problems working with a superior. Often those problems will reflect a subordinate's failure to adapt to working with a specific superior. In the case of a public-minded managerial leader as subordinate, perhaps that subordinate leader does not take direction easily, suffering from the problems many people have with authority figures. Leaders who struggle working with a specific superior might consider this possibility. Or, more generally, to return to the importance of emotional intelligence, these leaders might ask themselves whether their problems with superiors point to the need for additional self-awareness. Does some aspect of their own emotional makeup underlie problems experienced with superiors? If so, improving self-awareness might provide a route to resolving problems in a difficult superior-subordinate relationship.

Sometimes, though, the problems begin with a superior who does not handle the leadership role well and might simply not be prepared to lead. As discussed in earlier chapters, an unfortunate reality of organizational life finds many people landing in leadership roles that they have no idea how to perform. Promotions go to those who have shown high-quality technical performance, as if being a good technician (e.g., good engineer) implies anything about one's leadership potential, or leadership positions go simply to the next person in line, whoever has waited the longest for a promotion. Neither route bodes well for the resulting quality of leadership.

Different issues sometimes arise when the superior is elected rather than appointed. As Rainey (2014, 9) describes the potential problems,

> too often elected officials charged with overseeing public organizations show too little concern with effectively managing them. Elected officials have little political incentive to attend to "good government" issues, such as effective management of agencies. Some have little managerial background, and some tend to interpret managerial issues in ways that would be considered outmoded by management experts.

Those tendencies among both appointed and elected officials can undermine the development of effective leaders, potentially making for a difficult working environment for public-minded managerial leaders who work under their authority. Some counsel offered earlier may help, particularly the recommendation to learn and attempt to adapt to the styles, strengths, and weaknesses of the superior. The ability to engage in inquiry may also help, perhaps by eliciting a superior's preferences, in the process gaining direction for the subordinate leader. If these strategies do not prove effective, the subordinate public-minded managerial leader would be pardoned for pondering the possibility of seeking a different job.

Looking Outward I: Partners

When public-minded managers look outward—beyond the boundary of the entity they oversee—they see a range of relevant actors likely far more extensive and complex than their predecessors encountered. These actors are more extensive in their sheer numbers and in the types of interests they represent, including traditional interest groups, public interest groups, citizens, as well as related organizational entities (i.e., other parts of the same organization and other organizations with similar missions). They are more complex in the roles they play, with the most prominent of those roles being as partners, citizens, and customers.[2] Public-minded managerial leaders need to understand how to work with external actors in all three of these roles, beginning with partnering.

Partnering as Governance

Seldom can a single public or nonprofit agency achieve its goals without partnering with external actors, including community leaders, community organizations, various governmental and nonprofit entities, and members of the public. The provision of public and social services and the broader pursuit of public ends now occur mostly through networks of governments, private and nonprofit entities, and members of the public. This phenomenon has become known as "governance" (e.g., Bingham, Nabatchi, and O'Leary 2005), which has been described as the current "dominant model of public sector management" (Alford and Hughes 2008, 137).

Governance implies the relevance for public-minded managerial leaders of at least four forms of partnering. A first involves networking, communicating with various key actors, organizations, and informal and formal associations of those actors and organizations in a public or nonprofit agency's external environment. A second form entails formal partnerships with other agencies or even other parts of the same organization. The third form encompasses partnerships not with organizations, but with members of the

---

2. This discussion omits the mass media, not because they are unimportant to public-minded managerial leaders, but because they raise additional issues too extensive to cover adequately here.

public in producing public services. A final form also involves citizens, but as formal volunteers assisting in the delivery of public and social services. Public-minded managerial leaders, whether they work in the public, non-profit, or private sector, need some understanding of all four forms.

Networking

Networking for public-minded managerial leaders involves making contacts and developing relationships with external actors who may have a stake in those leaders' organizations. This networking might begin with a mapping of who a leader perceives as the relevant external actors as well as the role those actors play relative to the organization (for an example, see Thomas and Poister 2009). Taking time to map the important interests and entities in an organization's environment can suggest where and with whom the manager might want to network. Recalling the words of Bill Bolling, the founder and former executive director of the Atlanta Community Food Bank, "The community is the broad community, so you've got to map that community. There you're mapping the different sectors, the political, the business, the faith, academe, the nonprofit, and then individuals. That mapping is really important."

Network connections likely develop most effectively through the same kind of interactive communication by which managers can build relationships with subordinates or superiors. Those connections may then prove useful in many different ways, including for resources or for political support during times of conflict.

Lateral Partnerships

Effective networking with external interests will sometimes serve as the first step toward creating a formal lateral partnership. Lateral partnerships occur when different agencies work with each other, often in a nonhierarchical relationship, to deliver a public good or service. Two nonprofit agencies may partner with each other, as when a nonprofit private school for girls joined with a faith-oriented, international development organization to provide "international immersion experiences" for the school's students (Mendel and Brudney 2018, 64). Or, a public agency may contract with a nonprofit agency in a partnership where the latter provides a service that the former funds.

Most interorganizational partnerships likely begin with networking, before progressing with the help of the same kind of interactive communication by which public-minded managerial leaders can build positive relationships with subordinates and superiors. A leader who wants to explore the potential for a partnership might have the three-phase LMX model in mind at outset, recognizing that a relationship with the head of another organization will typically begin in the stranger phase before perhaps progressing to acquaintance or partner status. If the relationship appears to be moving along those lines, the leader might experiment with inquiry and advocacy and the integrative approach, first by asking informational questions before eventually proposing a partnership of some kind.

Bill Gibson illustrated how this process could work effectively in his time as Executive Director of the Southwestern Commission, a regional council of government in Western North Carolina. Seeing an "opportunity for significant value creation through collaboration," Gibson negotiated a number of large-scale partnerships among various governmental, nonprofit, and private sector entities (Morse 2012, 167–168). Gibson viewed all of the partnerships as having their roots in his networking, which helped him build "relationship capital" reflective of "trust of others' motives, actions, and words."

Developing an interorganizational partnership will likely require more work than building relationships with subordinates or superiors because the partnership is with an *organization,* not an individual. That work might focus on nurturing a number of additional elements that experienced nonprofit executives view as essential to successful partnerships. Specifically:

- The manager needs "a clear understanding of the strengths and capabilities of the partnering organization."
- The partnership should be built around those strengths.
- There must be "a commitment from the senior management from each partnering organization to make the partnership work," preferably a commitment from "the person at the top of the [other] organization."
- It is "essential to take the time necessary to develop relationships with your partner on all levels of the organization," not just with senior management (Mendel and Brudney 2018, 2–3, 169).

All that takes time. In the words of one nonprofit executive, "the benefits of partnership arise through incremental and time-consuming processes" (Mendel and Brudney 2018, 174). A successful process will often be "open-ended, adaptive, and flexible," much like the processes for building effective relationships with superiors and subordinates. Ultimately, the decision to partner should reflect "a careful and deliberative weighing of partnership pros and cons prior to engagement in partnership" (Mendel and Brudney 2018, 169).

Once developed, partnerships require ongoing monitoring. Someone, either the manager or the manager's designate, needs to monitor how the partnership functions once in operation. Ultimately, that monitoring should extend to whether the partnership succeeds, "weighing whether the return on investment rose to the level of partnership success" (Mendel and Brudney 2018, 169).

Coproducing with the Public

A third kind of partnership occurs with "coproduction" where governments partner with nongovernmental entities, often including members of the public, to produce services jointly that governments earlier produced on their own (e.g., Brudney and England 1983; Ostrom et al. 1978). With education, for example, government can fund classrooms and teachers, but educational effectiveness hinges on students also doing their part, preferably with the active support of their parents (Whitaker 1980).

Rethinking the service process. Successful coproduction requires first that many public-minded managerial leaders revisit their outlook on how services are best developed and delivered. Traditionally, many of these leaders have seen their agencies as service providers or experts, with the public as service recipients (e.g., Bryer 2009, 274). A more accurate perspective would cast governments and nonprofit agencies as the lead actors where service effectiveness requires that the public also contribute.

Starting from that recognition, public-minded managerial leaders in charge of a given public service might next ask what assistance they need from the public. That assistance could include hauling trash bags to the curb for waste collection, using knowledge from publicly-provided job training in interviewing for jobs, or quitting smoking in response to an anti-smoking public information campaign. In each case, members of the public contribute their efforts in some manner to an initiative of a governmental or nonprofit entity. In that spirit, contributions from the public may be desirable anywhere "across the full chain of service planning, design, commissioning, managing, delivering, monitoring, and evaluation activities" (Bovaird 2007, 847).

Facilitating coproduction. The task of engaging the public's assistance should be easiest when the citizen partner is the principal service beneficiary (e.g., Pestoff 2006, 508). In training programs for the unemployed, for example, since trainees receive the principal program benefits, they may be motivated to engage actively in the training and give their best in job interviews, thereby doing their part to coproduce (Alford 2009, 99).

Most services, though, lack clear principal beneficiaries, raising the need for other strategies. As a first option, public-minded managerial leaders might consider how to make the task easier for people to perform, as when postal authorities in Australia persuaded envelope manufacturers to add four empty boxes to all envelopes to simplify the public's entry of postal codes on outgoing mail (Alford 2009, 85–86).

Tasks can also be simplified by structuring choices better, an especially promising strategy given how social choices are often posed so poorly that people make many decisions counter to their own self-interest (Thaler and Sunstein 2008, 160). Where latitude is available, government—or the non-profit sector—should instead seek to structure choices in the manner "most likely to help and least likely to inflict harm" (Thaler and Sunstein 2008, 72). In the area of organ donations in the United States, for example, "most states use what is called an explicit consent rule, meaning that people have to take some concrete steps to demonstrate that they want to be donors," a requirement that appears to deter "otherwise willing donors from registering" to donate. By contrast, a "presumed consent" default choice, which requires people to opt out, attracts many more volunteers (Thaler and Sunstein 2008, 176–177).

A closely related approach involves enhancing the abilities of members of the public to coproduce (Alford 2009, 200). In that spirit, a local government in Aarhus, Denmark, experimented with providing language support to assist immigrant parents in developing their children's Danish-language abilities. The results showed the assistance had "a positive effect on coproduction for the families with the greatest need for the service. . . ." (Jakobsen 2013, 49).

Leaders can also encourage coproduction by activating social norms. The experience of the Sacramento (California) Municipal Utility District illustrates how this can work. In an effort to increase energy conservation, the district put "smiley faces" on bills for consumers whose energy usage fell below that of similar households. Presumably prompted by the positive reinforcement, "customers who received the personalized report reduced energy use by 2 percent more than those who got standard statements" (Kaufman 2009).

The role of incentives. By contrast, material or financial incentives have a poor record for increasing coproduction (Alford 2009, 192). By their nature, material rewards invoke a sense of precisely specified exchanges unlikely to motivate much coproduction because most coproductive work in the public sector "is difficult to specify in advance." Public-minded managerial leaders might better employ material incentives as part of a larger strategy, as when neighborhood residents in parts of California and Louisiana were persuaded to join in community environmental policing by a combination of an anticipated personal benefit of better air quality *and* the sense of contributing to their community (Laurian 2004).

Finally, sanctions also do not perform well as a primary incentive for coproduction because people often take offense at perceived threats, especially if they were already inclined to cooperate. Yet, sanctions serve two positive functions that make them a necessary element for many forms of coproduction (Alford 2009, 198–199). First, "when they are visibly wielded, sanctions deter the *resistant* clients from non-compliance, or punish them when they fail to contribute" (emphasis in original). Second, in so doing, sanctions also guarantee "to the potentially cooperative that the process to which they are contributing is fair"; that is, those who are likely to comply can see that they are not naively cooperating while others flout the law without consequence.

As these examples illustrate, coproduction represents an important new perspective on the services public and nonprofit agencies provide. Public-minded managerial leaders can serve their roles more effectively if they recognize that importance and strategize for how to increase the public's involvement in their agencies' service coproduction.

Volunteers

Volunteers, members of the public who contribute their time to public and community roles, represent a final form of partnering. Volunteers assist governmental and nonprofit agencies in all manner of functions: "from serving as board members of nonprofit organizations to serving on local government boards and commissions" to assisting "as coaches of nonprofit and municipality-sponsored sports and recreation activities" to serving in other roles with "myriad services in public and nonprofit cultural, educational, social service, and health care agencies" (Pynes 2013, 377). As with coproduction, volunteers "assist employees in meeting their agency's mission and thus become an important part of" the work of the public realm.

For public-minded managerial leaders, volunteers represent a potentially invaluable, yet inexpensive, resource for assisting in the work of their agencies. The presence or absence of an effective volunteer program can sometimes make an enormous difference in what public entities can achieve. For example, a vigorous volunteer program appeared to enable the City of Redlands, California to weather the Great Recession with only modest service cutbacks, while the absence of a similar program contributed to draconian cutbacks by the City of Colorado Springs, Colorado (see Buntin 2011; Patton 2010; Thomas 2012, 92–93).

Looking Outward II: Citizens

On occasion, public-minded managerial leaders will find value in involving the public in their administrative decision making. As two examples, the challenges of coproduction may recommend working with potential public partners in deliberating what services should be produced and how, or the potential impact of an agency program on the public may point to a need to ask the public for its views on what the program should look like. Here the public-minded managerial leader invites the public to assume the role a citizen plays in a democracy, sharing responsibility for determining the direction of governmental programming.

There are many reasons why public-minded managerial leaders might want to involve the public in their agencies' decision making. As with the involvement of subordinates in decision making (see Chapter 8), benefits of involving the public can include (1) better information, as when citizens contribute ground-level knowledge otherwise unavailable to decision makers (e.g., Beierle 2002, 746), (2) greater likelihood of the public accepting any decision it helped make, which can facilitate program implementation, (3) improved agency performance, as documented in such disparate venues as state departments of transportation in the United States (Neshkova and Guo 2011) and rural water supply projects in India (Prokopy 2005), and, perhaps, (4) increased citizen trust as a result of a rewarding involvement experience. The public can benefit, too, as from (1) a better fit of public policies and programs to community preferences, (2) improved capacity for other joint efforts with government or the nonprofit sector, and, ultimately, (3) a better quality of life in the community.

But public involvement brings problems, too. For one, those who become involved seldom constitute a cross-section of the population, often looking more like an odd lot of "the curious, the fearful, and the available" (McComas, Besley, and Trumbo 2006, 691–692). In addition, involvement can (1) require more time of public administrators to work with the public, (2) undermine necessary quality standards, and/or (3) raise program costs to meet the public's demands (e.g., Till and Meyer 2001, 377).

Public Involvement as a Contingent Issue

Fearing these problems, many public and nonprofit managers historically have sought to avoid public involvement. No truly public-minded managerial leader can afford to take that stance. They are better advised to view public involvement, like subordinate involvement, as a contingent proposition, desirable only under some circumstances, and, when desirable, best pursued with strategies that vary by issue. A handful of guidelines can help public-minded managerial leaders in understanding and responding appropriately to these contingencies.

To begin with, whenever an issue arises for a public or nonprofit agency, the public-minded managerial leader should ask first if public involvement in deliberating the issue could be desirable. That could be the case with the implementation of a new program, a perceived problem with an existing program, or any other community concern related to an agency's programs or mission. Faced with any of those issues, public-minded managerial leaders should ask if they need (1) information from the public to be able to make an informed decision and/or (2) public acceptance of the decision in order to facilitate its implementation (see also Bryson et al. 2013, 26; Thomas 1990).

Information needs could reflect managers not knowing what citizens want from a program or what the community context is like where a program would be implemented. A need for either kind of information provides grounds for engaging the public. Even stronger grounds for involving the public exist if (1) implementation of any decision would require the public's acceptance and (2) that acceptance cannot be assumed without the public's involvement. Some administrative decisions do not raise concerns about public acceptance; their impact may be so limited or so positive that acceptance either is unnecessary or can be assumed. For the most part, though, an administrative decision by a public or nonprofit agency that might substantially impact the public calls for extensive involvement if the agency hopes to gain the public acceptance necessary for implementation (Thomas 1990, 1993, 1995).

Absent either need, the public-minded managerial leader should, if possible, avoid public involvement as unnecessarily complicating decision-making. As Bryson et al. (2013, 25) have explained, issues without those needs may be "primarily technical or operational" and so of little interest to the public. To be sure, any judgment that an issue does not require public involvement should be viewed as tentative and subject to change if new evidence from the public suggests unexpected interest in the issue.

Planning Public Involvement

When needs for information and/or acceptance do imply the desirability of public involvement, public-minded managerial leaders should define any essential goals or constraints that their agency brings to the issue. Defining these constraints at the outset permits their assertion before commencing public involvement. At the same time, these leaders should try to minimize constraints, thus to open more aspects of the issue to public scrutiny and thereby give the public more reason to think its input will be used. Public managers have been known to assert "essential" constraints that ultimately proved nonessential (e.g., Manring 1993, 352). Time constraints are especially questionable since, as explained in Chapter 8, they can prove illusory if the public mobilizes and forces a delay in decision making (e.g., Thomas 1990, 441–442).

The effort to minimize constraints reflects a key principle of public involvement: Engaging that involvement means that decision-making authority must be shared with the public. Too many public involvement initiatives over the years have ignored this principle, limiting the public's role to commenting on a proposed decision that is essentially a fait accompli. Citizens who give their time to public involvement may reasonably expect their ideas to affect any eventual decision. Denied that influence, they may not support the decision, defeating the purpose for inviting their involvement in the first place.

The issue is not simply when to invite public involvement, but also how much authority to share. Sharing could extend to fully collaborative decision making, where the public works jointly with agency managers in making a decision. That has been termed a "public decision" approach, analogous to the group decision approach used with subordinates (see Thomas 2012, 130). Or, involvement could be limited to consultation, where the public-minded managerial leader seeks ideas from the public, but retains authority to make the decision. In general, fewer agency constraints recommend more sharing of authority (for more detailed guidelines, see Bryson et al. 2013; Thomas 2012, Chapters 7–9).

Planning for public involvement must also address how to obtain representative turnout. Achieving that goal typically requires (1) careful and thorough advance identification of possible relevant actors and groups and (2) aggressive recruitment of both. Although neither part of the task is easily accomplished, various techniques are available for pursuing both (e.g., Bryson et al. 2013; Thomas 2012, 147–157).

Public-minded managerial leaders must also choose specific vehicles for involving the public. In general, more diverse and more representative readings on public sentiments can be obtained by (1) using a number of techniques (e.g., public meetings, advisory committees, citizen surveys) and (2) providing multiple opportunities (e.g., public meetings at different sites and different times) (for a good illustration, see Denters and Klok 2010).

As a last crucial step before commencing public involvement, the public-minded managerial leader should confirm that any results are likely to be used. Sometimes the leader alone may be able to make that commitment, while on other occasions additional endorsements may be needed from higher-level managers or elected officials. Whatever the case, engaging the public in the absence of this commitment can waste everyone's time and nurture public distrust and skepticism (see also Bryson et al. 2013, 27).

Deliberating with the Public

Although public involvement requires extensive planning, the public-minded managerial leader is wise to begin actual involvement earlier rather than later. Earlier initiation reduces the potential for an issue to accumulate constraints before it reaches the public as well as decreasing the risk of the public wondering why their input was not invited earlier.

Public involvement initiatives will benefit from public-minded managerial leaders following a number of other practices, including:

- Encouraging participants to come with and maintain an open mind (Barabas 2004, 690).
- Arranging for both (1) agency education of citizen participants (McComas 2010, 180) and (2) communication of citizen perspectives to the agency (Beierle and Konisky 2000, 596).
- Structuring opportunities for face-to-face small-group interactions, typically nested within larger involvement mechanisms (Ostrom 1990, 90).
- Using a trained facilitator, preferably a neutral outsider (Baker, Addams, and Davis 2005, 297).

Finally, beyond public involvement per se, public-minded managerial leaders are well-advised to remain alert for possible emerging issues and, where desirable, to invite the public's involvement before any of those issues reaches a critical stage.

Looking Outward III: Customers

Public-minded managerial leaders and their agencies also interact extensively with the public as customers. People assume the role of customers when (1) they seek a discrete product or service for its personal value, not for its value for the larger community, and (2) a public or nonprofit agency is responsible for providing that good or service, sometimes for a price (e.g., the fee for a driver's license), just as often is the case with private businesses. The reasons for these contacts defy full enumeration. On the governmental side, they include (1) complaints about garbage not being collected, (2) reports of potholes on residential streets, (3) inquiries about public health insurance reimbursements, (4) questions from the elderly about late pension payments, and (5) requests for information on local recreation programs. With nonprofit agencies, they could include requests for information or referrals for social services in such areas as utility assistance, food, housing, child care, after school programs, elder care, and crisis intervention.

Based on this definition, more people probably interact with government as customers, seeking discrete goods and services for personal use, than in any other capacity. As one example, the city of Hampton, Virginia, reported 302,000 calls coming to its centralized 311 customer call center in 2003, a volume more than twice the city's population of 146,000 (311 Customer Call Center, Hampton, Virginia 2005). Even larger numbers may take their customer requests to the web. In the City of Tampa, Florida, "self-service research sessions," so called because they involve visitors exploring the City's website without municipal staff involvement, totaled 1,635,786 in 2005, more than five times the city's population (Steve Cantler, email message to author, July 5, 2006). Earlier data, before the coming of 311, suggested that the proportions of residents in the United States who contacted their municipal government in a given year with a customer-like "request for service or a complaint" ranged as high as 60–70 percent (see Coulter 1992, 306; Thomas and Melkers 1999), substantially exceeding the magnitude of any other involvement with government.

The Challenge of Access

Public-minded managerial leaders face a special challenge in providing good customer service: how to ensure that individuals who try to initiate contacts with their agencies can easily reach someone who can help. Making a request of government often raises questions that do not arise when contacting a private business, starting with the question of which government or governmental agency is responsible. Nonprofit agencies can similarly present a confusing array of options for people looking for assistance.

In response, many governments and nonprofit agencies have created centralized call centers and/or websites where individuals can bring requests. In the governmental realm, these have taken the form principally of 311 call centers for nonemergency local service issues. Since their inception in Baltimore, Maryland in 1997, 311 call centers have spread rapidly to many cities, counties, and even universities across the United States and Canada. In the nonprofit realm, comparable 211 call centers for social service issues have proliferated. Similar call centers are developing in other countries (e.g., Xin 2013).

More recently, internet-based contact points have become increasingly popular, understandably so since they can offer a richer information base and more ability to explore than is possible with 311 or 211 call centers; these are important advantages given that most inquiries from the public seek information only (e.g., Corker and Eichenthal 2006, 271). Mobile devices represent the latest frontier, giving people options to make requests through "smartphones" and other mobile devices and applications.

For public-minded managerial leaders, these developments carry an obvious implication: Any agency that interacts extensively with the public should develop centralized contacting options for receiving and responding to citizen requests. To maximize potential usage, public-minded managerial leaders should be sure that those options are relatively easy to remember and to reach (e.g., the 311 number, a brief website URL) as well as capable of responding to a broad range of service questions.

The Need for Quality Customer Service

Beyond facilitating access, public-minded managerial leaders should commit to their agencies providing high-quality customer service in interactions with members of the public. The specific elements of that service will vary to some extent depending on the functional area (e.g., Thomas and Poister 2009), but are likely to include:

- Listening carefully to any request or complaint,
- Helping to the extent possible,
- Personalizing responses,
- Responding promptly, and
- Responding courteously (Nel et al. 2000).

The "machine-like nature" of traditional bureaucracies sometimes complicates the task of providing good customer service. Bureaucracies "are developed to do a specific job," and often do that job well, but they "do not lend themselves easily to change," such as an enhanced customer orientation (Lovell 1992, 395). Frontline personnel may succumb to "an excessive reliance on rules," seeing themselves as "controlled and frustrated by" bureaucratic systems and unable to provide the personalized attention that good customer service entails (Lovell 1992, 396; for a case in point, see Hartmann and Khademian 2010). It is the responsibility of public-minded managerial leaders to see that these obstacles are addressed in the agencies they direct.

The results can be rewarding, as the experience of the U.S. Mint illustrates. In 1994, "If you called the Mint, it took on average two minutes before anyone answered, and if you sent a letter, you could wait forty-two days for an answer. If you actually ordered something, you could wait eight weeks or more to get it" (Carbone 2008, 267). All that changed after Philip Diehl became the Mint's director and, as a public-minded managerial leader himself, gave a high priority to improving customer service. In only five years Diehl was able to move the Mint to the highest ratings for customer satisfaction of any government agency. "Calls were answered on average in 17.5 seconds, letters in three days, and orders were filled in less than two weeks." Along the way, the Mint gained new support in Congress.

Learning from and About the Public

As the other side of working with the public as customers, public-minded managerial leaders should seek to learn about and from their agencies' publics (e.g., Osborne and Gaebler 1993, 173). "About" refers to who the customers are and what they want, while "from" encompasses what customers can tell the agency about its successes, failures, and overall performance. Both kinds of information can be gained from customer/citizen relations management (CRM) systems that utilize data from call centers and their online equivalents (Edwards and Thomas 2005; King 2007).

While these data on citizen contacts represent an important input to CRM systems, they should be interpreted cautiously since they may reflect more the opinions of middle- to higher-income users (Thomas and Melkers 2001, 1999). As Fountain (2001, 65) has argued, if public-minded managerial leaders give these contacts too high a priority, "what arrangements will ensure that they listen to those customers less able to exercise voice, who cannot or do not express their preferences well or clearly?"

The best CRM systems address this problem by incorporating a variety of other performance data, including (1) results of representative citizen surveys, (2) records of employee workload assignments, (3) employee reports on services and problems (e.g., crime reports, numbers of potholes filled), and (4) information from third parties (e.g., economic data) (e.g., National Performance Management Advisory Committee 2010; Swiss and Strauss 2008; Walker, Damanpour, and Devece 2011). Public-minded managerial leaders are wise to institutionalize regular monitoring of these various data to provide both a balanced perspective on service quality and alerts to emerging service problems (e.g., Edwards and Thomas 2005).

To promote the most effective use of these data, public-minded managerial leaders should consider two additional strategies: (1) providing staff training on analyzing CRM data and (2) scheduling regular meetings to discuss the data. As Behn (2005, 308–309) has observed, it takes "talented people" to make these systems work effectively; that talent is unlikely to develop without training. Training might be targeted especially to those staff who show a facility for analysis of these data, thus to enhance their abilities to move readily between different types of data in analyzing issues (for an illustration, see Thomas 2012, 67–68).

Regular meetings for their part offer public-minded managerial leaders an opportunity to facilitate different officials drawing on each other's tacit knowledge about a government's functioning to build better understanding of CRM-generated data (for an example, see Edwards and Thomas 2005, 374). Leaders who follow this strategy typically meet on a weekly, biweekly, or monthly basis for departmental level reviews, less frequently for reviews by higher-level elected officials (see Behn 2006).

Setting Priorities in Looking Upward and Outward

For anyone taking a new position as a public-minded managerial leader, the first question to answer in looking upward and outward may be where to direct one's finite energies among the almost infinite range of options. As an obvious starting place, new would-be leaders should probably give their first priority to developing productive relationships with superiors. Leaders are unlikely to be able to succeed in working externally without having first built a strong foundation of positive working relationships with superiors.

With that foundation in place or at least in development, public-minded managerial leaders can turn their attention to assessing their external environment. That effort might begin with a mapping of the environment, likely along the lines that Bill Bolling undertook in the early years of the Atlanta Community Food Bank. That mapping should identify the external actors, both individuals and organizations, who could be important to the work of the new public-minded managerial leaders. It should also help these leaders in assessing how much they will want to focus their energies externally as opposed to internally.

The good news is that many of the skills helpful in working externally and with superiors are the same skills recommended for working with subordinates. These are the skills of (1) interactive communication, where both parties learn from each other, (2) occasional use of inquiry and advocacy as part of the integrative approach for crafting solutions to issues, (3) knowing when and how to approach interpersonal conflict, and (4) being able to facilitate small-group meetings of peers. Public-minded managerial leaders who develop these skills should find them invaluable for all of their working relationships, whether internal or external.

Some aspects of working with the public as partner, citizen, and customer will pose additional challenges, but the ability to work with these several roles should be within the capacity of most public-minded managerial leaders and their employees. As Jos and Tompkins (2009, 1084) have argued, "Rightly or wrongly, public policy often requires administrators to serve the same person or group in different ways that reflect . . . multiple roles. Social workers must profile both professional job referrals and sanction those who violate rules; regulators must treat the regulated as both regulated subjects and citizen stakeholders cooperatively engaged in voluntary self-policing."

Here, though, given the breadth of issues around partners, citizens, and

customers, public-minded managerial leaders may want to limit their responsibilities to strategic leadership. In that capacity, these leaders might set
the agenda for how their agencies can nurture increased coproduction, engage public involvement as appropriate, and ensure high-quality customer
service, while delegating implementation of many necessary initiatives to
others. Those initiatives might include training of agency employees on, as
a few examples, the complexities of creating effective partnerships, the nature and importance of coproduction, and the value of sometimes sharing
authority with the public.

By these various means, public-minded managerial leaders can look
upward and outward in a manner likely to enhance the effectiveness of the
agencies they lead. In the process, they also develop the final elements for
potentially undertaking transformational organizational change, the subject of the next chapter.

Personal Leadership Exercise 10.1

Assess Your Relationship with Your Immediate Supervisor.

Criteria	Yes	Somewhat	No
Do you meet regularly?			
Does your superior facilitate more than direct conversations?			
Do you seek to meet your superior's needs?			
Does your superior give you regular feedback?			
Do you give your superior regular feedback?			
Do you assist in resolving problems or issues raised by your superior?			
Do you understand your superior's leadership style and needs?			
Does your superior have any blind spots where you help?			

If you have had any conflicts with your superior, do you perceive any aspect of your emotional intelligence being part of the problem?

Do you see any strategies you might use to improve this relationship?

Personal Leadership Exercise 10.2

Assess a Potential or Actual Interorganizational Partnership Your Agency Has or Might Have.

Criterion	Yes	Somewhat	No
Do you understand the strengths and capabilities of the other organization?			
Is the partnership built around those strengths?			
Is senior management of both organizations committed to making the partnership work?			
Have you and your organization developed relationships at all levels of the other organization?			

In light of your answers, how effective do you think the partnership is—or a possible partnership could be? Why?

What, if anything, might be done to improve the effectiveness of the partnership?

Personal Leadership Exercise 10.3

Assess Your Agency's Ability to Coproduce with Relevant Nongovernmental Entities, Including Members of the Public.

Criterion	Yes	Somewhat	No
Do you see your agency as the lead actor where effectiveness requires that the public also contributes?			
Have you examined what assistance you need from the public in producing services?			
Have you considered how to make the public's part of coproduction easier to perform?			
Have you considered how to enhance the public's abilities to coproduce?			
Have you considered how you to activate social norms to persuade the public to co-produce?			
Have you considered how to use sanctions to deter resistance to coproducing?			

In light of your answers, how do you rate the overall effectiveness of your agency's approach to coproduction? Why?

What changes, if any, would you recommend for how your agency approaches coproduction?

Personal Leadership Exercise 10.4

Assess Your Agency's Approach to Involving the Public in Relevant Administrative Decision Making.

Criterion	Yes	Sometimes	No
Does your agency involve the public when in need of additional information or public acceptance?			
When involving the public, does your agency:			
• Define relevant constraints in advance?			
• Share influence over the decision with the public?			
• Take care to obtain representative involvement?			
• Use multiple vehicles for engaging involvement?			
• Engage involvement as early as possible?			
• Arrange for both education of citizen participants and communication of citizen perspectives?			
• Arrange for some face-to-face small-group interaction?			
• Use a trained facilitator?			

In light of your answers, how do you rate your agency's approach to involving the public in administrative decision making? Why?

What changes, if any, would you recommend to how your agency involves the public?

Personal Leadership Exercise 10.5

Assess the Quality of Your Agency's Customer Service.

Criterion	Yes	Somewhat	No
Does your agency have a centralized contact point for receiving and responding to citizen requests?			
Do your agency's customer service representatives:			
• Listen carefully to requests?			
• Help to the extent possible?			
• Personalize responses?			
• Respond promptly?			
• Respond courteously?			

In light of your answers, how do you rate the overall quality of your agency's customer service? Why?

What changes, if any, would you recommend to your agency's customer service?

Chapter 11

The Ultimate Challenge: Leading Organizational Change

Organizations on occasion need dramatic change, change that can transform a struggling, stagnant entity into a renewed, reenergized force. Understandably, change of that magnitude does not come easily or often. This kind of major organizational change represents the ultimate leadership challenge, requiring effective use of all of the leadership skills profiled in earlier chapters.

Drawing from an extensive literature on successful—and unsuccessful—organizational change, this chapter proposes a two-part strategy for how public-minded managerial leaders can achieve that kind of major organizational change. The first part of the strategy involves transformational leadership, where one or more leaders follow the tenets of transformational leadership theory, a popular contemporary theory focused on changing organizations. The second part of the strategy entails a proven step-by-step approach that leaders can use in undertaking organizational change. Together, the two parts offer a road map for how leaders might best navigate an effort to institute major organizational change.

After an introductory review of what transformational organizational change involves and why it is difficult to achieve, the chapter explains the two-part strategy. To illustrate elements of the strategy, the discussion draws examples from a turn-of-the-century major organizational change at the U.S. Internal Revenue Service. The chapter concludes by considering when and where leaders should think about attempting major organizational change.

The Nature and Challenges of Organizational Change

The term organizational change refers to large-scale change in the direction, structure, major processes, and/or culture of an organization, a wholesale restructuring that extends to the goals, structures, working arrangements, power distribution, and symbols of organizations. That kind of change might be undertaken to address perceived internal dysfunction if, for example, leaders believe an organization has become inefficient and ineffective in the performance of its duties. Or, the change might be designed to respond to a changing environment, such as reduced demand for an organization's products or services.

As profiled by Rainey and Thompson (2006) and Rossotti (2005), the U.S. Internal Revenue Service (IRS) in the late 1990s serves as an illustrative case from the public realm. The IRS at the time "had problems to match its vast size and complexity, and for decades, controversy and legislative action had focused on them" (Rainey and Thompson 2006, 597). In part, those problems traced to the inherent competing demands the agency faced: "Congress and critics press the IRS to show less aggression toward taxpayers, but when tax revenues start to fall, the pendulum swings to the other extreme." Complicating matters, the agency had a poor record of customer service:

> In 1995, taxpayers received four hundred million busy signals when trying to call the IRS, more busy signals than there were people in the United States. . . . At the same time that taxpayers were having more and more trouble conducting business with the IRS, the service provided by private banking and credit card and mail-order businesses was getting better and better. (Rossotti 2005, 15)

Catalyzed by these difficulties, Congress launched a reform of the IRS, which they placed in the hands of a new IRS Commissioner, Charles Rossotti.

Organizational change by definition means *major* organizational change. The vision and goals of an organization must be reviewed and modified; parts of the organization may be eliminated or merged with other parts; employees may be laid off or transferred elsewhere in the organization; and, some products and services may be modified or terminated with others added. In the IRS case, for example, Rossotti's eventual modernization plan:

> proposed reorganizing the agency into four new "customer-oriented" operating divisions. The new divisions, which "stood up" in October 2000, replaced the 50-year-old structure of geographic districts and regions. Layers of management were reduced by half, top jobs were redefined, and managers were assigned new roles through a competitive process. (Rainey and Thompson 2006, 17)

Change of that magnitude inevitably proves extremely difficult to accomplish.

Opposition can be expected from many quarters and in many forms. If jobs are changed, employees will experience anxiety and uncertainty, leading to resistance to change and the possibility of declining rather than improving performance. The response from within the IRS to Rossotti's modernization initiative is illustrative:

> Many employees faced with the new structure and new procedures felt uncomfortable . . . . Some of the managers who had been successful in the old structure resented losing their positions and having to compete for new ones. Aggravating such concerns . . . was an atmosphere of distrust of management among IRS employees and distrust of IRS headquarters by managers and employees in the regions. (Rainey and Thompson 2006, 600)

When change arrives, there likely come organizational winners and losers, with the potential for the would-be losers mobilizing to fight the change, further complicating matters.

The challenges of organizational change become all the more daunting with the frequent leadership choice historically to impose organizational change in a top-down manner. In this scenario, new management arrives and relatively quickly—often without seeking the opinions of anyone already in the organization—announces a new organizational vision and a plan for its implementation. Having had no input, employees may resist, often because what they are asked to do does not fit what they know how to do or what they think is best for the organization. In the face of that resistance, organizational change initiatives frequently fail with the targeted organizations often worse for the effort (e.g., Bolman and Deal 2017, 368–369).

These problems notwithstanding, organizational change initiatives are not all doomed to failure; the IRS effort, as a case in point, appears to have mostly succeeded. Success does require strong leadership and careful attention by that leadership to the process of change. In most cases, that process begins with public-minded managerial leaders who adopt a transformational leadership approach.

Transformational Leadership Theory

Transformational leadership theory gained popularity in the last third of the twentieth century through the work of scholars such as James Mac-

Gregor Burns (2003) and Bernard Bass (1990). Burns and Bass profiled a number of well-known public and private sector leaders who, they argued, practiced an effective style of leadership not previously described in the leadership literature. They termed the style transformational leadership in the belief that leaders could transform organizations by transforming their followers. Transformation itself means radical change, as Burns (2003, 24) has explained:

> It is to cause a metamorphosis in form or structure, a change in the very condition or nature of a thing, a change into another substance, a radical change in outward form or inner character, as when a frog is transformed into a prince or a carriage maker into an auto factory. It is change of this breadth and depth that is fostered by transforming leadership.

Principles of Transformational Leadership

Transformational leadership theory is actually less a theory and more a recommended approach for leaders to take in running organizations. As its core concept, the approach argues for the value of inspiring and challenging employers or followers, motivating them to perform well beyond what they might otherwise have produced. The transformational leader supposedly "changes and transforms individuals" (i.e., employees and other followers) through specific leader behaviors, reshaping followers' emotions, values, ethics, and goals. These changes supposedly translate to dramatic improvements in an organization's performance, effectively transforming the organization.

Transformational leadership is often defined in contrast to traditional "transactional" leadership approaches, where leaders motivate followers through exchanges or transactions (see Bass 1990, 19–21). Those exchanges take two principal forms of rewarding obedience and punishing deviation. Rewarding obedience plays out through "contingent reward" where followers contribute their efforts in exchange for specific rewards. Punishing deviation, in turn, plays out through "management by exception," where the leader monitors subordinates for mistakes (i.e., exceptions), correcting them when they occur. The leader-member exchange (LMX) theory discussed in earlier chapters represents a prototypical example of a transactional approach.

By their nature, transactional approaches supposedly hold only a limited potential for motivating others. For one thing, the nature of an exchange may mean that leaders get only what they pay for, that is, employees may provide only the circumscribed behavior for which they will be rewarded. They may have no incentive to provide more since the reward will be the same regardless. Second, most leaders have only limited resources to offer as rewards anyway; few, if any, managers have the ability to give tangible rewards, such as a raise or a bonus, every time an employee does as directed. Third, most workers probably prefer not to work principally on an exchange basis. Employees in the public realm, in particular, are driven substantially by the intrinsic value of their work, such as the ability to help others or to contribute to the larger community, not by the promise of specific tangible rewards (see Chapter 6).

Transformational leadership theory addresses those problems by asserting several additional ways by which leaders can motivate. First, transformational leaders can inspire followers by communicating an attractive vision of what an organization can become, especially if followers join the cause. Second, transformational leaders can challenge followers, encouraging them to be creative and innovative in doing their part in pursuit of the organization's vision. Third, transformational leaders can serve as strong role models, exemplifying in their own behavior the values they ask their followers to embrace. Fourth, transformational leaders can listen carefully to the needs of followers, giving consideration to individualized needs, thereby providing a supportive environment (e.g., Bass 1990, 21–23; Moynihan, Pandey, and Wright 2012, 146–150).

The Centrality of a Vision

Implicit in all these elements is the idea of a compelling vision as essential to transformational leadership. It is the vision that supposedly inspires, challenges, and embodies the values that leaders model and followers emulate. To achieve all that, the vision must satisfy several criteria (see also Chapter 3). Most important, it must offer an attractive idealized picture of what an organization can and should become. In addition, the vision should (1) include proposed changes, (2) invoke values that appeal to key audiences (e.g., subordinates and other followers), (3) provide a map of how to get from the present to the vision's anticipated future, and (4) present a challenge to key audiences, a challenge designed in part to motivate (e.g., Bolman and Deal 2017, 205–206; Yukl 2013, 123–128, 340–343; see also Chapter 3). Finally, rather than seeming an idealistic fantasy, an effective vision must appear realistic and potentially achievable. As Bellé (2014, 128) has documented, "leaders can be effective only insofar as they succeed in making their messages credible."

Typically, a vision will also be grounded in the organization's history, promising a future that respects the past. As Goodsell (2011, 480, 486) has observed, "Celebration of an honored historical past builds organizational pride and contributes to the formation of its identity." Indeed, "Recollections of the past connect what is pressing at the moment to what happened before, transforming contemporary events into the latest episode of a lengthy saga."

The ideal vision must do all that while remaining concise. In Goodsell's (2011, 482, 490) description, the vision "needs to be short enough to be memorable and suitable for spot placement on documents and artifacts." Yet, essential for its ability to motivate, a vision should carry "an emotional punch" as a "lively, galvanizing utterance that symbolizes an important public cause." These characteristics are evident, for example, in the Peace Corps vision of "promoting world peace and friendship," the United States Park Service goal of leaving parks "unimpaired for future generations," and the National Weather Service focus on "saving lives and livelihoods."

Finally, effective visions should imply substantial changes for organizations and their employees. In the words of Jensen, Moynihan, and Salomonsen (2018, 353), "Visions alter established routines, meanings ascribed to existing behavior, and identities within an organization, altering the very objectives of an organization and subsequently the goals to be pursued by employees." This is major organizational change, *transformational* organizational change.

Evidence of Effectiveness

Judging from substantial research, transformational leadership can be effective in improving employee performance and, as a consequence, in improving overall organizational performance (e.g., Oberfield 2014). The evidence suggests specifically that managerial use of transformational leadership strategies leads to increased goal clarity and mission valence among employees, with those changes in turn leading to improved employee performance (e.g., Moynihan, Pandey, and Wright 2014). Use of transformational strategies also appears to result in employees perceiving their organization's culture as more innovative, which can translate to employees becoming more inclined to innovate (e.g., Kim and Yoon 2015, 160).

As such, transformational leadership behaviors appear to affect organizational performance indirectly through their direct effects on employees, as by changing employee perceptions of goal clarity, mission valence, and the innovativeness of the organization's culture. In other words, transformational leaders likely influence organizational outcomes as mediated through their influence on followers, with the followers themselves producing the improvements in organizational outcomes.

Recommendations for Leaders

For those who might aspire to transformational leadership, this discussion implies first support for Oberfield's (2014, 426) recommendation that public managers "should consider how they might satisfy their followers' 'higher order' needs via inspiration, individual attention, and intellectual stimulation." More specifically, in attempting major organizational change, public-minded managerial leaders might heed these several recommendations from transformational leadership theory:

1. Develop a vision for organizational change consistent with the criteria defined earlier.
2. Communicate that vision to followers, being clear about the goals the vision implies and their linkage to the organization's mission.
3. Challenge followers, encouraging them to be creative and innovative in pursuit of the organization's vision.
4. Serve as an exemplary role model, embodying values for followers to emulate.
5. Listen carefully and give individualized consideration to the needs of followers.

Transformational Leadership at the IRS

In undertaking organizational change at the IRS, Charles Rossotti pursued a strategy consistent with many of the precepts of transformational leadership theory. While skeptical about the value of a vision as such, Rossotti recognized the need for a plan that would function much like a vision. Ultimately:

> This plan included a new mission statement, a revision of the mission statement the IRS had used. The new one emphasized service to taxpayers and helping understand their responsibilities. . . . Rossotti embraced a new approach to taxation that emphasized service, support, and information for honest taxpayers rather than the threat of being caught and penalized for noncompliance (Rainey and Thompson 2006, 598).

In the area of communication, Rossotti (2005, 67) placed a premium on disseminating and winning support for his plan: "I met with groups of managers and employees in headquarters. I conducted back-to-back ninety-minute video conferences with thousands of IRS managers and union officials around the country." More generally, as Rainey and Thompson (2006, 599) summarized Rossotti's efforts, "He constantly met with every type of person or group associated with the IRS. Internally, he resolved to meet with 'every key person' who had a stake in the modernization plan, and he did so." He also met with union leaders and members, Congressional representatives and senators, and other stakeholders, often resulting in "meeting rooms so full of people from outside the IRS that participants stood against the walls."

Rossotti also served as a role model, as evidenced by the widespread admiration for his work: "Those around him saw Rossotti carrying out his role under pressure, scrutiny, and criticism with a high level of energy, skill, and commitment." No one could question his commitment to the cause given that, "After the long meetings, he would go home for the weekend and return the next week with a detailed written response" to issues raised at the meetings (Rainey and Thompson 2006, 601).

Rossotti also displayed the individualized consideration component of transformational leadership, drawing praise for how closely he listened to different perspectives on the agency's modernization efforts. One participant described him as "an excellent listener," someone who was "open to new ideas so it's not about him having . . . preconceived notions" (Rainey and Thompson 2006, 601).

A Step-by-Step Approach to Organizational Change

While having a transformational leader in place may be an essential first step, major organizational change requires more than that leader's inspiration alone. Leaders must also engage effectively in a step-by-step, day-by-day organizational change process. Scholarly research by, in particular, John Kotter (e.g., 2007) on the private sector and Sergio Fernandez and Hal Rainey (2006) on the public sector suggests a sequence of steps that enhance the likelihood of success.

Building the Framework

The sequence begins with a determination of whether there is a need for major change and, if so, the nature of the need and how to achieve it.

1. "Ensure the need" (Fernandez and Rainey 2006, 169): Launching an effort at organizational change only makes sense if extensive change appears necessary. It does not make sense when an organization is running smoothly and succeeding in the pursuit of its core purposes. In that scenario, everyone's energies are likely better directed to seeing that the organization continues to perform well. An essential first step in contemplating possible organizational change is consequently to build intelligence on organizational needs, including whether major change should be on the agenda.

2. Create "a sense of urgency" (Kotter 2007, 98): The starting place for a change initiative should be the leader's determination that major change is needed. That requires identifying and defining organizational problem areas, including the threats and opportunities central to strategic plans. Any case for a sense of urgency should also draw from organizational intelligence, tapping knowledge from within the organization. The leader who uses organizational intelligence to make the case for change will likely at the same time begin to build the necessary sense of urgency among those who provided the intelligence.

In the case of the IRS, the sense of urgency was already clear before Rossotti arrived. "Years of criticism and complaint led Congress to authorize a reform commission in 1996," which produced legislation in 1998 mandating a variety of reforms (Rainey and Thompson 2006, 597; see also Rossotti 2005, 15–16). Rossotti was fortunate to arrive early enough to be involved in formulating that legislation.

3. Form a guiding team with needed skills, credibility, and connections (Kotter 2007, 98): Once persuaded of the need for change, the leader needs to create a team to lead the change initiative. As a group, team members need to satisfy a number of criteria, including having the necessary skills, organizational credibility, and political connections (see also Chapter 9). That team can then begin the effort to build the widespread organizational buy-in necessary for a change initiative to succeed. Buy-in begins with team members themselves, but must shortly extend broadly across the organization, likely facilitated in part by the efforts of those members. The team subsequently becomes the principal infrastructure for overseeing the implementation of changes.

With the IRS change initiative, this team took the form of a Modernization Steering Committee that was tasked with coordinating the initiative. In Rossotti's (2005, 183) description, this "senior management team, combining people with experience outside and inside the IRS, was a unique experiment in the IRS and probably in government." The team created and supervised twenty-four additional teams, involving "people from all levels and many different subunits and geographic locations," which were charged with planning and implementing different aspects of the agency's many reforms (Rainey and Thompson 2006, 600).

4. Create uplifting vision and strategy (Kotter 2007, 98): Another of the team's early tasks is to define, as facilitated by the leader, the vision of what organizational change will be designed to achieve, the kind of vision that is central to transformational leadership. The team often functions as the decision-making body for defining the vision, but the goal of maximizing buy-in recommends involving others around the organization, too. At the same time, when current employees are involved in defining a vision, leaders must strike a balance between accommodating different perspectives and producing a clear, concise, energizing vision. The vision cannot be a kind of "pork barrel" statement reflecting special concessions given multiple different interests to gain their support.

Rossotti (2005, 108), of course, chose to develop a plan rather than a vision, probably because he recognized the risks in trying to define a vision. As he described his view of such an exercise:

> The process can become endless with committees and consultants. Or, the CEO can so dominate the process that nobody believes that his or her own views counted. The product can become so long and vague that it says nothing and inspires nobody. The content can become so divorced from reality that it produces cynicism or black humor.

A case can be made, though, that Rossotti's plan, with its goal of a more service-oriented, customer-friendly IRS focused on providing "service to taxpayers and helping them understand their responsibilities," had all the markings of a vision (Rainey and Thompson 2006, 598).

5. *"Provide a plan"* (Fernandez and Rainey 2006, 169): Along with the vision must come a plan for implementation, the map for how the organization can move from the present to the desired future. The plan reflects the vision as "transformed into a course of action or strategy with goals and a plan for achieving it." The plan potentially "aligns relatively well with the ubiquity of performance management," assuming leaders link goals to performance measurement targets (Moynihan, Pandey, and Wright 2014, 100). Charles Rossotti obviously strongly believed in the importance of such a plan, prioritizing it over a vision statement.

Implementing the Plan

6. *"Communicate the vision and strategy through words, deeds, symbols"* to *"build internal support for change"* (Fernandez and Rainey 2006, 170; Kotter 2007, 98): No matter how attractive the vision and the plan, extensive work will be necessary to make both known, understood, and embraced across the organization. In the language of transformational leadership, the leader and the change team must work to increase the goal clarity and mission valence of the vision and plan in the minds of employees. As the "words, deeds, symbols" phrasing implies, these efforts should have multiple dimensions, including: A first for words, seeing that everyone knows the meaning of the vision; a second for deeds, ensuring that the initial organizational changes in the plan become a reality; and a third for symbols, recasting organizational images to be consistent with the new vision and plan.

Even in an era of advanced communication technologies, the most effective technique for selling a vision appears to be face-to-face dialogue, the same dialogue that is central to the development of positive leader-employee relationships (see Chapter 7). That dialogue appears most effective when facilitated by a transformational leader on behalf of an attractive vision (Jensen, Moynihan, and Salomonsen 2018, 358). Consistent with research findings on transformational leadership, part of the leader's effort should focus on showing employees how their support of the vision can promote the achievement of important public values (e.g., Moynihan, Pandey, and Wright 2014), "impacting the well-being of other people and society at large" (Jensen 2018, 54).

The potential for using a face-to-face approach obviously decreases in larger organizations where leaders may be unable to meet personally with all or most of the workforce. Leaders in this scenario will need additional strategies. They might choose, for example, to ask members of the coordinating team to serve as surrogates in meeting face-to-face with different subgroups in the organization.

Faced with such a challenge in the sprawling IRS bureaucracy, Rossotti pursued a several-part strategy. He met personally with many different groups and people, often leaving Washington in order to do so: "To build relationships, I had to travel. I had to find opportunities to meet with people in settings that encouraged them to get below the surface—to tell me what was truly on their minds and to solicit their support on fixing the real problems we were facing in trying to change the IRS" (Rossotti 2005, 88). Going beyond what he could do on his own, Rossotti made strategic use of the many teams he had created. "According to those involved in the events, Rossotti's time at the IRS involved teams, groups, and participation to an extent exceeding anything observed up to that time in the agency" (Rainey and Thompson 2006, 600). Those teams appear to have functioned as forums for both explaining the modernization plans and planning their implementation. To further enhance communication and coordination, "the design teams met periodically with the entire Modernization Steering Committee" (Rainey and Thompson 2006, 600).

These efforts at communicating the vision must be ongoing rather than limited in duration, too. Repetition can help leaders in keeping employees focused on a vision and on how their work can contribute to making that vision a reality. In the words of Polly Trottenberg, Commissioner of Transportation for New York City and a 2018 *Governing* magazine Public Official of the Year: "Setting a bold goal really is transformational. It sounds corny. I'm not sure I would have believed it if I had not lived through it.

But it motivates people" (Vock 2018). But such goals motivate only if leaders ensure that they remain salient for followers.

7. *"Ensure top-management support and commitment"* (Fernandez and Rainey 2006, 171): Transformational leadership theory focuses principally on gaining the support of followers, a crucial constituency for any major organizational change. In so doing, though, it may slight other key constituencies. Most notably, in a world where almost every organization is part of a larger organization and may report to an elected political body, leaders need to gain support from higher organizational levels before moving very far on any change initiative (see also Chapter 10). The need is not simply to win that support at the outset either; leaders also risk failure if they do not keep their overseers in the loop as a change process progresses.

Consistent with this principle, Rossotti met extensively with Congressional representatives and senators in formulating the U.S. Internal Revenue Service Reform and Restructuring Act that set the parameters for the IRS modernization. Subsequently, he maintained a seemingly "endless series of meetings with senators and representatives" through the entire process" (Rainey and Thompson 2006, 600).

8. *"Gain necessary external support"* (Kotter 2007): Similarly, leaders are likely to need the support of external stakeholders, those actors in an organization's larger environment whose assistance could be crucial for organizational change to succeed. That requires both understanding who those stakeholders are and reaching out effectively to them (see also Chapter 10).

Rossotti (2005, 178) demonstrated a clear understanding of this need. For one thing, he recognized the crucial important of the employees' union: "We knew that, of all the stakeholders that could most help or hurt the effort, one of the most important was the employees union, known as the National Treasury Employees Union, or NTEU." With that in mind, Rossotti consulted with the leadership of the NTEU and gave the union "a say in appointments to the teams." The head of the NTEU described that choice "as a masterstroke because it encouraged the union to buy into the change process and support it" (Rainey and Thompson 2006, 601). Rossotti also met with tax-preparation professionals, former IRS commissioners, and a variety of other external stakeholders.

9. *"Obtain necessary resources"* (Fernandez and Rainey 2006, 172): Seldom can organizational change succeed without an infusion of new resources, including either or both financial and/or human resources. As they move through the previous steps, the leader and the change team should develop a reading on what additional resources they may need. This is the time to define exactly what those resources are and how to obtain them.

In the IRS case, Rossotti saw a need to hire new people, in part "to break down the agency's insular culture" (Rainey and Thompson 2006, 601). Having effectively cultivated support at higher levels, he readily won support for a request to hire forty so-called "critical-pay" personnel. In addition, the agency was granted "streamlined authority" to make those hires rapidly and "at salaries that were high by the standards of the federal government."

Persisting Across Time

At this point, the organizational change initiative may have reached the equivalent of halftime, implying the need to sustain the same "level of effort for the second half" (Elk 2017). To succeed, those who lead change initiatives must persist through a number of additional steps. As Colleen Jollie, a well-respected long time state tribal liaison at the Washington State Department of Transportation has observed, "The first wave of transformation [is] the easiest. When you get down to the deeper layers—the layers where people are resistant to change because it's the way things have always been done, the typical response of people is to resist change" (King and Beeby 2008, 1149). Faced with that resistance, public-minded managerial leaders can pursue three additional strategies.

10. *"Remove obstacles, overcome resistance, and empower people to move"* (Fernandez and Rainey 2006, 170; Kotter 2007, 98): Leaders and their change teams must keep their ears and eyes open to the sounds and sights of resistance, before strategizing and acting to overcome that resistance, in some cases by negotiating revisions to the planned changes. Indeed, every successful organizational change process needs flexibility sufficient to permit adaptation and modification in implementation.

The IRS modernization effort certainly encountered resistance, facing a "legacy of skepticism and criticism" as a result of the failure of earlier reforms. Rossotti appears to have fought and overcome most of the resistance through the use of tactics already described, including a highly participatory planning process, extensive use of teams, and a willingness to meet with all interested stakeholders.

At the same time, leaders sometimes anticipate more obstacles and resistance than actually materializes. On occasion, employees may welcome reforms as "unleashing" them from organizational constraints, perhaps especially in the frequently rule-bound public sector. The potential for winning over employees becomes even greater when leaders engage employees in planning how change will be implemented (e.g., Fernandez and Rainey 2006, 171).

11. *Plan for and create "early wins"* (Kotter 2007, 98): The process of organizational change will almost always be an uphill battle, with a higher

likelihood of failure than success. Facing those long odds, leaders are wise to plan strategically for early wins, for organizational changes that will suggest the process is working. Those initial successes could help to build optimism and sustain commitment through the steps that remain for real organizational change to come to fruition.

12. *"Pursue comprehensive change" and nurture and shape new culture* (Fernandez and Rainey 2006, 173; Kotter 2007): Achieving comprehensive change likely requires reshaping an organization's culture to be more consistent with the values of the organization's new vision. Organizational culture refers to a "pattern of shared basic assumptions that a group has learned as it solved its problems . . . and that has worked well enough to be considered valid and taught to new members," or, more succinctly, to "how we do things around here." Culture is not necessarily what is *written* (e.g., formal policies) but how it is actually *done*. Culture also tends to be deeply entrenched and consequently not easily changed, making culture change one of the difficult challenges in any change initiative (see, for example, Hartmann and Khademian 2010).

In the case of the IRS, Charles Rossotti was aware of a need to change the agency's "insular" culture, as evidenced by his hiring of the forty new employees to challenge that culture (Rainey and Thompson 2006, 601). Perhaps even more important, he achieved a major overhaul of the IRS workforce: "In the new organizational structure, about two thousand senior management jobs were abolished. About 20 percent of these jobs were eliminated outright, and the rest totally redefined so that they focused more specifically on producing quality work on taxpayer cases rather than on internal administration" (Rossotti 2005, 183–184).

The Path to Successful Organizational Change

A leader who follows the principles of transformational leadership and uses this step-by-step approach to organizational change should maximize the potential for achieving major organizational change. That kind of change requires, in other words, both a leader who can inspire followers and a detailed strategy which the leader systematically and carefully implements.

To be clear, success may not mean accomplishing all that was desired; too many factors affect the fates of organizations to be confident of comprehensive success for any major reform initiative. In the case of the IRS, some of the problems Rossotti identified at the outset remained when his five-year term as commissioner ended, and a new commissioner appeared poised to reverse some of Rossotti's reforms, casting doubt on the extent of the modernization's success. At the same time, enough of the changes endured that Rossotti and the IRS were viewed much more positively when he left than when he arrived. As one observer commented at Rossotti's go-ing-away party, "How often do you think you will hear such sincere praise, from every group or authority with which he dealt, for an agency head who led a major, challenging reorganization of that agency?" (Rainey and Thompson 2006, 596).

Where and When Transformational Change?

Transformational organizational change is an undertaking that is only sometimes appropriate. It is unlikely to be appropriate for organizations that are functioning well and facing no major threats from their environ-ments. Nor is it even appropriate for every organization that is *not* function-ing well, especially if any of the preconditions for successful organizational change is not met. It would likely be ill-advised, for example, if higher-level management does not support the effort. It might also be futile for organi-zations that are highly rule-constrained, as sometimes in the public sector (e.g., Goldsmith 2010), or that lack a substantial public-service motivated workforce. Given the time and energy required, leaders are well-advised to gauge the prevailing winds before launching any effort at transformational organizational change.

These qualifications notwithstanding, transformational organizational change may frequently be a very effective strategy in the public realm, in-cluding at least the public and nonprofit sectors. Most evidence suggests that transformational leadership strategies positively affect "individual-level follower performance" to an extent that cannot be achieved through trans-actional approaches alone (e.g., Trottier, Van Wart, and Wang 2008; Wang et al. 2011, 223). Moynihan, Pandey, and Wright (2014, 100) go so far as to suggest that we may be at "a transformational moment in the public sec-tor," a time with especially high promise for transformational approaches. It may not be a coincidence that the transformational leadership change "model has grown in popularity at a time of deepening cynicism about gov-ernment, unprecedented in some democracies." Working in that setting, "those providing public services" may "hear enough about what is wrong with government. Having a leader who can articulate why their work mat-ters and offering a way to channel their passion to help others may be just what the doctor ordered."

Transformational strategies are likely to be most appropriate in any public service setting where a broad range of stakeholders see substantial change as desirable. Nonprofit agencies may be particularly attractive en-vironments for transformational strategies given their typical commitment to public-serving values and likely fewer of the constraining rules that plague parts of the public sector. For the same reasons, transformational approaches may also work well for political, social, and religious movements. The public-serving cultures of all of these settings could provide fertile environments for transformational leaders to engage and inspire followers, including both employees and volunteers, through a galvanizing vision and an artful strategy.

The vision behind any organizational change initiative need not reach the rhetorical heights of, say, a major social movement. There is substantial evidence, in fact, that transformational leadership may hold *more* potential for smaller organizations where grand visions make a poor fit. The advantage in smaller organizations derives from the greater ability of leaders to reach more employees directly and in person (see Jensen, Moynihan, and Salomonsen 2018, 354). By contrast, the size of larger organizations limits the ability of leaders to interact one-on-one with many employees without sacrificing other priorities, and inspiration is typically easier to achieve one-on-one and face-to-face than when mediated through others.

Leaders should not view transformational strategies as their only tools. Ample research suggests that transactional approaches are also important for leadership effectiveness, as in negotiating compromises to overcome resistance to organizational change. Leader-member exchange (LMX) strategies actually appear to fit well with the transformational leadership approach, with the exchanges mostly along the lines of positive interactions rather than quid pro quo swaps (see Vigoda-Gadot and Beeri 2012, 590).

In practice, the most effective leaders appear to use both transformational and transactional approaches. Bill Bolling, for example, employed exchange and pressure tactics, tactics central to transactional approaches, in addition to many transformational tools (e.g., a compelling vision, inspirational appeals, high ethical standards), varying his tactics as situations might dictate (see Chapter 4). Charles Rossotti (2005, 78) implied a similar outlook when he remarked that, in his IRS modernization effort, sometimes "purity of management principles had to be tempered by political reality."

The Importance of Leadership

Transformational change initiatives only make sense, though, when the right leader comes along. That happened when Charles Rossotti came to the Internal Revenue Service in 1997. The agency obviously needed change, but change came only when Rossotti followed both the precepts of transformational leadership and the recommended step-by-step approach to organizational change. A different leader might not have known to attempt a similar strategy.

The "right leader" need not mean the classic stereotype of a larger-than-life figure who mesmerizes and inspires simply upon entering a room. Conventional wisdom might imply otherwise by emphasizing such transformational leaders as Martin Luther King Jr. and John F. Kennedy. Both King and Kennedy possessed charisma in the dictionary sense of a personality characteristic involving "compelling attractiveness or charm that can inspire devotion in others."

For successful organizational change, what may be more important than a compelling personality is the adroit use by leaders of their personal skills and strategies, as profiled in earlier chapters. Bernard Bass (1990, 22), one of the early scholars of transformational leadership, implied this perspective when he described a charismatic leader as someone who "provides vision and sense of mission, instills pride, gains respect and trust." Similarly, Javidan and Waldman (2003, 236) argued that charismatic leadership in the public sector entails four characteristics: (1) "energy and determination," (2) "vision," (3) "challenge and encouragement," and (4) "risk taking." All of the characteristics from Bass, Javidan, and Waldman fall within the framework of effective leadership traits and skills profiled elsewhere in this book.

Interestingly, women may actually hold more potential than men to play this kind of leadership role. In summarizing meta-analyses of leadership studies, Eagly (2013) reported that "women, more than men, combine feminine and masculine leader behaviors" in "a highly effective, androgynous style" consistent with transformational leadership. Further, "These contemporary cultural models of good leadership are less masculine than earlier models and are at least partially consistent with feminist visions of good leadership" (Eagly and Chin 2010, 216).

Viewed from this perspective, the right leader means someone who (1) understands how to pursue organizational change, (2) has developed the skills necessary to successfully execute the various steps in that pursuit, and (3) wants and chooses to engage in the pursuit. That person could be anyone who understands the strategies detailed in the earlier chapters of this book and has practiced the skills necessary to execute those strategies effectively, a description that could extend to a broad range of public-minded managerial leaders. Those leaders might find the task of transformational organizational change less daunting and more practical than it might initially appear.

Personal Leadership Exercise 11.1

Assuming You Are or Have Been a Manager, Rate Yourself As a Transformational Leader.

Did you:	Definitely	Somewhat	No
Develop a vision for the future of the agency (or your part of it)?			
Communicate that vision to subordinates, being clear about the goals it implies?			
Challenge subordinates to be creative and innovative?			
Model the values you wanted subordinates to emulate?			
Listen carefully and give individualized consideration to the needs of subordinates?			

In light of your answers, how do you rate yourself overall as a transformational leader? Why?

What, if anything, might you do differently in the future to be more of a transformational leader?

Personal Leadership Exercise 11.2

If You Have Been Part of an Organizational Change Process, Rate the Fit of the Process to the Recommended Step-by-Step Approach.

Criterion	Definitely	Somewhat	No
Ensuring the need?			
Creating a sense of urgency?			
Having a guiding team?			
Having an uplifting vision and strategy?			
Having an implementation plan?			
Communicating the vision through words, deeds, and symbols?			
Ensuring top-management support?			
Gaining necessary external support?			
Obtaining necessary resources?			
Removing obstacles & overcoming resistance?			
Creating early wins?			
Achieving comprehensive change?			

How do you rate the success of this organizational change process? Why do you believe it was successful or unsuccessful?

If you were to lead an organizational change process, what, if anything, might you do differently from how this process was managed?

Chapter 12

Conclusions

The Politically Skilled Public-Minded Managerial Leader

Popular stereotypes picture leaders barking orders that others readily obey. In this view, leaders know what to do and, acting on that knowledge, are not shy about making demands of subordinates. Those subordinates for their part move quickly to comply, recognizing that, were they to balk, they might shortly be poring through help-wanted ads, having lost their jobs due to insubordination.

Contemporary reality departs sharply from that stereotype. Leaders on their own seldom have knowledge sufficient to frame sensible orders, that is, orders which, if followed, they can be confident will enhance their organizations' performance. Nor typically do they hold enough formal authority to force others to comply. In a world where information is now widely dispersed, leaders must learn what others know if their decisions are to be well-informed. In a world where power is broadly shared, leaders must find techniques other than formal power to gain the support necessary for their decisions to be effectively implemented.

That description captures the dilemma that faces contemporary managerial leaders, including public-minded managerial leaders. To be effective in their work, these leaders must develop a range of political skills, including both latent political skills (i.e., the personal characteristics discussed mostly in Chapters 3 and 4) and manifest or operational political skills (i.e., the principal focus of Chapters 6–11). By way of concluding, this final chapter summarizes those skills, reviews how they can be developed, considers their value in the often-constrained public realm, and ponders why more public servants do not rise to the challenge of becoming public-minded managerial leaders.

The Political Skills of Managerial Leadership

As stipulated in Chapter 4, political skills encompass "the social astuteness and behavioral flexibility and adaptability necessary to effectively address the needs and aspirations of followers in ways that favorably influence their work reactions and behavior, and indeed, affect the climate of the work unit" (Ahearn et al. 2004, 314). The latent and manifest political skills of interest are briefly summarized and illustrated here, with the illustrations drawn from the stories of Bill Bolling and Charles Rossotti, two exemplary public-minded managerial leaders.

The Personal Foundation

Effective political skills require a strong personal foundation comprised of (1) high emotional intelligence, (2) a desire to serve, (3) a strong sense of specific public purposes one wants to achieve, and (4) a personal vision and, eventually in any leadership role, an institutional vision. In the area of emotional intelligence, for example, leaders need (1) self-awareness, an understanding of their own emotional makeup, and (2) self-regulation, the ability to maintain self-control and respond appropriately when under pressure, as well as empathy, social skills, and motivation. To be public minded, too, they must feel the desire to serve and have a sense of the public purposes they want to promote.

Charles Rossotti exemplified that kind of emotional intelligence during his work at the IRS. Amid a challenging reorganization effort, "He never responded to the pressures with rancor or discouragement." Although frequently criticized, "he displayed respect for all participants and stakeholders and a tolerance of their perspectives." As perhaps the ultimate evidence of his self-awareness and self-regulation, Rossotti always seemed to keep a positive outlook, with one IRS executive observing, "He is never down" (Rainey and Thompson 2006, 601).

Bill Bolling's story illustrates the importance of the desire to serve, a sense of purpose, and a personal vision. Uncertain in his late twenties what he wanted to do with his life, Bolling regularly visited the Ebenezer Baptist Church where Martin Luther King Jr. had preached and is buried. Once there, he repeatedly walked around the King tomb, meditating and asking, "God, what do you want me to do?" Eventually, Bolling found his answer, his initial personal vision, although, even then, as he recalls, "the answer wasn't go feed the hungry." Instead:

> It was to raise the consciousness, to change hearts and minds about our relationship with each other and God. And that everything is sacred.

If everything's sacred, that will inform how you treat things—animals, the trees, oceans, and other people . . . . That is what I came away with, and that was the call to start a community, to have this safe place for different faith groups, different people of different capacities, mental health capacities or whatever.

That personal vision eventually grew into the Atlanta Community Food Bank.

Preparation for a Political World

Managerial leaders will be severely limited in their potential effectiveness unless they recognize and embrace the political nature of the world they work in. For one reason, since they almost always face a substantial gap between the formal power they hold and the power they actually need, leaders need to strategize how they can supplement formal authority by building informal power and developing and applying political skills.

Knowing that he initially lacked *any* formal power, Bill Bolling built extensive informal power through a variety of means: his energy and public-serving ambition, his insatiable appetite for knowledge and expertise, excellent listening abilities, a strong sense of empathy for others, a tolerance for conflict, and being trustworthy. He made effective use of that power by developing and applying his many political skills, including political mapping, consulting, facilitation, negotiation, among others. In a similar fashion, Charles Rossotti built informal power and applied political skills at the IRS by consulting extensively, listening well when consulting, showing understanding (i.e., empathy) for other perspectives, managing conflict as necessary, developing a learning mind-set for relevant knowledge and expertise, and proving himself trustworthy.

Becoming a Manager

With this personal foundation and political preparation, would-be public-minded managerial leaders may be ready to assume managerial leadership positions. Chapter 5 examined the challenges likely to arise with the transition to this typically very different kind of work world, and suggested strategies new managerial leaders might employ in adapting to the new responsibilities and, potentially, new way of life. Their successes with the Internal Revenue Service and the Atlanta Community Food Bank imply that Charles Rossotti and Bill Bolling both made this transition seamlessly.

Managing and Motivating People

Managerial effectiveness depends on an organization's human resources: its employees. Gaining their support starts with a firm foundation of effective human resource management through (1) hiring the right people, (2) investing in employees after hiring, (3) rewarding good performers, (3) protecting the jobs of effective performers, (4) promoting from within to the extent possible, (5) avoiding in-breeding, (6) seeking diversity, and (7) empowering employees to do their jobs.

Managers also need to understand and be responsive to what motivates their employees. Are they driven principally by public service motivation, by the opportunity to serve others, or are they motivated more by (1) responsible professionalism, the desire to apply their professional skills effectively, or (2) rational economic self-interest, the desire for personal economic gain, or most likely, by (3) by some other factor or combination factors? Careful consideration of the different sources of motivation for specific employees can prove invaluable in strategizing for how to maximize employee and organizational performance.

Bill Bolling is well known for the caring he showed employees during his decades at the Atlanta Community Food Bank. In the words of a former member of the Food Bank's Board of Directors:

> When you walk through the warehouse of the Food Bank with him [Bolling], he knows the people in that warehouse, he knows their families, he knows their children, he knows what maladies they have suffered. And he's genuinely concerned about their well-being and what they did this past weekend and what they're working on, and he's thankful for their presence in that warehouse. And they're thankful for his presence in that warehouse.

It is, as the former board member added, "a leadership lesson on how to treat people" and, more generally, on how to manage human resources effectively.

In his work with the IRS, Charles Rossotti (2005, 183–184) showed a very different side of effective human resource management, a side that did not always include either "promoting from within" or "protecting jobs." To the contrary, his efforts led to the elimination of "about two thousand senior management jobs," but, even then, only "20 percent of these jobs were eliminated outright," with "the rest totally redefined so that they focused more specifically on producing quality work on taxpayer cases rather than on internal administration."

At the same time, Rossotti also demonstrated understanding of the value of selectively "hiring the right people" through his addition of forty critical-pay employees to assist in the reform initiative (Rainey and Thompson 2006, 601). To empower them, Rossotti (2005, 182) structured their job descriptions to be "comparable to executive jobs in other organizations," making it "possible to recruit outside senior people with relevant experience to work with the career executives." To further empower them, Rossotti paired each new hire with an experienced insider, thereby seeking to diffuse the newcomers' influence broadly across the agency. By following these human resource principles, Rossotti attempted to strike a difficult balance between protecting current employees and drawing energy from the hiring of new, expert employees.

Relationship Development and Conflict Management

Effective managerial leaders build relationships with subordinates through focused efforts at interactive communication, where managers and subordinates exchange information and engage in mutual influence. Given the inevitability of at least occasional conflict, these leaders must also be able to address disagreements, preferably through an approach based on a combination of inquiry and advocacy.

Bill Bolling exemplifies these principles in his approach to employees, featuring prominently strong listening abilities and a high value placed on empathy. At the same time, he does not duck conflict and takes pride in his ability to reframe in resolving conflicts. As a former colleague commented on Bolling: "He's not afraid of tough conversations, but he does it in a respectful way. . . . It's a direct communication style. It's a compassionate communication style, but if there's a controversial point, he doesn't avoid it. He raises it and he talks about it."

Charles Rossotti demonstrated commitment to the same principles by soliciting and listening to a broad range of perspectives on the IRS modernization. As Rossotti (2005, 88) recalls his efforts: "I had to find opportunities to meet with people in settings that encouraged them to get below the surface—to tell me what was truly on their minds and to solicit their support on fixing the real problems we were facing in trying to change the IRS."

Understanding When and How to Involve Others

The need to work with others necessitates an ability to determine when others should be involved, whether to involve them as individuals or as groups, and how much authority to share when others are involved. Too little involvement and the leader may neither obtain the necessary information nor nurture acceptance essential for implementing decisions; too much involvement and decision making may stall amid an excess of organizational democracy. Leaders must learn how to walk the fine line between the two extremes.

Charles Rossotti knew how to walk this line. He needed to work extensively with many stakeholders in planning and implementing changes at the IRS, so extensively with so many stakeholders that the process could easily have spun out of control. That it did not shows that Rossotti knew how to involve others appropriately in decision making. Further evidence comes from how he went about redefining the IRS's mission: He put one person in charge, instructed her to consult widely before proposing a set of options. He then held one senior management team meeting to discuss the options before making the decision himself. In short, he shared influence, but only *some*, while retaining and exercising the final authority.

Leading Small-Group Teams and Meetings

The growing popularity of organizational teams puts a premium on leaders being able to structure small-group teams and manage their meetings. With the former, leaders need to be able to determine when a team is needed, what capabilities it should have, who can best provide those capabilities, and how to develop that team as an effectively functioning entity. With the latter, leaders need skills for planning and facilitating small-group meetings, including skills for setting agendas, sequencing topics, facilitating discussions, addressing conflicts, and moving issues to resolution.

Charles Rossotti proved extremely skillful in his use of teams and meetings in the IRS modernization. He created and directed a senior management team charged with overseeing the modernization, authorized an additional twenty-four design teams with membership drawn from all across the IRS, and included a mechanism for the design teams to communicate occasionally with the senior management team (Rainey and Thompson 2006, 601). From all indications, Rossotti was also proficient at facilitating the various meetings he convened.

Bill Bolling appears to have been similarly effective at building teams and facilitating meetings. On the latter, consider this description from the former member of the Food Bank board of directors on how Bolling facilitated and negotiated a conflict between a CEO of a smaller food bank and one of that food bank's principal donors:

> There's an amazing dialogue going on where . . . this conversation is occurring, but it's directional. It's not a robust conversation, but by the end of the meeting it is. There was a bridge that had to be built, and he [Bolling] was building it. . . . Bill bridged the gap, and that relationship now is healing. It's better than what it was, and there's a dialogue.

Looking Upward and Outward

Managers also need skills for working with superiors and external stakeholders, people over whom they hold no formal authority. These include skills to gain "top-management support and commitment," which is a necessity of everyday management as well as a crucial step in the organizational change process. In an increasingly networked society, managers must also frequently gain support from actors outside the core organization, external stakeholders who function as the organization's customers, partners, and citizen-owners.

Charles Rossotti and Bill Bolling proved effective in both areas. Looking upward, Rossotti held a seemingly "endless series of meetings with senators and representatives," his legislative superiors, "through the entire process" (Rainey and Thompson 2006, 600). Looking outward, he consulted with a variety of external stakeholders, including "former commissioners and representatives of tax accountants and lawyers" (Rossotti 2005, 67). For his part, Bolling looked upward and outward at essentially the same time, building a supervisory board, his bosses, that included external stakeholders he could tap for assistance in customer service training (Ritz-Carlton Hotels) and programming of Food Bank pick-up and delivery trucks (United Parcel Service). He even found a way to build an alliance with conservative Republican Senator Saxby Chambliss around their overlapping interests in agriculture and food.

A Toolkit for Public-Minded Managerial Leaders

These are the personal characteristics and political skills that, once developed, serve as the principal tools of an effective public-minded managerial leader. The personal characteristics provide a foundation for leading, what might be thought of as the leadership personality, while the various political skills provide the means to realize that potential, the techniques for working effectively with others and persuading them to follow.

As the stories of Bill Bolling and Charles Rossotti illustrate, these characteristics and skills serve as the tools necessary for successful organization building and transformational organizational change. Bolling used his version of these tools for organization building, creating and shaping the now iconic Atlanta Community Food Bank as well as leading the national food bank movement. Rossotti employed his set of these tools to achieve transformational organizational change through the modernization of the Internal Revenue Service.

Other public-minded managerial leaders who develop enough of these political talents might similarly be able to build a significant nonprofit organization, as Bolling did, or transform a long-standing, but stagnant, governmental agency, as Rossotti did. Or, they might choose to use these tools simply to be effective leaders. While Bill Bolling and Charles Rossotti impressed with their feats of organization building and organizational change, most public-minded managerial leaders will likely be satisfied to do their jobs well without inducing dramatic change.

Ironically, as a byproduct of the effective use of these political skills, these leaders may create the potential for sometimes being able to "bark" orders—or at least issue orders—with a reasonable expectation that subordinates will comply. Subordinates can appreciate a leader's cultivation of partnership relationships of mutual influence so much that they will support an occasional departure from that norm. That potential serves as yet additional evidence of the effectiveness of these tools.

Developing the Toolkit

To develop these skills, would-be leaders might keep in mind a few basic principles, including:

1. *Develop understanding of what the different personal characteristics and political skills entail:* Herein lies the purpose of this book—to define clearly what is entailed in each of the political skills important for effective managerial leadership. This book will have succeeded if it significantly enhances this understanding for would-be or actual public-minded managerial leaders.

2. *Practice*: Working from that basic understanding, would-be managerial leaders need to practice the different principles, especially those where they may perceive themselves as deficient. Practice means, as a few examples, thinking about one's emotional intelligence, assessing the extent of one's informal power and political skills, weighing when and to what extent to involve others in decision making, and experimenting with facilitating small-group meetings.

3. *Observe and listen*: As practice plays out (e.g., facilitating meetings), leaders should observe the results as well as listen to what others say about their efforts. Practice by its nature will inevitably include elements that do not work well. On those occasions, leaders need to observe and listen to identify and understand what happened and why.

4. *Reflect and revise:* In addition to observing and listening, leaders are well-advised to reflect after the fact, continuing to think about what happened and why. As Warren Bennis has documented, most leaders report learning more from their mistakes than from their

successes. What lessons for going forward can the leader learn from disappointing outcomes? What might a leader learn, for example, from having facilitated a small-group meeting that felt frustrating for the leader or group members?

5. *Consult:* There are limits to what leaders can learn from self-reflection on their perceived successes and failures. They will sometimes err in those perceptions, believing they have succeeded or failed when others perceive the opposite. That risk, along with other factors, recommends regularly consulting, checking one's perceptions against others' perspectives. As more general counsel, leaders are wise to cultivate relationships with others who can serve as trusted confidantes when consultation may be desirable.

6. *Repeat:* The counsel typically included with shampoo instructions—"lather, rinse, repeat"—also applies to the development of leadership skills. After practicing, observing and listening, reflecting and revising, and possibly consulting, leaders can best learn by repeating the process. Repeating means, for example, facilitating another small-group meeting or attempting to resolve another interpersonal conflict via inquiry and advocacy as well as, in both cases, repeating the efforts to observe and listen, reflect and revise, and perhaps consult. Repeated experimentation and reflection provide the most effective route to mastery of any leadership skill.

Is More Needed?

But will effective use of these skills always result in successful leadership? Some authors suggest additional characteristics may also be needed. Former university president Nannerl Keohane (2012), in particular, argues persuasively for three other factors. A strong case can be made, though, that each should develop as a byproduct of cultivating the other political skills. Consider each in turn:

Rhetoric: The public-minded managerial leader needs to be able to "articulate ideas and policies persuasively" in order to persuade others to follow (Keohane 2012, 98). Leaders seem likely to develop this talent if, as recommended in earlier chapters, they (1) build their knowledge and expertise, giving them a firmer basis from which to speak, (2) learn to interact effectively with others, which itself will likely require developing rhetorical skills, and (3) become capable at framing and reframing, which also necessitates rhetorical skills.

Judgment: For Keohane (2012, 87), "The most valuable attribute leaders can possess in any context is good judgment." This attribute, too, seems likely to grow with the development of other political skills. Good judgment likely rests on a combination of knowledge, understanding of others' perspectives, and, again, the ability to frame and reframe. The better a leader understands how an organization and its members work, the better the judgment that leader may be able to apply to organizational issues.

Courage: Leaders also need courage. As Keohane (2012, 111) has written, "Leaders need courage to make tough and unpopular decisions, stand up for principles they believe in, and face the loneliness that sometimes comes with holding power." Mark Funkhouser (2018, 57), editor of *Governing* magazine and former mayor of Kansas City, Missouri, agrees, arguing that, "It is [the] test of moral courage that separates real leaders from those who merely hold positions of authority."

The development of political skills might not necessarily nurture courage, but it could well reduce the difficulty of showing courage in the face of opposition. After all, leaders who have earned trust through the adroit use of political skills may in the process gain the latitude to make difficult, courageous decisions without undermining that trust. Leaders can demonstrate their courage more confidently if they do not anticipate that doing so will undermine their standing with others.

Leaders *Can* Make a Difference in the Public Realm

The many challenges of working in the public realm, as detailed in Chapter 2, could cast doubt on the value of developing these skills. That is, why develop leadership skills if even the most proficient public-minded managerial leader will not be able to make a difference in the often highly-constrained public and nonprofit sectors?

Evidence documented across this book should by now have made clear that proficient public-minded managerial leaders can make a difference in the public realm, if not always or everywhere, at least frequently enough and in a sufficiently wide range of settings that the value of political leadership skills cannot be questioned. Strong anecdotal evidence comes from the stories of Bill Bolling and Charles Rossotti. Despite starting with no formal power and having to struggle continuously with the resource stringency that is characteristic of the nonprofit world, Bolling built the enormously successful Atlanta Community Food Bank and served as one of the principal leaders in the development of the national food bank movement. Working in an agency that was likely subject to as many of the challenges of the public realm as any public agency ever faces, Rossotti for his part spearheaded a successful transformation of the U.S. Internal Revenue Service.

Broader studies reinforce the point that motivated public-minded managerial leaders can produce positive change in the public realm. Borins (2000, 503), for one, has documented the success of many governmental innovators, public-minded managerial leaders by another name, in achieving "creative solutions to public-sector problems." Most succeeded only by persisting in the face of many obstacles, gaining "support for their ideas from many sources, both inside and outside the public sector" (Borins 2000, 503). They succeeded, in other words, by deftly employing the political toolkit (e.g., persuasion, consultation, negotiation) of public-minded managerial leaders to overcome the challenges characteristic of the public realm.

Public-minded managerial leaders are also helped by seldom, if ever, having to confront *all* of the challenges of the public realm at once. Instead, most probably need to deal with only *some* of the challenges at any given time. Consistent with that idea, Wright and Pandey (2010, 75) concluded from their research that, "the structure of these [public-sector] organizations may not be as bureaucratic as commonly believed," and, "some bureaucratic characteristics had little, if any, adverse effect on the prevalence or practice of transformational leadership behaviors." The emphasis on constraints can also obscure how public-minded managerial leaders will sometimes be able to counter constraints by drawing on the unique resources of the public realm, resources such as public service motivation, the authority of democratic government, and the unique legitimacy of the nonprofit sector.

To be sure, success does require that leaders adapt their approach to the specific constraints and resources they face in any given leadership role as well as to the current political climate. As Keohane (2012, 85) has observed, "Leaders who adapt their behavior to the times will prosper, and those whose policies clash with the demands of the times do not." Still, between the unique resources of the public realm and the less burdensome than anticipated constraints, public-minded managerial leaders appear likely to find substantial latitude for exercising political skills to make a difference in the public realm.

Why the Reluctance to Lead?

The enormous potential for making a difference as a public-minded managerial leader in the public realm could raise a question of why so few rise to the task. What author and management trainer Bruce Tulgan (2013) says of middle managers in the private sector likely applies equally to the public realm: "They want the business card [of being a manager], but they don't want the day-to-day hassle of managing" (CollaborativeAgency, 2013).

One obvious reason may be the radical difference in the nature of work that comes with taking a leadership role. As described in Chapter 5, managerial work can be "almost the diametric opposite of the studied, analytical, persisting work pattern of the professional who expects and demands closure: the time to do a careful and complete job that will provide pride of authorship" (Sayles 1979, 17). Many professionals may prefer to stay with their methodical "work pattern," fearing the "hectic and fragmented" life of a managerial leader.

While that may be part of the story, it seems unlikely to be the full story. A larger part of the story may lie in the perceived difficulty of successfully performing the work of a public-minded managerial leader. That work, after all, requires a wide range of skills beyond what professional work usually requires. Those are, of course, the political skills that have been the subject of this book: developing a vision, building informal power, cultivating political skills, learning how to manage and motivate subordinates, knowing when and how to involve others in decision making, forming teams and facilitating small-group meetings, and working effectively with superiors and external stakeholders.

It may not be the perceived difficulty alone either, but also the perceived *mystery* around these skills. Politics and power in organizations can hold substantial mystery, with many people neither understanding how they work nor wanting to understand. Included in their number, unfortunately, are many managerial leaders whose positions place them, like it or not, at the center of organizational politics. For them and for many others in organizations, the political world and the political skills for its navigation can seem both mysterious and difficult.

As a core argument of this book, leaders, would-be leaders, and others in organizations would be wise to confront any personal distaste for the political skills of leadership, whether based on perceived difficulty, mystery, or other factors. Overcoming that distaste and being willing to practice these political skills can transform many hesitant would-be leaders into effective public-minded managerial leaders. For others who still choose to decline leadership roles, a better understanding of the necessary political skills can still enhance their comfort and satisfaction with that work. Anyone can benefit from understanding better how and why their workplace functions as it does.

References

311 Customer Call Center, Hampton Virginia. 2005. Memorandum, City Hall.

Ahearn, Kathleen K., Gerald R. Ferris, Wayne A. Hochwarter, Ceasar Douglas, and Anthony P. Ammeter. "Leader political skill and team performance." *Journal of Management* 30, no. 3 (2004): 309–327.

Ajmera, Maya. "Conversations with Maya: Dr. Edward Thorp." *Science News*, November 17, 2017.

Alford, John. *Engaging public sector clients: From service-delivery to co-production*. London: Palgrave Macmillan, 2009.

Alford, John, and Owen Hughes. "Public value pragmatism as the next phase of public management." *American Review of Public Administration* 38, no. 2 (2008): 130–148.

Alford, John, and Janine O'Flynn. *Rethinking public service delivery: Managing with external providers*. Basingstoke: Palgrave Macmillan, 2012.

Allison, Graham T. "Public and private administrative leadership: Are they fundamentally alike in all unimportant respects." In *Leadership and organizational culture: New perspectives on administrative theory and practice*, edited by James L. Perry and Kenneth L. Kraemer, 72–92. Palo Alto: Mayfield Publishing, 1983.

American Society for Public Administration. "Code of ethics." Accessed May 21, 2019. https://www.aspanet.org/ASPA/Code-of-Ethics/Code-of-Ethics.aspx.

Ammeter, Anthony P., Ceasar Douglas, William L. Gardner, Wayne A. Hochwarter, and Gerald R. Ferris. "Toward a political theory of leadership." *The Leadership Quarterly* 13, no. 6 (2002): 751–796.

Anderson, Cameron, Sandra E. Spataro, and Francis J. Flynn. "Personality and organizational culture as determinants of influence." *Journal of Applied Psychology* 93, no. 3 (2008): 702.

Andrews, Rhys, George A. Boyne, and Richard M. Walker. "Dimensions of publicness and organizational performance: A review of the evidence." *Journal of Public Administration Research and Theory* 21, no. suppl_3 (2011): i301–i319.

Argyris, Chris. *Integrating the individual and the organization*. New York: Wiley, 1964.

Argyris, Chris, and Donald A. Schön. *Organizational learning II: Theory, method and practice*. Reading: Addison-Wesley Publishing, 1996.

Atlanta Community Food Bank. Accessed May 17, 2017. www.acfb.org.

Axelrod, Robert. *The evolution of cooperation*. New York: Basic Books, 1984.

Baker, William H., H. Lon Addams, and Brian Davis. "Critical factors in enhancing municipal public hearings." *Public Administration Review* 65, no. 4 (2005): 490–499.

Banks, George C., Kelly Davis McCauley, William L. Gardner, and Courtney E. Guler. "A meta-analytic review of authentic and transformational leadership: A test for redundancy." *The Leadership Quarterly* 27, no. 4 (2016): 634–652.

Barabas, Jason. "How deliberation affects policy opinions." *American Political Science Review* 98, no. 4 (2004): 687–701.

Barbuto, John E., Susan M. Fritz, Gina S. Matkin, and David B. Marx. "Effects of gender, education, and age upon leaders' use of influence tactics and full range leadership behaviors." *Sex Roles* 56, no. 1–2 (2007): 71–83.

Barrett, Katherine, and Richard Greene. "Tennessee takes on telework." *Governing*, January 2019, 55.

Bass, Bernard M. "From transactional to transformational leadership: Learning to share the vision." *Organizational Dynamics* 18, no. 3 (1990): 19–31.

Behn, Robert D. "The varieties of CitiStat." *Public Administration Review* 66, no. 3 (2006): 332–340.

Behn, Robert D. "The psychological barriers to performance management: or why isn't everyone jumping on the performance-management bandwagon?" *Public Performance & Management Review* 26, no. 1 (2002): 5–25.

Beierle, Thomas C. "The quality of stakeholder-based decisions." *Risk Analysis* 22, no. 4 (2002): 739–749.

Beierle, Thomas C., and David M. Konisky. "Values, conflict, and trust in participatory environmental planning." *Journal of Policy Analysis and Management* 19, no. 4 (2000): 587–602.

Bellé, Nicola. "Leading to make a difference: A field experiment on the performance effects of transformational leadership, perceived social impact, and public service motivation." *Journal of Public Administration Research and Theory* 24, no. 1 (2014): 109–136.

Bennis, Warren. *On becoming a leader*. Reading: Addison-Wesley Publishing, 1994.

Bennis, Warren, and Burt Nanus. *Leaders: Strategies for taking charge*. New York: Harper Business, 2007.

Beu, Danielle S., and M. Ronald Buckley. "This is war: How the politically astute achieve crimes of obedience through the use of moral disengagement." *The Leadership Quarterly* 15, no. 4 (2004): 551–568.

Bingham, Lisa Blomgren, Tina Nabatchi, and Rosemary O'Leary. "The new governance: Practices and processes for stakeholder and citizen participation in the work of government." *Public Administration Review* 65, no. 4 (2005): 547–558.

Blass, Fred R., and Gerald R. Ferris. "Leader reputation: The role of mentoring, political skill, contextual learning, and adaptation." *Human Resource Management* 46, no. 1 (2007): 5–19.

Blumenthal, W. Michael. "Candid reflections of a businessman in Washington: Interview with Secretary of the Treasury." In *Public management: Public and private perspectives*, edited by James L. Perry and Kenneth L. Kraemer, 22–33. Palo Alto: Mayfield Publishing, 1983.

Bolman, Lee G., and Terrence E. Deal. *Reframing organizations: Artistry, choice, and leadership*. 7th ed. San Francisco: Jossey-Bass, 2017.

Borins, Sandford. "What border? Public management innovation in the United States and Canada." *Journal of Policy Analysis and Management* 19, no. 1 (2000): 46–74.

Bovaird, Tony. "Beyond engagement and participation: User and community coproduction of public services." *Public Administration Review* 67, no. 5 (2007): 846–860.

Boyne, George A. "Public and private management: What's the difference?" *Journal of Management Studies* 39, no. 1 (2002): 97–122.

Bozeman, Barry. *Public values and public interest: Counterbalancing economic individualism*. Washington: Georgetown University Press, 2007.

Bozeman, Barry, and Japera Johnson. "The political economy of public values: A case for the public sphere and progressive opportunity." *American Review of Public Administration* 45, no. 1 (2015): 61–85.

Brewer, Gene A., Sally Coleman Selden, and Rex L. Facer II. "Individual conceptions of public service motivation." *Public Administration Review* 60, no. 3 (2000): 254–264.

Brudney, Jeffrey, and Robert England. "Toward a definition of the co-production concept." *Public Administration Review* 43, no. 1 (1983): 59–65.

Bryant, Adam. "How to run a more effective meeting." *New York Times*, April 25, 2017.

Bryer, Thomas A. "Explaining responsiveness in collaboration: Administrator and citizen role perceptions." *Public Administration Review* 69, no. 2 (2009.): 271–281.

Bryson, John M. "What to do when stakeholders matter: Stakeholder identification and analysis techniques." *Public Management Review* 6, no. 1 (2004): 21–53.

Bryson, John M., Barbara C. Crosby, and Laura Bloomberg. "Public value governance: Moving beyond traditional public administration and the new public management." *Public Administration Review* 74, no. 4 (2014): 445–456.

Bryson, John M., Kathryn S. Quick, Carissa Schively Slotterback, and Barbara Crosby. "Designing public participation processes." *Public Administration Review* 73, no. 1 (2013): 23–34.

Buchanan, James M., and Gordon Tullock. *The calculus of consent*. Ann Arbor: University of Michigan Press, 1962.

Buntin, John. "Voluntary force." *Governing*, April, 2011, 36–43.

Burns, James MacGregor. *Leaders who changed the world*. London: Penguin, 2003.

Burns, James MacGregor. *Transforming leadership: A new pursuit of happiness.* New York: Grove Press, 2004.

Caillier, James Gerard. "Towards a better understanding of public service motivation and mission valence in public agencies." *Public Management Review* 17, no. 9 (2015): 1217–1236.

Caplow, Theodore. *Managing an organization.* 2nd ed. New York: Holt, Rinehart and Winston, 1983.

Carbone, Lou. 2008. "Engineering experiences that build trust in government." In *The Trusted Leader: Building the relationships that make government work,* edited by Terry Newell, Grant Reeher, and Peter Ronayn, 267–285. Washington: CQ Press.

Charles, J. Brian. "Learning to cheat." *Governing,* September 2018, 25–30.

Chira, Susan. "Why women aren't CEOs, according to women who almost were." *New York Times,* July 21, 2017.

Choi, Sungjoo. "Diversity in the US federal government: Diversity management and employee turnover in federal agencies." *Journal of Public Administration Research and Theory* 19, no. 3 (2008): 603–630.

Choi, Sungjoo, and Hal G. Rainey. "Organizational fairness and diversity management in public organizations: Does fairness matter in managing diversity?" *Review of Public Personnel Administration* 34, no. 4 (2014): 307–331.

Christensen, Robert K., Laurie Paarlberg, and James L. Perry. "Public service motivation research: Lessons for practice." *Public Administration Review* 77, no. 4 (2017): 529–542.

Cloke, Kenneth, and Joan Goldsmith. *Resolving conflicts at work: Ten strategies for everyone on the job.* 3th ed. San Francisco: Jossey-Bass, 2011.

CollaborativeAgency. "Bruce Tulgan on generational shifts in the workplace— Speaker bureau." YouTube video, 11:32. Posted [September 4, 2013]. https://www.youtube.com/watch?v=PjG1R6GDiyE.

Corker, Bob, and David Eichenthal. 2006. "Applying innovations in midsized cities: 311 and Chattanooga's results." In *Innovations in e-government: The thoughts of governors and mayors,* edited by Erwin A. Blackstone, Michael L. Bognanno, and Simon Hakim, 266–275. Lanham, MD: Roman and Littlefield.

Coulter, Philip B. "There's a madness in the method: Redefining citizen contacting of government officials." *Urban Affairs Quarterly* 28 , no. 2 (1992): 297–316.

Covey, Stephen R. *The 7 habits of highly effective people: Powerful lessons in personal change.* New York: Free Press, 1989.

Cronin, Thomas E., and Michael A. Genovese. *Leadership matters: Unleashing the power of paradox.* Abingdon: Routledge, 2015.

Crosby, Barbara C., and John M. Bryson. *Leadership for the common good: Tackling public problems in a shared-power world.* San Francisco: Jossey-Bass, 2005.

Cullen, Kristin L., Alexandra Gerbasi, and Donna Chrobot-Mason. "Thriving in central network positions: The role of political skill." *Journal of Management* 44, no. 2 (2018): 682–706.

Daft, Richard L. "First, lead yourself." In *Contemporary issues in leadership*, edited by William L. Rosenbach, Robert L. Taylor and Mark A. Youndt, 7th ed, 125–133. Boulder: Westview Press, 2012.

Davis, Mark. "Food Bank's CEO is stepping down." *Atlanta Journal-Constitution*, June 30, 2015, D1 and D4.

Denters, Bas, and Pieter-Jan Klok. "Rebuilding Roombeek: Patterns of citizen participation in urban governance." *Urban Affairs Review* 45 no. 5 (2010): 583–607.

Doig, Jameson W., and Erwin C. Hargrove, eds. *Leadership and innovation: Entrepreneurs in government*. Baltimore and London: Johns Hopkins University Press, 1990.

Doyle, Michael, and David Straus. *How to make meetings work: The new interaction method*. New York: Jove Books, 1982.

Duhigg, Charles. "What Google learned from its quest to build the perfect team." *New York Times Magazine*, February 25, 2016.

Eagly, Alice H. "Women as leaders: Leadership style versus leaders' values and attitudes." In *Gender and work: Challenging conventional wisdom*, 4–11. Cambridge: Harvard Business School Press, 2013.

Eagly, Alice H., and Linda L. Carli. "Women and the labyrinth of leadership." In *Contemporary issues in leadership*, edited by William L. Rosenbach, Robert L. Taylor and Mark A. Youndt, 7th ed, 147–162. Boulder: Westview Press, 2012.

Eagly, Alice H., and Jean Lau Chin. "Diversity and leadership in a changing world." *American Psychologist* 65, no. 3 (2010): 216–224.

Edwards, David, and John Clayton Thomas. "Developing a municipal performance-measurement system: Reflections on the Atlanta Dashboard." *Public Administration Review* 65, no. 3 (2005): 369–376.

Eldor, Liat. "Public service sector: The compassionate workplace—The effect of compassion and stress on employee engagement, burnout, and performance." *Journal of Public Administration Research and Theory* 28, no. 1 (2018): 86–103.

Elk, Sarah. "How to reenergize your transformation for its second half." *Forbes*, November 6, 2017, https://www.forbes.com/sites/baininsights/2017/11/06/how-to-reenergize-your-transformation-for-its-second-half/#48ca036e1ec5.

Ellen III, B. Parker, Gerald R. Ferris, and M. Ronald Buckley. "Leader political support: Reconsidering leader political behavior." *The Leadership Quarterly* 24, no. 6 (2013): 842–857.

Elsesser, Kim M., and Janet Lever. "Does gender bias against female leaders persist? Quantitative and qualitative data from a large-scale survey." *Human Relations* 64, no. 12 (2011): 1555–1578.

Ely, Robin J. "A field study of group diversity, participation in diversity education programs, and performance." *Journal of Organizational Behavior: The International Journal of Industrial, Occupational and Organizational Psychology and Behavior* 25, no. 6 (2004): 755–780.

Fernandez, Sergio, and Hal G. Rainey. "Managing successful organizational change in the public sector." *Public Administration Review* 66, no. 2 (2006): 168–176.

Ferris, Gerald R., and Darren C. Treadway, eds. *Politics in organizations: Theory and research considerations*. Abingdon: Routledge, 2012.

Fountain, Jane E. "Paradoxes of public sector customer service." *Governance* 14, no. 1 (2001): 55–73.

Funkhouser, Mark. " On leadership: The quality you can't learn: Anyone can learn to lead. Not everyone has the courage to do it." *Governing*, November 2018, 57.

Furst, Stacie A., and Daniel M. Cable. "Employee resistance to organizational change: Managerial influence tactics and leader-member exchange." *Journal of Applied Psychology* 93, no. 2 (2008): 453.

Gabarro, John J., and John P. Kotter. "Managing your boss". *Harvard Business Review* 71, no. 3, 150–157, 1993.

Gardner, John W. "The antileadership vaccine." In *Contemporary issues in leadership*, edited by William L. Rosenbach, Robert L. Taylor and Mark A. Youndt, 7th ed., 287–295. Boulder: Westview Press, 2012.

Getha-Taylor, Heather. "Managing the 'new normalcy' with values-based leadership: Lessons from Admiral James Loy." In *Serving the public interest: Profiles of successful and innovative public servants*, edited by Norma M. Riccucci, 116–124. Armonk: M.E. Sharpe, 2012.

Goldsmith, Stephen. "How rules demean public workers." *Governing*, November 2010, 56–57.

Goleman, Daniel. *Working with emotional intelligence*. New York: Bantam Books, 1998.

Goleman, Daniel. "What makes a leader." *Organizational Influence Processes* (2003): 229–241.

Goodsell, Charles T. "Invited essay: Mission mystique: Strength at the institutional center." *American Review of Public Administration* 41, no. 5 (2011): 475–494.

Graen, George B., and Mary Uhl-Bien. "Relationship-based approach to leadership: Development of leader-member exchange (LMX) theory of leadership over 25 years: Applying a multi-level multi-domain perspective." *The Leadership Quarterly* 6, no. 2 (1995): 219–247.

Greenleaf, Robert K. "The servant as leader." In *Corporate ethics and corporate governance*, edited by Walther C. Zimmerli and Klaus Richter, 72–92. Berlin: Springer, 2007.

Grillo, Jerry. "Feeding the hungry: 2012 Georgian of the Year." *Georgia Trend*, January, 2012, 18–23.

Haar, Jarrod M., Marcello Russo, Albert Suñe, and Ariane Ollier-Malaterre. "Outcomes of work–life balance on job satisfaction, life satisfaction and mental health: A study across seven cultures." *Journal of Vocational Behavior* 85, no. 3 (2014): 361–373.

Harris, Kenneth J., K. Michele Kacmar, Suzanne Zivnuska, and Jason D. Shaw. "The impact of political skill on impression management effectiveness." *Journal of Applied Psychology* 92, no. 1 (2007): 278.

Hartmann, Jim, and Anne M. Khademian. "Culture change refined and revitalized: The road show and guides for pragmatic action." *Public Administration Review* 70, no. 6 (2010): 845–856.

Hassan, Shahidul. "The importance of ethical leadership and personal control in promoting improvement-centered voice among government employees." *Journal of Public Administration Research and Theory* 25, no. 3 (2015): 697–719.

Hassan, Shahidul, and Deneen M. Hatmaker. "Leadership and performance of public employees: Effects of the quality and characteristics of manager-employee relationships." *Journal of Public Administration Research and Theory* 25, no. 4 (2015): 1127–1155.

Hassan, Shahidul, Bradley E. Wright, and Gary Yukl. "Does ethical leadership matter in government? Effects on organizational commitment, absenteeism, and willingness to report ethical problems." *Public Administration Review* 74, no. 3 (2014): 333–343.

Headlee, Celeste. *We need to talk: How to have conversations that matter.* New York: HarperCollins, 2017.

Hefetz Amir, and Mildred Warner. "Privatization and its reverse: Explaining the dynamics of the government contracting process." *Journal of Public Administration Research and Theory* 14, no. 2 (2004): 171–190.

Heinrich, Carolyn J., and Gerald Marschke. "Incentives and their dynamics in public sector performance management systems." *Journal of Policy Analysis and Management* 29, no. 1 (2010): 183–208.

Herrera, Tim. "4 ways to be more effective in meetings." *New York Times,* March 6, 2017.

Hicklin, Alisa, and Kenneth J. Meier. "Race, structure, and state governments: The politics of higher education diversity." *Journal of Politics* 70, no. 3 (2008): 851–860.

Hill, Linda A. *Becoming a manager: How new managers master the challenges of leadership.* 2nd ed. Cambridge: Harvard Business School Press, 2003.

Hill, Linda A. "Becoming the boss." *Harvard Business Review* 85, no. 1 (2007): 48.

Hirschman, Albert O. *Exit, voice, and loyalty: Responses to decline in firms, organizations, and states.* Cambridge: Harvard University Press, 1970.

Homberg, Fabian, Dermot McCarthy, and Vurain Tabvuma. "A meta-analysis of the relationship between public service motivation and job satisfaction." *Public Administration Review* 75, no. 5 (2015): 711–722.

House, Robert J. "Path-goal theory of leadership: Lessons, legacy, and a reformulated theory." *The Leadership Quarterly* 7, no. 3 (1996): 323–352.

Jacobsen, Christian Bøtcher, and Lotte Bøgh Andersen. "Is leadership in the eye of the beholder? A study of intended and perceived leadership practices and organizational performance." *Public Administration Review* 75, no. 6 (2015): 829–841.

Jakobsen, Morten. "Can government initiatives increase citizen coproduction? Results of a randomized field experiment." *Journal of Public Administration Research and Theory* 23 (2013): 27–54.

Javidan, Mansour, and David A. Waldman. "Exploring charismatic leadership in the public sector: Measurement and consequences." *Public Administration Review* 63, no. 2 (2003): 229–242.

Jay, Antony. "How to run a meeting." *Harvard Business Review*, March-April 1976, 43–57.

Jensen, Ulrich Thy. "Does perceived societal impact moderate the effect of transformational leadership on value congruence? Evidence from a field experiment." *Public Administration Review* 78, no. 1 (2018): 48–57.

Jensen, Ulrich Thy, Donald P. Moynihan, and Heidi Houlberg Salomonsen. "Communicating the vision: How face-to-face dialogue facilitates transformational leadership." *Public Administration Review* 78, no. 3 (2018): 350–361.

Jin, Myung H., Bruce McDonald, and Jaehee Park. "Does public service motivation matter in public higher education? Testing the theories of person–organization fit and organizational commitment through a serial multiple mediation model." *American Review of Public Administration* 48, no. 1 (2018): 82–97.

Jonason, Peter K., Sarah Slomski, and Jamie Partyka. "The dark triad at work: How toxic employees get their way." *Personality and individual differences* 52, no. 3 (2012): 449–453.

Jørgensen, Torben Beck, and Barry Bozeman. "Public values: An inventory." *Administration & Society* 39, no. 3 (2007): 354–381.

Jos, Philip H., and Mark E. Tompkins. "Keeping it public: Defending public services values in a customer service age." *Public Administration Review* 69, no. 6 (2009): 1077–1086.

Kahneman, Daniel. *Thinking, fast and slow.* New York: Farrar, Straus and Giroux, 2011.

Kark, Ronit, Ronit Waismel-Manor, and Boas Shamir. "Does valuing androgyny and femininity lead to a female advantage? The relationship between gender-role, transformational leadership and identification." *The Leadership Quarterly* 23, no. 3 (2012): 620–640.

Kaufman, Leslie. "Utilities turn their customers green, with envy." *New York Times*, January 31, 2009.

Kellerman, Barbara, and Deborah L. Rhode. "Viable options: Rethinking women and leadership." In *Contemporary issues in leadership*, edited by William L. Rosenbach, Robert L. Taylor and Mark A. Youndt, 7th ed. 135–145. Boulder: Westview Press, 2012.

Kelley, Katherine M., and Ryan S. Bisel. "Leaders' narrative sensemaking during LMX role negotiations: Explaining how leaders make sense of who to trust and when." *The Leadership Quarterly* 25, no. 3 (2014): 433–448.

Keohane, Nannerl O. *Thinking about leadership*. Princeton: Princeton University Press, 2012.

Killian, Jerri, and Mary Wenning. "Are we having fun yet? Exploring the motivations of MPA and MPP program directors in the United States." *Journal of Public Affairs Education* 23, no. 3 (2017): 799–810.

Kim, Chulwoo, and Hindy Lauer Schachter. "Exploring followership in a public setting: Is it a missing link between participative leadership and organizational performance?" *American Review of Public Administration* 45, no. 4 (2015): 436–457.

Kim, Soonhee. "Participative management and job satisfaction: Lessons for management leadership." *Public Administration Review* 62, no. 2 (2002): 231–241.

Kim, Soonhee, and Gyunsoo Yoon. "An innovation-driven culture in local government: Do senior manager's transformational leadership and the climate for creativity matter?" *Public Personnel Management* 44, no. 2 (2015): 147–168.

King, Cheryl Simrell, and Megan Beeby. "Colleen Jollie, state tribal liaison: A story of transformational change." *Public Administration Review* 68, no. 6 (2008): 1142–1150.

King, Stephen F. "Citizens as customers: Exploring the future of CRM in UK local government." *Government Information Quarterly* 24, no. 1 (2007): 47–63.

Kotter, John P. *Power and influence*. New York: Free Press, 1985.

Kotter, John P. "Leading change." *Harvard Business Review* 85, no. 1 (2007): 96–103.

Kouzes, James M., and Barry Z. Posner. "Leadership begins with an inner journey." *Leader to Leader* 2011, no. 60 (2011): 22–27.

Krislov, Samuel and David H. Rosenbloom. *Representative bureaucracy and the American political system*. New York: Praeger, 1981.

Lafair, Sylvia. "Top 10 reasons why teams fail and what you can do to stay strong." *Inc.*, September 18, 2015, https://www.inc.com/sylvia-lafair/top-10-reasons-why-teams-fail-and-what-you-can-do-to-stay-strong.html.

Lambright, W. Henry. "Leadership and change at NASA: Sean O'Keefe as administrator." In *Serving the public interest: Profiles of successful and innovative public servants*, edited by Norma M. Riccucci, 68–80. Armonk: M.E. Sharpe, 2012.

Land, Deborah. "Local school boards under review: Their role and effectiveness in relation to students' academic achievement." *Review of Educational Research* 72, no. 2 (2002): 229–278.

LaPorte, Todd R. "The recovery of relevance in the study of public organizations." *Toward a new public administration: The Minnowbrook Perspective* (1971): 17–48.

Laurian, Lucie. "Public participation in environmental decision making: Findings from communities facing toxic waste cleanup." *Journal of the American Planning Association* 70, no. 1 (2004): 53–65.

Lee, Hyun Jung. "How emotional intelligence relates to job satisfaction and burnout in public service jobs." *International Review of Administrative Sciences* 84, no. 4 (2018): 729–745.

Linos, Elizabeth. "More than public service: A field experiment on job advertisements and diversity in the police." *Journal of Public Administration Research and Theory* 28, no. 1 (2017): 67–85.

Liu, Yongmei, James G. Combs, David J. Ketchen Jr, and R. Duane Ireland. "The value of human resource management for organizational performance." *Business Horizons* 50, no. 6 (2007): 503–511.

Lovell, Roger. "Citizen's charter: The cultural challenge." *Public Administration* 70, Autumn (1992): 395–404.

Lowe, Zach. "Brad Stevens and the Celtics have a special brand of toughness." *ESPN*, May 11, 2018, http://www.espn.com/nba/story/_/id/23465885/zach-lowe-boston-celtics-toughness-nba-playoffs.

Maciag, Mike. "Work happy." *Governing*, August 2013, 52–55.

Malone, Clare. "Americans don't trust their institutions anymore." *Five ThirtyEight*, November 16, 2016, https://fivethirtyeight.com/features/americans-dont-trust-their-institutions-anymore/.

Manring, Nancy J. "Reconciling science and politics in Forest Service decision making: New tools for public administrators." *American Review of Public Administration* 23, no. 4 (1993): 343–359.

March, James G. "How we talk and how we act: Administrative theory and administrative life." In *Leadership and Organizational Culture*, edited by Thomas J. Sergiovanni and John E. Corbally, 18–35. Urbana: University of Illinois Press, 1981.

McComas, Katherine A. "Citizen satisfaction with public meetings used for risk communication." *Journal of Applied Communication Research* 31, no. 2 (2010): 164–184.

McComas, Katherine A., John C. Besley, and Craig W. Trumbo. "Why citizens do and do not attend public meetings about local cancer cluster investigations." *Policy Studies Journal* 34, no. 4 (2006): 671–698.

Mendel, Stuart C., and Jeffrey L. Brudney. *Partnerships the nonprofit way: What matters, what doesn't*. Bloomington: Indiana University Press, 2018.

Morse, Ricardo S. "Bill Gibson and the art of leading across boundaries." In *Serving the public interest: Profiles of successful and innovative public servants*, edited by Norma M. Riccucci, 160–172. Armonk: M.E. Sharpe, 2012.

Moss, Sherry E., and Juan I. Sanchez. "Are your employees avoiding you? Managerial strategies for closing the feedback gap." *Academy of Management Perspectives* 18, no. 1 (2004): 32–44.

Moynihan, Donald P. "Advancing the empirical study of performance management: What we learned from the program assessment rating tool." *American Review of Public Administration* 43, no. 5 (2013): 499–517.

Moynihan, Donald P., Sanjay K. Pandey, and Bradley E. Wright. "Setting the table: How transformational leadership fosters performance information use." *Journal of Public Administration Research and Theory* 22, no. 1 (2012): 143–164.

Munyon, Timothy P., James K. Summers, Katina M. Thompson, and Gerald R. Ferris. "Political skill and work outcomes: A theoretical extension, meta-analytic investigation, and agenda for the future." *Personnel Psychology* 68, no. 1 (2015): 143–184.

National Performance Management Advisory Commission. *A performance management framework for state and local governments.* Chicago: NPMAC, 2010.

Nel, Deon, Tom Athron, Leyland F. Pitt, and Michael T. Ewing. "Customer evaluations of service complaint experiences in the public sector." *Journal of Nonprofit & Public Sector Marketing* 7, no. 3 (2000): 3–30.

Neshkova, Milena, and Hai Guo. "Public involvement and organizational performance: Evidence from state agencies." *Journal of Public Administration Research and Theory* 22, no. 2 (2011): 267–288.

Newport, Cal. 2016. *Deep work: Rules for focused success in a distracted world.* New York: Grand Central Publishing.

Niskanen, Jr. *Bureaucracy and representative government.* Chicago: Aldine Atherton, 1971.

Northouse, Peter G. *Leadership: Theory and practice,* 8th ed. Thousand Oaks: Sage Publications, 2018.

Oberfield, Zachary W. "Public management in time: A longitudinal examination of the full range of leadership theory." *Journal of Public Administration Research and Theory* 24, no. 2 (2012): 407–429.

Oberfield, Zachary W. *Becoming bureaucrats: Socialization at the front lines of government service.* Philadelphia: University of Pennsylvania Press, 2014.

Osborne, David, and Ted Gaebler. *Reinventing government: How the entrepreneurial spirit is transforming the public sector.* New York: Penguin Books, 1993.

Osborne, Stephen P., Zoe Radnor, and Greta Nasi. "A new theory for public service management? Toward a (public) service-dominant approach." *American Review of Public Administration* 43, no. 2 (2013): 135–158.

Ostrom, Elinor. "A behavioral approach to the rational choice theory of collective action: Presidential address, American Political Science Association, 1997." *American Political Science Review* 92, no. 1 (1998): 1–22.

Ostrom, Elinor. *Governing the commons: The evolution of institutions for collective action.* New York and Cambridge: Cambridge University Press, 1990.

Ostrom, Elinor, Roger Parks, Gordon Whitaker, and Stephen Percy. "The public service production process: A framework for analyzing police services." *Policy Studies Journal* 7, December (1978): 381–389.

Paarlberg, Laurie E., and Bob Lavigna. "Transformational leadership and public service motivation: Driving individual and organizational performance." *Public Administration Review* 70, no. 5 (2010): 710–718.

Patton, Zach. "Doing less with less." *Governing,* September, 2010, 20–27.

Pearce, Craig L. "Follow the leaders." In *Contemporary issues in leadership*, edited by William L. Rosenbach, Robert L. Taylor and Mark A. Youndt, 7th ed., 95–100. Boulder: Westview Press, 2012.

Pedersen, Mogens Jin, and Justin M. Stritch. "Internal management and perceived managerial trustworthiness: Evidence from a survey experiment." *American Review of Public Administration* 48, no. 1 (2018): 67–81.

Perry, James L., and Lois Recascino Wise. "The motivational bases of public service." *Public Administration Review* (1990): 367–373.

Pestoff, Victor. "Citizens and co-production of welfare services." *Public Management Review* 8, no. 4 (2006): 503–519.

Peters, Thomas J., and Robert H. Waterman. *In search of excellence: Lessons from America's best-run companies.* New York: Warner, 1982.

Pfeffer, Jeffrey. "Building sustainable organizations: The human factor." *Academy of Management Perspectives* 24, no. 1 (2010): 34–45.

Pfeffer, Jeffrey. *Power: Why some people have it and others don't.* 3rd ed. New York: HarperCollins, 2010.

Pitts, David. "Diversity management, job satisfaction, and performance: Evidence from US federal agencies." *Public Administration Review* 69, no. 2 (2009): 328–338.

Prokopy, Linda Stalker. "The relationship between participation and project outcomes: Evidence from rural water supply projects in India." *World Development* 33, no. 11 (2005): 1801–1819.

Pynes, Joan E. *Human resources management for public and nonprofit organizations: A strategic approach.* San Francisco: Jossey-Bass, 2013.

Radin, Beryl A. "Qualified to learn the job: Donna Shalala." In *Serving the public interest: Profiles of successful and innovative public servants*, edited by Norma M. Riccucci, 26–39. Armonk: M.E. Sharpe, 2012.

Rainey, Hal G. "Perceptions of incentives in business and government: Implications for civil service reform." *Public Administration Review* 39, no. 5 (1979): 440–448.

Rainey, Hal G. (2014). *Understanding and managing public organizations.* 5th ed. San Francisco: Jossey-Bass.

Rainey, Hal G., and Barry Bozeman. "Comparing public and private organizations: Empirical research and the power of the a priori." *Journal of Public Administration Research and Theory* 10, no. 2 (2000): 447–470.

Rainey, Hal G., and James R. Thompson. "Leadership and the transformation of a major institution: Charles Rossotti and the Internal Revenue Service." *Public Administration Review* 66, no. 4 (2006): 596–604.

Riccucci, Norma M. *Serving the public interest: Profiles of successful and innovative public servants.* Armonk: M.E. Sharpe, 2012.

Rosenbach, William E., Thane S. Pittman, and Earl H. Potter. "What makes a follower?" In *Contemporary issues in leadership*, edited by William L. Rosenbach, Robert L. Taylor and Mark A. Youndt, 7th ed., 77–87. Boulder: Westview Press, 2012.

Rosenthal, Seth A. *National leadership index 2012: A national study of confidence in leadership.* Cambridge: Center for Public Leadership, Harvard Kennedy School, 2012.

Rossotti, Charles O. *Many unhappy returns: One man's quest to turn around the most unpopular organization in America.* Cambridge: Harvard Business School Press, 2005.

Sachs, Justin. "The power of persistence." *Forbes*, May 24, 2016, https://www.forbes.com/sites/forbescoachescouncil/2016/05/24/the-power-of-persistence/#3d462d252a70.

Salamon, Lester M. "The changing context of nonprofit leadership and management." In *The Jossey-Bass handbook of nonprofit leadership and management*, 3th ed, edited by David O. Renz, 77–99, San Francisco: Jossey-Bass, 2010.

Sawyer, Keith. *Group genius: The creative power of collaboration.* New York: Basic Books, 2017.

Sayles, Leonard R. *Leadership, what effective managers really do and how they do it.* New York: McGraw-Hill, 1979.

Schachter, Hindy Lauer. "Lillian Borrone: Weaving a web to revitalize port commerce in New York and New Jersey." In *Serving the public interest: Profiles of successful and innovative public servants*, edited by Norma M. Riccucci, 59–67. Armonk: M.E. Sharpe, 2012.

Schelling, Thomas C. "The strategy of conflict. Prospectus for a reorientation of game theory." *Journal of Conflict Resolution* 2, no. 3 (1958): 203–264.

Selden, Sally Coleman, Patricia Wallace Ingraham, and Willow Jacobson. "Human resource practices in state government: Findings from a national survey." *Public Administration Review* 61, no. 5 (2001): 598–607.

Sell, Samantha. "Running an effective school district: School boards in the 21st century." *Journal of Education* 186, no. 3 (2006): 71–97.

Sparrowe, Raymond T., Budi W. Soetjipto, and Maria L. Kraimer. "Do leaders' influence tactics relate to members' helping behavior? It depends on the quality of the relationship." *Academy of Management Journal* 49, no. 6 (2006): 1194–1208.

Spillane, James P. *Distributed leadership.* San Francisco: Jossey-Bass, 2006.

Stivers, Camilla. "The listening bureaucrat: Responsiveness in public administration." *Public Administration Review* 54, no. 4 (1994): 364–369.

Sturm, Rachel E., Dusya Vera, and Mary Crossan. "The entanglement of leader character and leader competence and its impact on performance." *The Leadership Quarterly* 28, no. 3 (2017): 349–366.

Sunstein, Cass R., and Reid Hastie. *Wiser: Getting beyond groupthink to make groups smarter.* Cambridge: Harvard Business Press, 2015.

Surowiecki, James. *The wisdom of crowds.* New York: Doubleday, 2005.

Swiss, James E., and Stephen K. Straus. "Implementing results-based management in local government." In *Leading performance management in local government,* edited by David N. Ammons, 85–101. Washington: ICMA Press, 2008.

Taylor, Scott N., and Jacqueline N. Hood. "It may not be what you think: Gender differences in predicting emotional and social competence." *Human Relations* 64, no. 5 (2011): 627–652.

Thaler, Richard H., and Cass R. Sunstein. *Nudge: Improving decisions about health, wealth, and happiness.* New Haven & London: Yale University Press, 2008.

Thomas, John Clayton. "Public involvement in public management: Adapting and testing a borrowed theory." *Public Administration Review* 50, no. 4 (1990): 435–445.

Thomas, John Clayton. "Public involvement and governmental effectiveness: A decision-making model for public managers." *Administration & Society* 24, February (1993): 444–469.

Thomas, John Clayton. *Public participation in public decisions: New skills and strategies for public managers.* San Francisco: Jossey-Bass, 1995.

Thomas, John Clayton. *Citizen, customer, partner: Engaging the public in public management.* Abingdon: Routledge, 2012.

Thomas, John Clayton. "Theory to practice: Citizen, customer, partner: Re-thinking the place of the public in public management." *Public Administration Review* 73, no. 6 (2013): 786–796.

Thomas, John Clayton. "Practicing a virtuous politics: Bill Bolling and the Atlanta Community Food Bank." *Public Administration Review* 77, no. 6 (2017): 933–941.

Thomas, John Clayton, and Julia E. Melkers. "Citizen contacting of municipal officials: Choosing between appointed administrators and elected leaders." *Journal of Public Administration Research and Theory* 11, no. 1 (2001): 51–71.

Thomas, John Clayton, and Julia E. Melkers. "Explaining citizen-initiated contacts with municipal bureaucrats: Lessons from the Atlanta experience." *Urban Affairs Review,* 34, no. 5 (1999): 667–690.

Thomas, John Clayton, and Theodore H. Poister. "Thinking about stakeholders of public agencies: The Georgia Department of Transportation stakeholder audit." *Public Organization Review* 9, no. 1 (2009): 67–82.

Till, John E., and Kathleen R. Meyer. "Public involvement in science and decision making." *Health Physics* 80, no. 4 (2001): 370–378.

Tropman, John E. *Effective meetings: Improving group decision making.* 3rd ed. Thousand Oaks: Sage, 2014.

Trottier, Tracey, Montgomery Van Wart, and XiaoHu Wang. "Examining the nature and significance of leadership in government organizations." *Public Administration Review* 68, no. 2 (2008): 319–333.

Ury, William. *Getting past no: Negotiating your way from confrontation to cooperation.* New York: Bantam, 1993.

U.S. Government Accountability Office. *Managing the supplier base in the 21st Century.* GAO-06-533SP. Washington, DC, 2015. Accessed January 31, 2015. https://www.gao.gov/assets/250/249592.pdf.

Van der Voet, Joris. "Change leadership and public sector organizational change: Examining the interactions of transformational leadership style and red tape." *American Review of Public Administration* 46, no. 6 (2016): 660–682.

Van der Voet, Joris, Ben S. Kuipers, and Sandra Groeneveld. "Implementing change in public organizations: The relationship between leadership and affective commitment to change in a public sector context." *Public Management Review* 18, no. 6 (2016): 842–865.

Van Wart, Montgomery. "Book review: The role of trust in leadership." *Public Administration Review* 72, no. 3 (2012): 454–457.

Van Wart, Montgomery. "Lessons from leadership theory and the contemporary challenges of leaders." *Public Administration Review* 73, no. 4 (2013): 553–565.

Van Wart, Montgomery. *Leadership in public organizations: An introduction.* Abingdon: Routledge, 2014.

Vigoda-Gadot, Eran, and Itai Beeri. "Change-oriented organizational citizenship behavior in public administration: The power of leadership and the cost of organizational politics." *Journal of Public Administration Research and Theory* 22, no. 3 (2012): 573–596.

Vock, Daniel. "Polly Trottenberg: Commissioner of Transportation, New York City." *Governing*, December 2018, 41.

Vroom, Victor H., and Arthur G. Jago. *The new leadership: Managing participation in organizations.* Englewood Cliffs: Prentice-Hall, 1988.

Vroom, Victor H., and Philip W. Yetton. *Leadership and decision-making.* Pittsburgh: University of Pittsburgh Press, 1973.

Walker, Richard M., Fariborz Damanpour, and Carlos A. Devece. "Management innovation and organizational performance: The mediating effect of performance management." *Journal of Public Administration Research and Theory* 21, no. 2 (2011): 367–386.

Wang, Gang, In-Sue Oh, Stephen H. Courtright, and Amy E. Colbert. "Transformational leadership and performance across criteria and levels: A meta-analytic review of 25 years of research." *Group & Organization Management* 36, no. 2 (2011): 223–270.

Westphal, James D., and Ithai Stern. "The other pathway to the boardroom: Interpersonal influence behavior as a substitute for elite credentials and majority status in obtaining board appointments." *Administrative Science Quarterly* 51, no. 2 (2006): 169–204.

Whitaker, Gordon P. "Coproduction: Citizen participation in service delivery." *Public Administration Review* 40, no. 2 (1980): 240–246.

Wholey, Joseph S. "Exploratory evaluation." In *Handbook of practical program evaluation*, 3rd ed. Edited by Joseph S. Wholey, Harry P. Hatry, and Kathryn E. Newcomer, 81–99. San Francisco: Jossey-Bass, 2010.

Wise, Lois Recascino. "Social equity in civil service systems." *Public Administration Review* 50, no. 5 (1990): 567–575.

Wise, Lois Recascino. "Bureaucratic posture: On the need for a composite theory of bureaucratic behavior." *Public Administration Review* 64, no. 6 (2004): 669–680.

Workfront. *The state of work: 2018–2019 edition.* Accessed January 30, 2019. https://www.workfront.com/sites/default/files/files/2018-09/Report _2018-2019-State-of-Work-report-FINAL.pdf.

Wright, Bradley E., and Sanjay K. Pandey. "Transformational leadership in the public sector: Does structure matter?" *Journal of Public Administration Research and Theory* 20, no. 1 (2010): 75–89.

Wright, Bradley E., Sanjay K. Pandey, and Donald P. Moynihan. "Transformational leadership in the public sector: Empirical evidence of its effects." In *Public Administration Reformation,* edited by Yogesh K. Dwivedi, Mahmud Shareef, Sanjay K. Pandey, and Vinod Kumar, 87–104. Abingdon: Routledge, 2013.

Xin, Chen. "Two during the 12319 Hotline smooth 24 hours." Accessed February 22, 2013. http://www.tianjinwe.com/tianjin/tjcj/201209/t20120924 _6436239.html.

Yukl, Gary A. *Leadership in organizations.* 8th ed. New York: Pearson Education, 2013.

Yukl, Gary. "Chapter 17, Use power effectively." In *The Blackwell handbook of principles of organizational behavior,* edited by Edwin A. Locke, 242–256. Oxford: Blackwell Publishers, 2000.

Yukl, Gary, and J. Bruce Tracey. "Consequences of influence tactics used with subordinates, peers, and the boss." *Journal of Applied Psychology* 77, no. 4 (1992): 525.

Index

Italic page references indicate tables and personal exercises.

Active listening, 102
Advocacy and conflict management, 63, 108, 110–112
Aesthetes' motivation, 86
Affirmative action, 18
Agency processes purposes, 9
Ahearn, Kathleen K., 49–50
Allison, Graham, 16
"Amateur" political overseers, 21
Ambition and informal power, 53
American Society for Public Administration (ASPA) principles, 39
Ammeter, Anthony P., 49
Argyris, Chris, 63, 104
Assertive approach to conflict management, 105–106
Atlanta Community Food Bank (ACFB), 1, 3, 42–44, 51, 64. *See also* Bolling, Bill
Atlanta Journal-Constitution, 56
Atlanta Prosperity Campaign, 51
Attrition, 82
Authority, 19–20. *See also* Power
Axelrod, Robert, 112–114

Balancing work-life, 91–92
Bass, Bernard, 189
Bay of Pigs fiasco, 145–146
Becoming a manager. *See* Transition to management
Behn, Robert D., 178
Bellé, Nicola, 190
Bennis, Warren, 2, 6–7, 35, 38, 58

Big Star (grocery store), 51, 56, 58
Bolling, Bill
    Atlanta Community Food Bank startup by, 50–52
    conflict management tactics of, 108, 110
    as example of public minded managerial leader, 1–3, 30
    informal power and, 10, 52–59
    networking partnership and, 167
    organizational change and, 201
    organizational politics and, 50–52, 65–66
    partnerships and, 179
    personal vision of, 42
    political skills of, 59–65, 73, 206–212
    transformational change and, 1–3, 30, 214
Bolman, Lee, 104–105, 156
Borins, Sandford, 30, 215
Borrone, Lillian, 98–99
Boyne, George A., 15
Bozeman, Barry, 39
Brudney, Jeffrey L., 59–60
Bryson, John M., 8, 103, 173
Buckley, M. Ronald, 49–50
Burns, James MacGregor, 38, 188–189
Bush, George W., 23–24

Careerism, 49
Caring, committing to, 80
Center for Public Leadership, 27
Challenger space shuttle disaster, 146
Chambliss, Senator, 64
Character, 35
Chief Financial Officers Act (CFO) (1990), 23

Choi, Sungjoo, 84–85

Christensen, Robert K., 87

Citizen partnerships

as contingent issue, 172–173

coproduction and, 169–171, *183*

deliberation and, 174–175

incentives in, 170–171

Personal Leadership Exercise, *184*

planning, 173–174

priorities in, setting, 179–180

public-minded managerial leaders and, 169, 171–172, 179

reasons for, 171–172

service process and, rethinking, 169

volunteers, 171

Citizenry, 27–29

Cloke, Kenneth, 102, 104, 107, 120, 152

Coaching leadership style, 116

Collaboration, 139, 144–145, 157. *See also* Partnerships

Communication, 99–100, 103. *See also* Interactive communication

Communitarians' motivation, 86

Compassion, 102

Conflict

decision-making strategies and subordinates, 125

ducking, 104–105

over employee performance, 109–110

informal power and tolerance for, 57

with peer, 114–115

Conflict management

advocacy and, 63, 108, 110–112

assertive approach, 105–106

Bolling's tactics in, 108, 110

ducking, 104–105

inquiry and advocacy approach, 63, 104–109, *105*

integrative approach to, 106–112

overview, 11, 103–104

passive approach, 105

political skills and, building, 209

reflection, 74–75

win-lose approach, 115

win-win approach, 115

Consent of the governed, 19, 170

Consultation, 61

Coproduction with the public, 169–171, *183*

Courage, 214

Covey, Stephen, 41

Credibility of manager, building, 99

Crosby, Barbara C., 8, 103

Culture, organizational, 199

Customer/citizen relations management (CRM), 178

Customer partnerships

access and, challenge of, 176–177

customer service and, need for quality, 177

government interaction and, 175–176

learning from, 178–179

Personal Leadership Exercise, *185*

priorities in, setting, 179–180

public-minded managerial leaders and, 175, 179

311 call centers and, 175–177

Customer service, need for quality, 177

Daft, Richard L., 75

DailyWorth, 41–42

Deal, Terrence, 104–105, 156

Decision-making strategies

acceptance of decision and, 124

conflict among subordinates and, 125

delegated decision, 126–127, 132–133

"forced-choice" decision and, 123

group consultation, 126, 130–131

group decision, 126, 131–132

group development as goal and, 133

individual consultation, 126, 128–130

involving others, 121–122

involving others sometimes, 122–126

mistakes in involving (and not involving) others, 135–136

modified unilateral, 127–128

overview, 12, 121

Personal Leadership Exercise, *137*

political skills and, building, 209–210

principles, core, 135

public decision approach, 174

public-minded managerial leaders and, 120–121

quality of decision and, 123

selecting, 126–127

structured choices and, 123–124

uncertainty about issue characteristics and, 133–134

unilateral, 126–127

Decision quality, 123

Declaration of Independence, 38

"Deep work," 75

Defection of employees, 112–114

Delegated decision-making strategy, 126–127, 132–133

Delegating leadership style, 116

Deliberating with public, 174–175

Democratic government, authority of, 19–20

Democratic theory, believing in, 17

Desire to serve, 10, 36–37, 75

Diehl, Philip, 177

Directive leadership style, 115

Disney, Walt, 102

Distrust, pervasive public, 27

Diversity

English as a Second Language programs, 84

public realm's value for, 18

pursuing, 83–85

Downsizing, 82

Doyle, Michael, 153

Ducking conflict, 104–105

Eagly, Alice H., 202

Ebenezer Baptist Church, 42

Economic self-interest, 89–91

Egalitarians' motivation, 86

Ellen, B. Parker III, 49–50

Emotional intelligence (EI)

components of, 33–35

developing, 45, 75

empathy and, 34

motivation and, 34–35

as personal foundation for leadership, 10, 32–35

personal vision and identifying elements needing attention to reach goals, 41

self-awareness and, 33

self-regulation and, 33–34

social skill and, 34

Empathy, 34, 54–55

Employees. See also Manager-employee relationships; Motivating people

buffering of, 99

compassion for, 102

conflict over performance of, 109–110

defection of, 112–114

empowering, 85

hiring the right, 80–81

importance of work of, communicating, 99–100

investing in, 81–82

job security for, providing, 82

nurturing, 85

poorly motivated, 92

promoting from within, 82–83

representation of, 99

rewarding good performance of, 82

Empowering employees, 85

Energy and informal power, 52–53

English as a Second Language programs, 84

Environmentalists' motivation, 86

Equal Employment Opportunity, 18

Ethical sensitivity, improving, 103

Ethics and organizational politics, 5, 49

Evolution of Cooperation, The (Axelrod), 112

Exchange and pressure tactics, 64–65, 110

Expertise and informal power, 56–57

Explicit consent rule, 170

External actors, relationship with, 12–13, 161. See also Partnerships

Facilitation skills, 61–62

Feedback-avoiding behavior, 101–103

Feedback, pursuing, 102–103

Fernandez, Sergio, 193

Ferris, Gerald R., 49–50

Financial austerity, 26

Financial constraints, 25–27, 28–29

Fish bowl, working in, 27–28, 70

Flattery as persuasion tool, 110

Flexibility in rules, 95

Flexible hours, 91–92

Focus and informal power, 53–54

Follett, Mary Parker, 99

"Forced-choice" decision, 123

Formal authority, 20

Formal power, 69

Forums, access to, 20

Fountain, Jane E., 17, 178

Framing/reframing ideas, 62–63

Freedom of information, 27–28

Funkhouser, Mark, 214
Furloughs, 82

Gabarro, John J., 163
Gaming the new systems, 24
Gardner, John, 3–4
Gibson, Bill, 168
"Gig economy," 92
Globalization, 139–140
Goals
    problematic, 22–23, 28
    of public realm, 16–18
    public-serving, 16–17, 19, 28
Goldsmith, Joan, 102, 104, 107, 120, 152
Goldsmith, Stephen, 25
Goleman, Daniel, 32–35, 53
Goodsell, Charles T., 190–191
Google, 150
Governance partnerships, 166–167
Government. *See also* Political leadership;
    Public realm
    in Aarhus (Denmark), 170
    authority of democratic, 19–20
    customer partnerships and interaction of,
        175–176
    democratic theory and, believing in, 17
    governance partnerships and, 166–167
    managers, 16
    in Sacramento (California), 170
Government Performance and Results Act
    (GPRA) (1993), 23
Greenleaf, Robert, 36, 45
Group consultation decision-making strategy,
    126, 130–131
Group decision-making strategy, 126,
    131–132
Group development, goal of, 133
Group think, 145–146
Guiding purpose, 38

Hampton (Virginia) 311 calls, 175–177
Happiness, value of pursuit of, 38
Harris, Joe Frank, 20, 101–102
Harvard Kennedy School, 27
Hassan, Shahidul, 95
Hastie, Reid, 141, 148
Hatmaker, Deneen M., 95
Hill, Linda, 69, 71, 73–74

Hiring the right employees, 80–81
Human resource management (HRM)
    caring, committing to, 80
    diversity, pursuing, 83–85
    empowering employees, 85
    flexibility in rules and, 95
    hiring the right people, 80–81
    inbreeding in organization, risks of, 83
    investing in employees, 81–82
    job security, providing, 82
    manager-employee relationships and
        following principles, 95
    overview, 11, 79
    Personal Leadership Exercises, *96–97*
    principles, overview, 11, 79–80
    promoting from within, 82–83
    rewarding good performance, 82
    strategic, 79
Humanitarians' motivation, 86

Ideas, framing/reframing, 62–63
In-groups, 101
In Search of Excellence (Peters and Waterman),
    102
Inbreeding in organization, risks of, 83
Individual consultation decision-making
    strategy, 126, 128–130
Inexperience, 21
Informal authority, 20
Informal power
    ambition and, 53
    Bolling and, 10, 52–59
    building skills of, 75–76
    conflict and, tolerance for, 57
    empathy and, 54–55
    energy and, 52–53
    expertise and, 56–57
    focus and, 53–54
    knowledge and, 56–57
    listening ability and, 55–56
    other sources of, 59
    persistence and, 58
    self-knowledge and, 58–59
    self-reflection and, 58–59
    sources, 52–59
    tolerance for conflict and, 57
    in transition to management, 73–74
    trustworthiness and, 57–58

Ingraham, Patricia Wallace, 95
Ingratiation as persuasion tool, 110
Inquiry and advocacy approach to conflict
    management, 63, 104–109, *105*
Inspirational appeals, 63–64, 110
Integrative approach to conflict management,
    106–112
Interactive communication
    ethical sensitivity and, improving, 103
    feedback-avoiding behavior and, challenge
        of, 101–103
    functions of, 99–103
    leader-member exchange theory and,
        100–101
    manager-employee relationships and,
        building, 98–103
    succession planning and, assisting with,
        103
    three-step evolution of, 100–101
Internal Revenue Service (IRS), 1, 187, 194,
    197. *See also* Rossotti, Charles
Inter-organizational partnerships, 167–169
Intra-organizational purposes, 9
Investing in employees, 81–82

Jacobson, Willow, 95
Jago, Arthur, 122, 125
Javidan, Mansour, 202
Jensen, Ulrich Thy, 191
Job security, providing, 82
Jollie, Colleen, 40, 198
Jørgensen, Torben Beck, 39
Jos, Philip H., 179
Judgment, 213–214

Kahneman, Daniel, 35
Kennedy, John F., 202
Keohane, Nannerl, 3–4, 8, 120, 213–215
Kids In Need, 51
King, Martin Luther Jr., 42, 202
Knowledge and informal power, 56–57
Knowledge, tacit, 144
Kotter, John P., 65, 163, 193

Laissez-faire leadership style, 115
Lateral partnerships, 167–169
Leader-management exchange (LMX) theory,
    162, 167–168

Leader-member exchange (LMX) theory,
    100–101, 189, 201
Leadership. *See also* Managerial leadership;
    Personal foundation for leadership; Public-
    minded managerial leaders
    importance of, 201–202
    people as core of, 79, 94–95
    reluctance to take on, 215–216
    styles, 115–116
Learning mind-set, 102
Liberty, value of, 38
Life, value of, 38
Listening ability, 55–56
Liu, Yongmei, 94
Looking upward and outward. *See*
    Partnerships; Superiors, relationship with
Loy, James, 38
Lundgren, Terry, 153

Management by wandering around (MBWA),
    102
Manager-employee relationships
    conflict in, addressing, 103–112
    cooperation, failure of, 112–115
    defection and, responding to, 112–114
    feedback-avoiding behavior and, challenge
        of, 101–103
    human resource management principles
        and, following, 95
    interactive communication in building,
        98–103
    leader-member exchange theory and,
        100–101
    leadership styles and, 115–116
    overview, 11, 98
    Personal Leadership Exercises, *117–119*
    public-minded managerial leaders'
        effectiveness and, 98
Managerial leadership. *See also* public-minded
    managerial leaders
    constraints on, 4–5
    context and, 15
    fantasy versus reality, 4–5, 205
    focus on management and leadership
        and, 3
    motivating people and, 8
    nature versus nurture, 6–7
    people skills and, 7–8

Managerial leadership (*continued*)
  politics and, 7–9
  promotion to, typical, 5
  purpose skills and, 7, 9
  sine qua non of, 8, 32–35
  stereotype, 4, 205
  stewardship and, 3
Managerial work
  doing more than reflecting, 68–69
  fantasy versus reality, 5
  illusion of authority/control, 69
  insider versus outsider, 70–71
  transition to management and, 68–71
Mapping, political, 59, 73
March, James G., 103
Market exposure, increased, 26–27
Master of public administration (MPA),
  92–93, *93*
Master of public policy (MPP), 92–93, *93*
Mendel, Stuart C., 59–60
Modified unilateral decision-making strategy,
  127–128
Motivating people. *See also* Human resource
  management (HRM)
  balance of work-life, 91–92
  for director's positions in master of public
    administration and public policy
    Program, 93, *93*
  managerial leadership and, 8
  motives, 11
  multiple motivations, 92–94
  nurturing motivations and, 90–91
  overview, 11, 79, 85
  political skills and, building, 207–209
  poorly motivated employees and, 92
  professionalism, responsible, 88–89
  public-minded managerial leaders and, 79
  public service motivation, 85–88
  self-interest, economic, 89–91
  working with people and, 94–95
Motivation. *See also* Public service motivation
  (PSM)
  of asthetes, 86
  of communitarians, 86
  of egalitarians, 86
  as emotional intelligence component,
    34–35
  of environmentalists, 86

  of humanitarians, 86
  multiple, 92–94
  nurturing, 90–91
  of patriots, 86
  of Samaritans, 86
Moynihan, Donald P., 191, 200
Mutual dependence of superiors and
  managers, 163–165

Nanus, Burt, 2
National Treasury Employees Union (NTEU),
  197
National Weather Service (NWS), 43, 191
Negotiation skills, 61–62
Networking, 59–61
Networking partnerships, 167
"Neutral competence," 88
New Public Management (NPM), 26
Newport, Cal, 75
Nonprofit agency purposes, 9
Nonprofit sector. *See also* Public realm; *specific
  nonprofit*
  financial constraints, 28–29
  movement from producer to consumer
    subsidies in, 29
  performance assessment difficulties, 28
  private giving and, tepid growth of, 29
  problematic goals, 28
  public service motivation in, 28
  public-serving goals, 28
  skeptical citizenry and, 29
  social legitimacy and, 28
  unique challenges, 28–29

Obama, Barack, 23–24
Oberfield, Zachary W., 191–192
O'Keefe, Sean, 124
Omnipotent managerial leaders, fantasy of, 5
Open communication, 103
Organizational change. *See also*
  Transformational change
  Bolling and, 201
  challenges of, 186–188
  framework, building, 193–195
  Internal Revenue Service, 187, 194
  nature of, 186–188
  overview, 13, 186
  persisting across time, 198–199

Personal Leadership Exercises, *203–204*
plan, implementing, 195–198
public-minded managerial leaders and,
    186
Rossotti and, 187–188, 192–201
step-by-step approach to, 193–200
successful, 199–200, 202
transformational change and, 13
transformational leadership theory and,
    188–193
Organizational culture, 199
Organizational politics. *See also* Political skills
    accepting, 8
    Bolling and, 50–52
    debate over political leadership and,
        48–50
    embracing, 9450
    ethics and, 5, 49
    informal power sources, 52–59
    literature on, 49–50
    overview, 10, 48
    perception of, 49
    Personal Leadership Exercise, *67*
    political skills and, building, 207
    political skills for exercising power, 59–65
    public-minded managerial leaders and, 48
    skill domains, 7–9
    virtuous politics, practicing, 65–66
Organizational vision, 10, 40, 43–45
Ostrom, Elinor, 154
Out-groups, 101

Paarlberg, Laurie, 87
Pandey, Sanjay K., 200, 215
Participative leadership style, 116
Partners, defining, 100
Partnerships. *See also* Citizen partnerships;
    Customer partnerships; Public
    partnerships
    Bolling and, 179
    coproduction with public and, 169–171,
        183
    governance, 166–167
    inter-organizational, 167–169
    lateral, 167–169
    networking, 167
    overview, 12–13, 161
    Personal Leadership Exercises, *182–185*

political skills and, building, 211
public-minded managerial leaders and,
    166, 179
with superiors, 161–163
Passive approach to conflict management, 105
Patriots' motivation, 86
Peace Corps, 43, 191
Pedersen, Jim, 98
Peer conflict, 114–115
People skills, 7–8
Performance assessment
    conflict over employee, 109–110
    correcting flawed systems, 90
    difficulties, 23–24, 28
    rewarding good, 82
Perry, James L. (Jim), 85–87
Persistence and informal power, 58
Personal exchange as persuasion tool, 110
Personal foundation for leadership
    desire to serve, 10, 36–37
    emotional intelligence, 10, 32–35
    overview, 10, 32
    Personal Leadership Exercise, *47*
    political skills and, building, 206–207
    public-minded managerial leaders and, 32
    public purposes, sense of, 10, 37–40
    transition to management and, drawing
        on, 72–73
    vision, personal and organizational, 10,
        40–45
Personal Leadership Exercises
    coproduction with public, *183*
    customer partnerships, *185*
    decision-making strategies, *137*
    human resource management, *96–97*
    manager-employee relationships, *117–119*
    organizational change, *203–204*
    organizational politics, *67*
    partnerships, *182–185*
    personal foundation for leadership, *47*
    public partnerships, *184*
    public realm, *31*
    small-group teams and meetings, *159–160*
    superiors, relationships with, *181*
    transition to management, *77–78*
Personal values, 38
Personal vision, 10, 40–43, 46, 75
Persuasion, tools for, 110–112

Pfeffer, Jeffrey, 52–53, 57–59
Pittman, Thane S., 100
Pitts, David, 85
Political leadership. *See also* Political skills
  debate over, 48–50
  effective managers and, 48
  flawed, 20–22, 29
Political mapping, 59, 73
Political skills. *See also* Organizational politics
  of Bolling, 59–65, 73, 206–212
  building, 75–76, 206–212
  conflict management and, 209
  consultation, 61
  courage, 214
  decision-making strategies and, 209–210
  distaste for, confronting personal, 216
  embracing organizational politics and, 7–9
  exchange and pressure tactics, 64–65
  facilitation, 61–62
  framing/reframing ideas, 62–63
  inspirational appeals, 63–64
  judgment, 213–214
  motivating people and, 207–209
  negotiation, 61–62
  networking, 59–61
  organizational politics and, 207
  other skills needing to be developed, 213–214
  partnerships and, 211
  personal foundation for leadership and, 206–207
  political mapping, 59
  power and, exercising, 59
  rhetoric, 213
  of Rossotti, 206–212
  small-group teams and meetings and, 210
  superiors and, relationships with, 211
  toolkit for, 211–213
  transition to management and, 207
Politics, 7–9, 48–49. *See also* Organizational
  politics; Political skills
Poorly motivated employees, 92
Potter, Earl H., 100
Power. *See also* Informal power
  attraction to, 49
  of democratic government, 19–20
  empowering employees and, 85
  fantasy of managerial leadership and, 4

  formal, 69
  political skills for exercising, 59–65
Power (Pfeffer), 52
Presumed consent, 170
Principles of public administrators, 39
Private giving, tepid growth of, 29
Private sector, 4, 15
Problematic goals, 22–23, 28
Process, public realm's priority on, 17
Professionalism, responsible, 88–89
Promoting from within, 82–83
Public decision approach decision-making
  strategy, 174
Public distrust, pervasive, 27
Public involvement. *See* Citizen partnerships;
  Customer partnerships
Public-minded managerial leaders. *See also*
  specific issue
  advice for new, 76
  Bolling as example of, 1–3, 30
  citizen partnerships and, 169, 171–172, 179
  customer partnerships and, 175, 179
  decision-making strategies and, 120–121
  defining, 2–4
  developing, 13–14
  dilemmas facing, 205
  first steps for, 45–46
  manager-employee relationships and
    effectiveness of, 98
  motivating people and, 79
  networking partnerships and, 167
  organizational change and, 186
  organizational politics and, 48
  overview, 9–13
  partner relationships and, 166
  partnerships and, 166, 179
  personal foundation for leadership and, 32
  in private sector, 4
  public partnerships and, 169, 171–172, 179
  public realm and, 15
  Rossotti as example of, 1–3, 30
  small-group teams and meetings and, 138
  successful, 30, 32
  superiors and, relationships with, 161–162
  toolkit for, 211–213
  transformational change and, 30
  transformative change and, 30

Public partnerships
  as contingent issue, 172–173
  coproduction and, 169–171, *183*
  deliberation and, 174–175
  incentives in, 170–171
  Personal Leadership Exercise, *184*
  priorities in, setting, 179–180
  public-minded managerial leaders and,
    169, 171–172, 179
  reasons for, 171–172
  service process and, rethinking, 169
  volunteers, 171
Public purposes, sense of, 9–10, 37–40
Public realm
  authority of democratic government and,
    19–20
  challenges of, 20–30
  citizenry and, skeptical, 27–28
  defining, 10
  diversity and, value for, 18
  financial constraints and, 25–27
  as fish bowl, 27–28
  goals of, 16–18
  hiring right employees in, 81
  latitude for leadership and, 29–30
  leaders making a difference in, 214–215
  overview, 10, 15
  performance assessment difficulties,
    23–24
  Personal Leadership Exercise, *31*
  political leadership and, flawed, 20–22
  private sector and, blurring, 15
  problematic goals and, 22–23
  process and, priority on, 17
  public-minded managerial leaders and, 15
  public service motivation in, 86
  public-serving goals of, 16–17
  representativeness and, value for, 18
  resources of, special, 19–20
  self-regulation and, 24–25
  transformational change in, 200
  uniqueness of nonprofit sector and, 28–29
Public service motivation (PSM)
  in motivating people, 85–88
  in nonprofit sector, 28
  in public realm, 6
  public-serving goals and, 19
Public-serving goals, 16–17, 19, 28

Public values, 16, 38–40, 46
Purpose skills, 7, 9
Pynes, Joan E., 79–80, 83–84

Quality of decision, 123

Rainey, Hal G., 16, 22–23, 56, 70, 84–86,
  165, 187, 192–193
Reflection, 74–75
Relationship-oriented leadership style,
  115–116
Representation of employees, 99
Representativeness, public realm's value for,
  18. *See also* Diversity
Resources of public realm, special, 19–20
Responsibility for well-being of others, 3
Responsible professionalism, 88–89
Rewarding good performance, 82
Rhetoric, 213
Rosenbach, William E., 100
Rossotti, Charles
  as example of public-minded managerial
    leader, 1–3, 30
  Internal Revenue Service and, taking over
    by, 1–3, 30
  listening skills of, 193
  management by wandering around and,
    102
  organizational change and, 187–188,
    192–201
  political skills of, 206–212
  transformational change and, 1–3, 30,
    214

St. Luke's Episcopal Church, 50, 54
Salomonsen, Heidi Houlberg, 191
Samaritans' motivation, 86
Sawyer, Keith, 148
Sayles, Leonard R., 5, 68, 73
Schön, Donald, 63, 104
School boards, local, 21
Selden, Sally Coleman, 95
Self-awareness, 10, 33
Self-interest, economic, 89–91
Self-knowledge, 58–59
Self-questioning, 41
Self-reflection, 58–59, 74–75
Self-regulation, 10, 24–25, 29, 33–34

Servant-leadership theory, desire to serve and, 36–37
Servant nature of leadership roles, recognizing, 36, 45
Service process, rethinking, 169
7 Habits of Highly Effective People, The (Covey), 41
Shalala, Donna, 73
Sine qua non of managerial leadership, 8, 32–35
Small-group teams and meetings
    accountability and, collective, 145, 157
    agenda-setting for meeting, 148–149
    benefits of, 144–145, 157–158
    "boss" as facilitator and, 153–154
    challenges, 155–158
    collaboration and, 139, 144–145, 157
    commitment and, common, 144, 157
    defining, 138–140
    domination by a minority and, 145, 156
    effective, building, 157
    facilitating, principles for, 146–147
    globalization and, 139–140
    group development and, 144–145
    group member as facilitator and, 155
    group think and, 145–146, 156–157
    information-only meeting and, 145, 156
    limiting information, 150–152
    malfunctions, 145–146, 156–157
    overview, 12, 138
    Personal Leadership Exercises, *159–160*
    planning, 146
    political skills and, building, 210
    popularity of, growing, 139–140
    public-minded managerial leaders and, 138
    purposes for, 147–148
    sequencing topics, 146–147, 149–150
    skills needed for, 6
    soliciting information, 147, 150–152
    starting, 141–143, 155–156
    summarizing/deciding, 147, 152–153
    tacit knowledge and, 144
    trivial and, preoccupation with, 145, 156
    unnecessary, 146, 157
    virtual meetings, challenge of, 154–155
Social legitimacy, 28
Social skill, 34

Steinberg, Amanda, 41–42
Stevens, Brad, 109–110
Stewardship, 3
Stivers, Camilla, 55
STOP approach, 75
Strategic human resources management (SHRM), 79
Straus, David, 153
Stritch, Justin, 98
Structured choices, 123–124
Subordinates. *See* Employees; Manager-employee relationships
Succession planning, 103
Sunstein, Cass R., 141, 148
Superiors, multiple, 22
Superiors, relationships with
    difficulties in, 165–166
    goal of, 161–163
    mutual dependence and, implications of, 163–165
    overview, 12–13
    partnership, 161–163
    Personal Leadership Exercise, *181*
    political skills and, building, 211
    priorities in, setting, 179–180
    public-minded managerial leaders and, 161–162
Supportive leadership style, 115–116
SWOT analysis, 73

Tacit knowledge, 144
Task-oriented leadership style, 115
Teleworking, 91
Temporary Assistance to Needy Families (TANF) program, 23
Thompson, James R., 187, 192
Thorp, Edward, 37–38
311 call centers (Hampton, Virginia), 175–177
Time management, 74
Tolerance for conflict and informal power, 57
Tompkins, Mark E., 179
Toolkit for public-minded managerial leaders, 211–213
Tracey, J. Bruce, 64, 110
Transformational change. *See also* Organizational change
    appropriateness of, 200

Bolling and, 1–3, 30, 214
at Internal Revenue Service, 192–193
leadership and, importance of, 201–202
"moment" for, 200
organizational change and, 13
public-minded managerial leaders and, 30
in public realm, 20
Rossotti and, 1–3, 30, 214
strategies, 200–201
Transformational leadership theory
Bass and, 189
Burns and, 188–189
defining, 189
effectiveness, evidence of, 191
organizational change and, 188–193
popularity of, 188–189
principles of, 189–190
recommendations for leaders, 191–192
vision and, centrality of, 190–191
Transition to management
doing more than reflecting, 68–69
fishbowl and, working in, 70
formal power and, 69
illusion of authority/control, 69
informal power in, 73–74
insider versus outsider, 70–71
managerial work and, 68–71
overview, 10–11, 68
personal foundation and, drawing on, 72–73
Personal Leadership Exercises, *77–78*
political skills and, building, 207
starting, 71–75
strong beginning, strategy for, 75–76
time management, 74
Transparency
factors underlying greater, 27–28
of manager's behavior, 70
motivating people with economic self-interest and, 90

Tropman, John E., 142, 146, 150, 152
Trottenberg, Polly, 196–197
Trustworthiness and informal power, 57–58
Tulgan, Bruce, 215

Uncertainty about issue characteristics, 133–134
Unilateral decision-making strategy, 126–127
U.S. Internal Revenue Service (IRS), 1, 187, 194, 197. *See also* Rossotti, Charles
U.S. Mint, 177
U.S. Park Service, 191

Values
personal, 38
public, 16, 38–40, 46
Van Wart, Montgomery, 49
Virtual meetings, challenge of, 154–155
Virtuous politics, practicing, 65–66
Vision
organizational, 10, 40, 43–45
personal, 10, 40–43, 46, 75
transformational leadership theory and centrality of, 190–191
Volunteers, 171
Vroom, Victor, 122, 125

Waldman, David A., 202
Win-lose approach to conflict management, 115
Win-win approach to conflict management, 115
Wise, Lois Recascino, 19, 85–86
Work-life balance, 91–92
Working with people, 94–95
Wright, Bradley E., 200, 215

Yetton, Philip, 122
Yukl, Gary, 2–4, 53, 59, 63–64, 107, 110, 132

About the Author

John Clayton Thomas is a professor of public management and policy in the Andrew Young School of Policy Studies at Georgia State University in Atlanta. He has taught courses on leadership and organizational behavior for more than twenty years, and has served in leadership roles at three universities and with several national scholarly organizations.

This is Thomas's sixth book along with more than sixty articles on different aspects of public management and public policy. His research has appeared in *Public Administration Review*, the *Journal of Public Administration Research and Theory*, *Administration & Society*, *Urban Affairs Review*, and the *Journal of Urban Affairs*, among other journals. He also served for thirty years as editor of *The American Review of Public Administration*, one of the elite journals in public administration.

Dr. Thomas has consulted and conducted training for state and local governments and nonprofit agencies in Colorado, Georgia, New York, South Carolina, Pennsylvania, Texas, and Missouri. He holds a Ph.D in political science from Northwestern University and a B.A. (magna cum laude) and M.A. in journalism and mass communications from the University of Minnesota.